Supporting Course and Programme Leaders in Higher Education

Offering research- and evidence-based approaches that explore the essential components of programme leadership in higher education, this book is designed to define, develop and support the programme leadership role and all those who undertake it.

The book is split into three parts, taking into account the three different lenses through which programme leaders and their professional practice and relationships are generally viewed: the institution, the individual and the programme team. Chapters and case studies address key elements crucial to the holistic development of programme leadership and programme leaders. These include:

- Understanding and developing programme leadership in context
- Developing organisational structures and processes so programme leaders can thrive
- Growing programme leaders' educational leadership, team working and communication

Crucial reading for programme leaders, as well as academic and educational developers and leaders working across faculties and whole institutions, this text includes contributions from teaching- and research-focused higher education institutions, as well as established and modern college- and university-based providers in both the northern and southern hemispheres.

Jenny Lawrence is a Reader in Higher Education and the Head of the Teaching Excellence Academy at the University of Hull, UK.

Sue Morón-García is a writer, researcher and educational developer with over 35 years of combined experience in higher, adult and secondary education where she has designed, led and advised on a variety of programmes.

Rowena Senior is a Reader in Higher Education within the School of Education, University of Hertfordshire, UK.

The Staff and Educational Development Series
Series Editor: James Wisdom

Written by experienced and well-known practitioners and published in association with the Staff and Educational Development Association (SEDA), each book in the series contributes to the development of learning, teaching and training and assists in the professional development of staff. The books present new ideas for learning development and facilitate the exchange of information and good practice.

Recent and forthcoming titles in the series:

Advancing Practice in Academic Development
Edited by David Baume and Celia Popovic

Developing Intercultural Practice
Academic Development in a Multicultural and Globalizing World
David Killick

Delivering Educational Change in Higher Education
A Transformative Approach for Leaders and Practitioners
Edited by Jackie Potter and Cristina Devecchi

A Handbook for Student Engagement in Higher Education
Theory into Practice
Edited by Tom Lowe and Yassein El Hakim

Supporting Course and Programme Leaders in Higher Education
Practical Wisdom for Leaders, Educational Developers and Programme Leaders
Edited by Jenny Lawrence, Sue Morón-García and Rowena Senior

Developing Expertise for Teaching in Higher Education
Implications for Professional Learning and Development
Edited by Helen King

For more information about this series, please visit: https://www.routledge.com/SEDA-Series/book-series/SE0747

Supporting Course and Programme Leaders in Higher Education

Practical Wisdom for Leaders, Educational Developers and Programme Leaders

Edited by Jenny Lawrence, Sue Morón-García and Rowena Senior

LONDON AND NEW YORK

Cover image: Getty Images

First published 2022
by Routledge
2 Park Square, Milton Park, Abingdon, Oxon OX14 4RN

and by Routledge
605 Third Avenue, New York, NY 10158

Routledge is an imprint of the Taylor & Francis Group, an informa business

© 2022 selection and editorial matter, Jenny Lawrence, Sue Morón-García and Rowena Senior; individual chapters, the contributors

The right of Jenny Lawrence, Sue Morón-García and Rowena Senior to be identified as the authors of the editorial material, and of the authors for their individual chapters, has been asserted in accordance with sections 77 and 78 of the Copyright, Designs and Patents Act 1988.

All rights reserved. No part of this book may be reprinted or reproduced or utilised in any form or by any electronic, mechanical, or other means, now known or hereafter invented, including photocopying and recording, or in any information storage or retrieval system, without permission in writing from the publishers.

Trademark notice: Product or corporate names may be trademarks or registered trademarks, and are used only for identification and explanation without intent to infringe.

British Library Cataloguing-in-Publication Data
A catalogue record for this book is available from the British Library

Library of Congress Cataloging-in-Publication Data
Names: Lawrence, Jenny (Writer on education and training) editor. | Morón-García, Sue, editor. | Senior, Rowena, editor.
Title: Supporting course and programme leaders in higher education : practical wisdom for leaders, and programme leaders / Edited by Jenny Lawrence, Sue Morón-García, Rowena Senior.
Description: Abingdon, Oxon ; New York, NY : Routledge, 2022. | Series: Seda series | Includes bibliographical references and index.
Identifiers: LCCN 2021040956 (print) | LCCN 2021040957 (ebook) | ISBN 9780367610388 (hardback) | ISBN 9780367650155 (paperback) | ISBN 9781003127413 (ebook)
Subjects: LCSH: Educational leadership. | Education, Higher–Management. | Curriculum planning.
Classification: LCC LB2806 .S85 2022 (print) | LCC LB2806 (ebook) | DDC 371.2/011 dc23/eng/20220124
LC record available at https://lccn.loc.gov/2021040956
LC ebook record available at https://lccn.loc.gov/2021040957

ISBN: 978-0-367-61038-8 (hbk)
ISBN: 978-0-367-65015-5 (pbk)
ISBN: 978-1-003-12741-3 (ebk)

DOI: 10.4324/9781003127413

Typeset in Galliard
by KnowledgeWorks Global Ltd.

This book is dedicated to those leading programmes of study in Higher Education and the educational developers and leaders who support their important work.

Contents

List of contributors   xi
Foreword   xxiii
List of acronyms and abbreviations   xxv
Acknowledgements   xxvi

Introduction: Supporting course and programme leaders in higher education: Positioning programme leadership as central to HE success   1
JENNY LAWRENCE, SUE MORÓN-GARCÍA AND ROWENA SENIOR

PART I
Institutional development of programme leadership and programme leaders: Understanding and developing the role   11

Introduction   13
JENNY LAWRENCE

1 A national approach: Foregrounding programme leadership in Scotland   15
MARTHA CADDELL, SAM ELLIS, CHRISTINE HADDOW AND KIMBERLY WILDER-DAVIS

Practitioner response: Considering Canadian programme leadership   27
ANDREA S. WEBB

2 Understanding and defining programme leadership in a large institution   29
RACHEL FORSYTH AND STEPHEN POWELL

Practitioner response: Understanding and defining programme leadership in a South African context   40
NOSISANA MKONTO

3 Developing programme leadership in an Australian university: An institutional approach to professional learning and development 41
LOUISE MADDOCK, SAMANTHA CARRUTHERS AND
KAREN VAN HAERINGEN

Practitioner response: Reviewing the programme leadership strategy in an Australian university: Could it be adapted in the Greek context? 53
MARIANTHI KARATSIORI

Case study 1: Developing a role statement for programme leadership 55
LOUISE MADDOCK, SAMANTHA CARRUTHERS, KAREN VAN
HAERINGEN, HELEN MASSA AND CHRISTOPHER LOVE

4 A collaborative and comprehensive approach to designing a cross-institutional development programme for programme leaders 60
PETIA PETROVA

Practitioner response: Considering co-constructing a Programme Leadership Development Programme in a research-intensive HEI 71
DEANNE GANNAWAY

5 Harnessing the potential of formal networks and informal communities to support the holistic development of programme leaders 73
GRAHAM SCOTT AND JENNY LAWRENCE

Practitioner response: It's a good start: Reflections through indigenous eyes on a holistic approach to supporting course and programme leadership 84
PIKI DIAMOND

Case study 2: Academic almanac: A practical workshop for programme leaders to plan the academic yearly cycle 86
JULIET EVE

PART 2
Individual programme leaders: The development of leadership through experience and collaboration 91

Introduction 93
SUE MORÓN-GARCÍA

6	Programme leaders as educational and academic leaders: A question of influence – relationships, behaviour and commitment DOUG PARKIN	95
	Practitioner response: A sympathetic approach and practical strategies SVITLANA KALASHNIKOVA AND OLENA ORZHEL	109
7	'It can be a lonely job sometimes': The use of collaborative space and social network theory in support of programme leaders MAEVE O'DWYER AND REBECCA SANDERSON	111
	Practitioner response: Social support for programme leaders – Building an interdisciplinary community MAYARA DA MOTA MATOS	123
8	Empowering programme leaders: Developing relational academic leadership SARAH MOORE	124
	Practitioner response: Leadership as collaboration – Taking a less individualistic approach OSCAR JEREZ YAÑEZ	136
	Case study 3: Honesty and the power of open approaches that foster trust JESSIE JOHNSON AND FRANCES KALU	137
	Case study 4: Reflecting on the transition from traditional to blended programmes: Six critical messages to manage change EMMA O'BRIEN, CAROL O'SULLIVAN AND GWEN MOORE	140
	Case study 5: Leading joint and combined honours programmes: Amplified complexity DAWNE IRVING BELL AND SUE MORÓN-GARCÍA	144
	Case study 6: Taking the lead: Creating an undergraduate environmental science programme to meet the benchmarks and expectations BETHAN L. WOOD	148

PART 3
The practice of programme leadership: Leading programme teams   151

    Introduction   153
    ROWENA SENIOR

9 The collaborative programme leader: Embedding meaningful collaboration into a programme culture   155
    EVELYN JAMIESON

    Practitioner response: Using our disciplines to improve our leadership approaches   165
    LUCÍA PIQUERO ÁLVAREZ

    Case study 7: A team-based retreat for programme development   166
    SARAH MOORE

    Case study 8: Coordinating programme design through 'Assessment Therapy'   170
    DOMINIC HENRI

10 In pursuit of excellence: A collaborative and interdisciplinary framework for reconceptualising programme leaders   174
    JACQUELINE HAMILTON AND CHRISTOPHER DONALDSON

    Practitioner response: The importance of framing the curriculum as a living system   186
    CATHERINE M. MILLETT

    Case study 9: Leading successful programme transformation   188
    SHARON ALTENA AND KAREN THEOBALD

    Case study 10: Facilitating educational leadership: Building and sharing an understanding amongst the programme team   191
    EVA MALONE AND STEPHEN YORKSTONE

    Conclusion: Championing programme leadership for success in higher education   195
    ROWENA SENIOR, SUE MORÓN-GARCÍA AND JENNY LAWRENCE

    Index   203

Contributors

Editors

Jenny Lawrence
University of Hull, UK
Dr Jenny Lawrence, AFSEDA, PFHEA, NTF, is a Reader in Higher Education and the Head of the Teaching Excellence Academy at the University of Hull, UK. She has driven multiple change initiatives in universities across the four nations, with a specific focus on creating a higher education (HE) environment inclusive to staff and students from groups under-represented in HE. Her research interests include wellbeing in HE, educational and programme leadership.

Sue Morón-García
Oxford Brookes University, UK
Dr Sue Morón-García, SFHEA, is a writer, researcher and tech savvy educational developer with a PhD in Educational Technology. She has over 35 years of experience working in higher, adult and secondary education and is passionate about collaborative endeavour and supporting colleagues' teaching and learning at different career stages. Her own highlights include contributing to the first iteration of the ISSoTL collaborative writing groups, 2010, Hamilton, Canada, co-writing the International Journal of Academic Development article of the year for 2015, facilitating an invited workshop on "What is SoTL?" in Spanish at EuroSoTL 2019 and working with colleagues in Chile to develop their institutional educational development approach.

Rowena Senior
University of Hertfordshire, UK
Dr Rowena Senior is Reader in Higher Education within the School of Education, University of Hertfordshire, UK. Rowena has led Programme Leadership support initiatives and has consulted on and provided workshops for a number of institutions on supporting Programme Leaders. Rowena is an active researcher particularly in the domain of academic leadership. Rowena has led a number of strategic projects including curriculum redesign and the development of educational and pedagogic research.

Authors

Sharon Altena
Queensland University of Technology, Australia
Sharon Altena, SFHEA, is Senior Curriculum and Learning Designer in the Learning and Teaching unit at Queensland University of Technology. She has worked in curriculum and learning design for the past 30 years across the secondary, vocational education and higher education sectors. In her current role, Sharon leads course teams to re-imagine their curriculum and implement evidence-based digital learning practices. She has diverse research interests including: third space workers, online learning, curriculum and technology. Sharon is a member of the Digital Learning for Change Research Group and is currently studying for a Doctor of Education at Griffith University.

Martha Caddell
Heriot-Watt University, UK
Professor Martha Caddell, PFHEA, is Director of the Learning and Teaching Academy and Professor of Higher Education Policy and Pedagogy at Heriot-Watt University in Edinburgh, Scotland. She leads on university policy and practice in learning and teaching, support for academic development, and pedagogic research, scholarship and evaluation. Martha was Deputy Chair of the QAA Scotland Enhancement Theme (2017–2020) on Evidence for Enhancement: Improving the Student Experience. She is a Principal Fellow of the Higher Education Academy.

Samantha Carruthers
Griffith University, Australia
Samantha Carruthers, SFHEA, is Senior Consultant – Leadership for Learning, at Griffith University's Learning Futures, Queensland, Australia. An experienced psychologist, specialising in group and organisational change, with a Masters in Organisational Psychology, she is currently studying a Master of Information Technology. Her role in co-leading Griffith University's Building Program Leadership Strategy was acknowledged when the team received the Vice Chancellor's Award for Excellence in 2019. She ponders what capabilities might be important for program leaders to develop, in order to influence the design and development of technology-based information systems, which increasingly contribute to the quality of students' experiences in their university programs.

Piki Diamond
Auckland University of Technology, NZ
Piki Diamond is Māori (indigenous to Aotearoa New Zealand) a descendant of Ngāti Tūwharetoa and Ngāpuhi tribes. She is an academic developer and doctoral candidate at Auckland University of Technology, and co-designed Ako Aronui (an indigenous alignment to the UKPSF). The phrase "honouring te Tiriti o Waitangi (the Treaty of Waitangi)" is at the heart of her research and teaching, a decolonising approach focused on bringing awareness of the relationship between moral values and the values held within the system of the

University. Creatively Piki, re-members staff and students to practice Māori values of aroha (love and attentiveness), tika (justice and doing the right thing) and pono (self-collective truth) within their teaching.

Christopher Donaldson
York University, Canada

Chris Donaldson, MBA, BEd, is an innovative leader in quality assurance and teaching and learning excellence who emphasises the importance of the learner experience in his work. He is the Manager of Quality Assurance and Accreditation at the Lassonde School of Engineering at York University (Ontario, Canada), where he leads a dynamic team in support of continuous program improvement and academic excellence in program design and curriculum development. He teaches quality assurance and instructional design in the Ontario College system, and was formerly the Manager, Academic Programs at the University of Guelph.

Sam Ellis
Royal Conservatoire of Scotland, UK

Dr Sam Ellis, SFHEA, is Associate Head of the BMus (Bachelor of Music) degree programme at the Royal Conservatoire of Scotland. He plays a key role in ensuring the continued academic and professional relevance of the curriculum, as well as teaching across a range of subjects including history, analysis, theory, harmony and research skills. He was previously a senior lecturer at Glasgow Caledonian University, specialising in professional learning and the pursuit of expert practice. He is a Senior Fellow of the Higher Education Academy.

Juliet Eve
University of Brighton, UK

Juliet Eve is the Head of the Learning and Teaching Hub at the University of Brighton. She has led the institutional Postgraduate Certificate for new lecturers, and established the CPD Scheme which awards HEA Fellowships. In 2011, she developed CPD sessions for programme leaders, and continues to lead this annual series of workshops. Her research interests include programme leadership and assessment and feedback.

Rachel Forsyth
Manchester Metropolitan University, UK

Dr Rachel Forsyth, PFHEA, is Head of the University Teaching Academy at Manchester Metropolitan University. She began her career as a lecturer in physics and then moved into academic development via distance and e-learning production. Her research interests focus on institutional change, particularly in relation to inclusive learning communities and assessment in higher education, and she teaches on the University's PGC in Learning and Teaching in Higher Education and MA in Higher Education. As Editor-in-Chief of the Student Engagement in Higher Education Journal, she is an active member of the Researching, Advancing, Inspiring Student Engagement (RAISE) network.

Deanne Gannaway
University of Queensland, Australia
Dr Deanne Gannaway, ALTF, is an academic developer and curriculum transformation expert with twenty years' experience in Australian universities. She is currently the Academic Lead (Professional Learning) in the Institute of Teaching and Learning Innovation (ITaLI) at the University of Queensland (UQ). Her teaching and scholarship focus on continuing professional learning for university teachers and professional education for students. Her reputation as a leader of change in learning and teaching is grounded in her research on curriculum and transfer of innovation and practice in the professional learning of university educators.

Christine Haddow
Edinburgh Napier University, UK
Dr Christine Haddow, FHEA, is Lecturer and Programme Leader of the BA (Hons) Criminology programme at Edinburgh Napier University. She is a Fellow of the Higher Education Academy. Christine's interests in education and pedagogy focus on the role of programme leaders, community and belonging at university, and education in custodial settings. In her current role, she oversees the curriculum design of the programme, embedding employability and enhancing the student experience. She also teaches a social research methods course to people in custody in the Scottish Prison Service.

Karen van Haeringen
Griffith University, Australia
Karen van Haeringen is Principal Advisor, Strategy and Innovation at Griffith University with 32 years' experience in higher education, including 18 as Head of the Secretariat and 7 years as Deputy Academic Registrar. Karen's leadership in Australian higher education has been recognised nationally with the award of a 2006 Carrick Citation and a 2010 Australian Learning and Teaching Council Citation for outstanding contributions to student learning. Karen led the nationally funded 2011 Queensland Promoting Excellence Network (QPEN) and was a member of the Office for Learning and Teaching 2013 Exemplary Academic Integrity and 2016 Contract Cheating and Assessment Design Projects.

Jacqueline Hamilton
University of Guelph, Canada
Jackie Hamilton, MEd, is Senior Manager of Learning, Assessment and Accreditation at the Lang School of Business and Economics at the University of Guelph (Ontario, Canada). She is passionate about learner-centred education and is responsible for the School's accreditation, quality assurance, and teaching and learning strategic operations. She works collaboratively with faculty and other stakeholders by leading people through efficient and meaningful processes. She has given invited talks on the importance of providing intentional faculty support and presented on creative curriculum solutions. Jackie also instructs in the first-year seminar program, where she provides active learning opportunities to her students.

Dominic Henri
University of Hull, UK

Dr Dominic Henri, NTF, is Senior Lecturer in the University of Hull's Department of Biological and Marine Sciences. Director of Studies and Deputy Head for the department since 2019, he has worked with programme directors on all aspects of current student attainment, retention, satisfaction and graduate prospects, and leads multiple modules on conservation biology and ecology. He is a prominent member of the Biosciences Education Research Group, a community of biology lecturers involved in pedagogic research on student employability, equality, and wellbeing and a founding member of the Royal Society of Biology's Early Career Lecturer forum, leading on the Academic Wellbeing working group.

Dawne Irving-Bell
Edge Hill University, UK

Dr Dawne Irving-Bell, PFHEA, is Senior Learning and Teaching Fellow (Reader) at Edge Hill University. She is an award-winning educator, dedicated to raising the profile of SoTL. She enjoys lecturing on visual thinking and advocates for technology and design education. Dawne established The National Teaching Repository and leads AdvanceHE's Social Media for Learning Group. She edits the Journal of Social Media for Learning and is a member of ISSOTL's Recognition Committee. Dawne leads her University's GTA teaching-programme, the PGCert Teaching in Higher Education Research module, and as a PFHEA leads on university-wide strategies to enhance student learning.

Evelyn Jamieson
University of Chester, UK

Dr Evelyn Jamieson, SFHEA, is an Associate Professor and Programme leader for MA Dance and MA Drama at the University of Chester. Previously head of department at the Liverpool Institute for Performing Arts and subject leader at University College Bretton Hall, she has a BA in Creative Arts, an MA in Educational Theatre and completed her PhD in 2016. Her professional experience includes performing for Wayne McGregor's Random Dance and as co-director with Leigh Landy of Idee Fixe Experimental Sound and Movement Theatre. Her research focuses on collaborative practice with publications, international conference presentations and a plethora of choreographic work, commissions and projects.

Oscar Jerez Yañez
University of Chile, Santiago, Chile

Dr Oscar Jerez has a PhD in Psychology and Education and is the Director of the Centre for Teaching and Learning of the Faculty of Economics and Business, and Professor of the Department of Health Sciences Education at the University of Chile in Santiago. He is a senior advisor to LASPAU, affiliated with Harvard University, and multiple higher education institutions in Latin America and the Caribbean. He is the Founder of LatinSoTL.

Jessie Johnson
University of Calgary, Canada in Qatar
Dr Jessie Johnson is a member of the faculty of Nursing, University of Calgary in Qatar. She holds a position as an assistant professor and teaches in both the undergraduate and graduate nursing program. She has served in the role of graduate program coordinator for the last two years. Jessie's research interests span across diverse modalities including that of interprofessional collaboration, health literacy, palliative care, immunisations and chronic disease management.

Svitlana Kalashnikova
National Academy of Educational Sciences of Ukraine, Ukraine
Professor Svitlana Kalashnikova has 25 years of experience in higher education in Ukraine, including 20 managing over 30 international education projects. She was the National Coordinator of the TEMPUS Project "ELITE – Education for Leadership, Intelligence and Talent Encouraging" and of the British Council's Ukraine Higher Education Leadership Development Programme. She was Advisor to the Minister of Education and Science of Ukraine (2016–2018, pro bono). Svitlana is a member of the National HE Reform Experts Team (Erasmus+ Office in Ukraine), has more than 130 publications to her name and is Co-founder and Leading Expert of the NGO "Institute for Leadership, Innovation and Development".

Frances Kalu
University of Calgary, Canada in Qatar
Dr Frances Kalu is a faculty member and Teaching and Learning Specialist at the Centre for Teaching and Learning, University of Calgary in Qatar. She is currently in Qatar on a secondment from the Taylor Institute for Teaching and Learning, University of Calgary, where she holds the position of a tenure-track Educational Development Consultant. As part of her role, Frances consults with faculties, curriculum committees and review teams on curriculum development and review projects. She also provides evidence-based educational development opportunities for faculty members to build capacity in, teaching and learning, innovations in education, the scholarship of teaching and learning, as well as curriculum.

Marianthi Karatsiori
University of Macedonia, Greece
Marianthi Karatsiori teaches "Globalisation and Intercultural Education", a postgraduate course in the department of Educational and Social Policy at the University of Macedonia, Greece. She has held various educational posts: an education programme expert at the Ministry of Education, Research and Religious Affairs, a lecturer in the teaching of English as a Foreign/International language on the MEd, at the Hellenic Open University, and as an ESP teacher at several Greek higher education institutions. Her role in the Technical Assistance Programme of the International Bureau of Education

(UNESCO, IBE) provided support to governmental representatives improving quality education. Her interests are teacher education and professional development, educational policy guidance and reform.

Christopher Love
Griffith University, Australia

Dr Chris Love, SFHEA, is Senior Lecturer in Biochemistry and Molecular Biology in the School of Environment and Science at Griffith University. He is a passionate STEM educator, teaching biochemistry in the Bachelor of Science and Bachelor of Biomedical Science programs at Griffith University, and teaches molecular biology at the Nanjing University of Chinese Medicine, China. Chris' teaching and learning interests are centred on student-staff partnerships; active, authentic and personalised learning; technology-enhanced learning; and, as first-year coordinator, improving student success and the student experience. His scientific research is focused on the structure and function of proteins in neuronal cell signalling and Parkinson's disease.

Louise Maddock
Griffith University, Australia

Louise Maddock, SFHEA, is Senior Learning & Teaching Consultant in the Centre for Learning Futures and lecturer in the Graduate Certificate in University Learning and Teaching at Griffith University, Australia. She is the Program Leader of the Curriculum Design for Learning professional learning program (HEA Fellowship pathway) and co-leads the Building Program Leadership Strategy, Program Directors' Leadership Series, and program development participatory action research projects. Louise is a member of the Griffith Institute of Educational Research and her PhD research focused on examining the academic middle leading practices of program development through a critical-social Theory of Practice Architectures lens.

Eva Malone
Edinburgh Napier University, UK

Eva Malone is Associate Professor within the School of Applied Sciences at Edinburgh Napier University. She leads a suite of biological sciences undergraduate programmes accredited by the Royal Society of Biology (RSB) and contributes to the immunology teaching within the suite and overseas on a sister programme. She is a Senior Fellow of the Higher Education Academy, a member of the RSB and represented Scottish Biology Teachers in a RSB national initiative to promote careers in Biology. Her research interests include exercise immunology, nanotoxicology and interdisciplinary learning.

Helen Massa
Griffith University, Australia

Associate Professor Helen Massa (AAUT, SFHEA) is nationally and internationally recognised for her sustained Learning and Teaching excellence and leadership, both within her anatomy/physiology discipline and more widely for supporting tertiary student recruitment and graduate success. Helen was instrumental in championing peer support for improving educator teaching practice, course and program design and review at Griffith University and is an Innovative Research Universities (IRU) peer reviewer. Helen led the School of Anatomy development for Griffith University and its vital role in establishing professional Health programs. Helen is currently Health Group Employability Lead and Senior Fellow of the Griffith Learning and Teaching Academy.

Mayara da Mota Matos
Universidade Federal de Alfenas, Brazil

Dr Mayara Matos is Academic and Educational Support Administrator at Universidade Federal de Alfenas (UNIFAL/MG) Poços de Caldas campus, Brazil. Her main research interests include health, quality of life, self-efficacy, self-regulation and other psychological variables influencing Brazilian Lecturers' work.

Catherine M. Millett
Educational Testing Service, USA

Catherine Millett is a senior research scientist and strategic advisor in the Policy Evaluation and Research Center at ETS. Her research focuses on factors leading to postsecondary readiness, access, success and completion for students at the undergraduate and graduate level. She has experience leading applied research projects and conducting policy research and program evaluations. She was a visiting lecturer, Princeton School of Public and International Affairs at Princeton University. She is a Fellow of the Salzburg Global Seminar, a member of the Karanga Global Steering Committee and chairs the Global Access to Postsecondary Education (GAPS) Executive Board.

Nosisana Mkonto
Cape Peninsula University of Technology, South Africa

Dr Nosisana Mkonto of the Cape Peninsula University of Technology is the Head of Student Development at the Fundani Centre for Higher Education Development. She has been heading the First Year Experience project since 2014. She began her career as a teacher, then a lecturer and academic development. Her research interests cover issues around student access, retention, support and development, learning styles, organisation development, first year experience and peer support. She has presented papers at conferences both national and international and published articles in journals and book chapters.

Gwen Moore
Mary Immaculate College, Ireland

Dr Gwen Moore is Director of Teaching and Learning and Senior Lecturer in Music Education at Mary Immaculate College, Limerick. In her role as Director, Gwen provides strategic leadership in the development of Teaching, Learning, Assessment and Feedback across the College. As senior lecturer, she has coordinated the MA in Music Education and serves on several international editorial boards including: International Journal of Music Education, Music Education Research, British Journal of Music Education and two book series, Popular Music Matters and Studies in Irish Music Education. Prior to her appointment at MIC, Gwen taught music at primary, secondary and higher levels of education.

Sarah Moore
Sheffield University, UK

Dr Sarah Moore is Academic Professional Development Manager at The University of Sheffield, responsible for the team who provides support for those who teach across the institution at any stage of their career. As part of this role, she is Director of the PGCert in Teaching for Learning in Higher Education and Director of the University's Learning and Teaching Professional Recognition Scheme. She is currently working with colleagues to develop a suite of development activity for aspiring academic leaders.

Emma O'Brien
Mary Immaculate College, Ireland

Dr Emma O'Brien is Academic Developer in Technology Enhanced Learning in Mary Immaculate College where she teaches, researches and supports programme teams in the area of digital pedagogies. Emma has over 40 peer reviewed publications in the areas of digital learning, workplace learning, and transformative pedagogies and has been awarded over 1 million Euro for her research in the area. She has worked in the field of digital learning since 2000 during which time she has successfully led several EU projects in partnership with a variety of higher education institutions, professional bodies, programme teams and disciplines.

Maeve O'Dwyer
Trinity College Dublin, Ireland

Dr Maeve O'Dwyer was an educational developer and third space professional based at the University of Lincoln, working with the Lincoln Academy of Learning and Teaching (LALT) to support colleagues across the institution when she undertook this work. Her role was Programme Manager HEA, leading the university's internal programme accredited by AdvanceHE to award UKPSF recognition. She has a keen interest in pedagogical support and development, including the importance of recognising and sharing best practice. Her own research interests vary from higher education pedagogy and educational development to her doctoral work in eighteenth-century art history, and she welcomes communication from colleagues in other institutions.

Olena Orzhel
National Academy of Educational Sciences of Ukraine, Ukraine

Dr Olena Orzhel is an experienced university teacher with expertise ranging from English for special purposes to EU studies and educational reform. A significant part of her experience is linked to EU educational programmes (Tempus, later Erasmus+). Working from 2009 to 2017 as a monitoring manager on these National programmes she was exposed to the daily challenges Ukrainian universities face. She is a competent researcher: her post-doctoral research dealt with EU policies and European governance. Her current focus, as a researcher at the Institute of Higher Education of the NAES, Ukraine, is on university social responsibility, community engagement and social cohesion.

Carol O'Sullivan
Mary Immaculate College, Ireland

Dr Carol O'Sullivan is a former Head of Department and former lecturer in SPHE in Mary Immaculate College (MIC), Limerick. She is currently Course Leader of the M.Ed in Leadership of Wellbeing in Education at MIC. Her research interests include educational policy development and analysis, the implementation of the SPHE curriculum in Irish Primary Schools, Teacher Wellbeing, Citizenship Education, Innovation in Teaching, and Health Promotion in college settings. She has contributed to a number of research publications and conferences and to the development of programme materials in SPHE and Wellbeing.

Doug Parkin
AdvanceHE, UK

Doug Parkin, PFHEA, is currently Principal Adviser for Leadership and Management at Advance HE, based in the UK (formerly the Leadership Foundation for Higher Education), where he is responsible for a range of national open programmes as well as undertaking bespoke consultancy assignments for universities both in the UK and around the world. A specialist in both leadership development and educational development, Doug was previously Head of Staff and Educational Development at the London School of Hygiene and Tropical Medicine (University of London). He is also an independent author on higher education, a recognised conference speaker and a qualified executive coach.

Petia Petrova
University of the West of England, UK

Dr Petia Petrova, SFHEA, is Associate Director of Academic Practice, at the University of the West of England, Bristol. Petia has been involved in academic and educational development for the last 15 years. She has taught on postgraduate certificates in academic practice, supported those making claims and reviewed applications for HEA fellowships. Petia has taken part in, and led, research, scholarship and change initiatives in the areas of employability, research-informed teaching, academic communities, curriculum design and the development of programme leadership skills and capabilities.

Lucía Piquero Álvarez
University of Malta, Malta

Dr Lucía Piquero Álvarez trained in classical ballet and read for a BSc in Psychology in Spain. She then followed contemporary dance training at The Place, London, an MA in Choreography at Middlesex University, and completed her PhD at Roehampton University in 2019. She is currently head of the Dance Studies Department at the University of Malta. She researches embodied and enactive cognition and the experience of emotion in dance. She has presented her research and her choreographic work internationally, including several conferences, commissions, residencies, and collaborations. She has also directed several choreographic practice-as-research projects.

Stephen Powell
Manchester Metropolitan University, UK

Dr Stephen Powell, PFHEA, is Associate Head of the University Teaching Academy at Manchester Metropolitan University where he is responsible for taught provision and the UKPSF recognition scheme for academic staff. He has worked in education for over 30 years, initially as a teacher in the compulsory school sector, and then in Higher Education. He has particular experience in curriculum design and development. He has developed and managed numerous projects in higher education working with colleagues to develop new taught provision and improve institutions' educational systems and processes using action research and systems thinking approaches.

Rebecca Sanderson
University of Lincoln, UK

Rebecca Sanderson works within the Lincoln Higher Education Research Institute as an institutional researcher and evaluator for the University of Lincoln Access and Participation Plan. She supports colleagues in academic and professional service departments through providing research and evaluation of organisational development, student experience and equality and diversity projects and interventions.

Graham Scott
University of Hull, UK

Professor Graham Scott, PFHEA, NTF, is Director of the Teaching Excellence Academy at the University of Hull. He is an experienced field biologist and has taught students in the classroom and in the field for more than 25 years. His teaching excellence, innovative teaching practice and support for both his students and his peers have been recognised by the wider higher education sector. He was awarded a National Teaching Fellowship (2009), won the Ed Wood Prize (renamed as UK Higher Education Bioscience Teacher of the Year) (2010) and was recognised as a Principal Fellow of the Higher Education Academy in 2013.

Karen Theobald
Queensland University of Technology, Australia

Associate Professor Karen Theobald, PFHEA, is Academic Lead Education in the School of Nursing, the largest school in the Faculty of Health at Queensland University of Technology. Karen has extensive experience in teaching and supporting student learning across undergraduate and postgraduate nursing and allied health programs. Her leadership and passion in her work with colleagues and students, for curriculum renewal, implementation and evaluation is well recognised. Karen's research centres on nursing Workforce Preparation. She also enjoys supporting a number of higher degree students to undertake important impactful research.

Andrea S. Webb
The University of British Columbia, Canada
Dr Andrea S. Webb spent a decade as a classroom teacher and department head before returning to higher education as a teacher educator. Her research interests lie in teaching and learning in higher education and she is the co-chair and academic program director for the University of British Columbia's International Program for the Scholarship of Educational Leadership (SoEL): UBC Certificate on Curriculum and Pedagogy in Higher Education. She is actively engaged in research related to Threshold Concepts, the Scholarship of Teaching and Learning and social studies Teacher Education.

Kimberly Wilder-Davis
University of Glasgow, UK
Dr Kimberly Wilder-Davis, FHEA, is Academic and Digital Development Advisor at the University of Glasgow. She specialises in curriculum development with a focus on programmatic assessment and feedback literacy for staff and students. She is a 2019 Collaborative Award Teaching Excellence Winner and a Fellow of the Higher Education Academy.

Bethan L. Wood
University of Glasgow, UK
Dr Bethan L. Wood, FRSB, CBiol, PFHEA, is Senior Lecturer at the Dumfries Campus, University of Glasgow. She has created, and led, two degree programmes (undergraduate and postgraduate) at the School of Interdisciplinary Studies. Her research interests include employability and graduate attributes - primarily through credit-bearing placements.

Stephen Yorkstone
Edinburgh Napier University
Steven Yorkstone is an internal consultant for Edinburgh Napier University. He facilitates; convenes a community of practice; delivers consultancy, coaching and training. He authored "Lean Universities" in the Shingo Prize Winning 'Routledge Companion to Lean Management' (2016); edited 'Global Lean for Higher Education: A Themed Anthology of Case Studies, Approaches and Tools' (2019); and lead authored "Lean as a Framework for Humanisation in Higher Education" in 'Humanising Higher Education: A Positive Approach to Enhancing Wellbeing' (2020). Steve chairs Lean HE the worldwide continuous improvement community for universities, chairs the International Association of Facilitators (Scotland), and co-hosts a weekly facilitation vlog: #BærekraftigFacilitation.

Foreword

One of the foundation concepts underlying the work of the Staff and Educational Development Association (SEDA) and its predecessor organisations is the insistence that the act of teaching is susceptible of improvement. It can be studied, researched, practiced in a variety of ways, reflected upon, and is capable of contributing to scholarly endeavour. Despite encouraging words in the Robbins report of 1963, many voices were still claiming that good teachers were born, not made, and very little was done in the way of training academic staff new to teaching beyond perhaps a couple of sessions during an induction process. The assumption was that if you were an expert in your subject, you could probably teach it. In his evidence to the National Committee of Inquiry into Higher Education (the Dearing Inquiry 1997) on SEDA's behalf, David Baume asserted that students deserved more than that – they were entitled to benefit from good teaching.

In SEDA, this focus on teacher performance became one element in a wider movement to study students' experiences of learning. Even rudimentary questionnaires at the end of a course were capable of raising questions and pedagogical issues, and a developing emphasis on the evaluation of courses and modules generated fruitful research. Combined with the more thorough grounding in pedagogy that SEDA developed, in most cases leading to a post-graduate certificate in teaching and learning in higher education, significant improvements could be made to the design of modules and their practical delivery by subject experts.

But any student's experience is multi-faceted, and when practitioners studied the holistic experience of the programme for students, two features emerged as central – the notion (whether explicit or not) of the programme team, and the critical role of the programme leader. It is also these two agencies who are frequently expected to convert into practice those policies devised by institutions when responding to external and internal pressures for change. Despite this, in many institutions and many departments, this role has traditionally been considered an administrative chore of modest significance. This cannot continue.

SEDA's purpose is "Supporting and Leading Educational Change" and we are proud of the work that SEDA has done in recent years to raise the profile of the programme leader, in particular through the work of the three editors of this volume. We are sure this book will contribute to the revaluation of that most pivotal role in higher education – leading, in its full complexity, the programme of study.

James Wisdom, Series Editor, and Steve Outram,
Higher Education Consultant

List of acronyms and abbreviations

BA   Bachelor of Arts - first degree in a predominantly science field
BSc   Bachelor of Science - first degree in a predominantly arts or humanities field
HE   Higher education
HEA   Higher Education Academy

(Precursor to Advance HE - UK based Advance HE is a member-led, sector-owned charity that works with institutions and higher education across the world to improve higher education for staff, students and society.)

HEI   Higher education institution
PL   Programme leader
UKPSF   UK professional standards framework
FHEA   Fellow of the Higher Education Academy (recognition against Descriptor 2 of the UKPSF
SFHEA   Senior Fellow of the Higher Education Academy (recognition against Descriptor 3 of the UKPSF
PFHEA   Principal Fellow of the Higher Education Academy (recognition against Descriptor 4 of the UKPSF

Acknowledgements

We are grateful to all the authors who have contributed to this work for their dedication to this edition, a dedication made more impressive given we have been writing during the global COVID-19 pandemic. In a period of intense adversity, when the demands on HE leaders, educational developers and programme leaders are high our authors continued with rigour: we managed to keep to our original publishing schedule (established before the pandemic) because of their professionalism. We were heartened by the great interest shown in contributing to the book, so our thanks also goes to those whose stories we could not accommodate: we hope you found other outlets for your work.

Thank you to Kathryn Tweddle who efficiently attended to so much of the book's administration and has been an invaluable clerical support for Jenny.

Thanks must also go to the SEDA Series Associate Editors Steve Outram and James Wisdom, who have been generous and encouraging throughout, as have the SEDA community, their commitment to educational development has sustained us.

Thank you to our loved ones for giving us leave to attend to this work.

And finally we wish to celebrate with a virtual group hug our new and strengthened collaborative partnership in the face of all the travails life has thrown at us during the development and creation of this book. We couldn't have done it without each other and it is richer as a consequence.

Introduction

Supporting course and programme leaders in higher education: Positioning programme leadership as central to HE success

Jenny Lawrence, Sue Morón-García and Rowena Senior, UK

This book contributes to an emerging culture where programme leaders are recognised and rewarded for their crucial role in higher education (HE), where programme leadership is embraced as central to a successful, contemporary, academic career and where institutions invest in developing programme leaders (PLs) and programme leadership. The contributors have taken a strategic and scholarly approach that draws on the lived experience of those who work in our institutions. You will find examples of successful work by and with PLs that provide models and strategies for success.

This introduction begins with a clarification of the terminology used throughout. We then outline why this book is important and explain its genesis. Finally, we explain the structure and provide a brief guide to the contents of the three parts.

A note on terminology: Programme leaders, academic units and institutions

We use the term programme leader (PL) to denote the individual who leads a coherent programme of study, typically a named award programme, at undergraduate or postgraduate level within higher education (HE). While this is the term most commonly used for individuals doing the same or comparable roles, other terms in use are programme convenor, manager or director, academic programme manager, course leader, director of academic programmes, academic programme leaders, and academic programme directors (Mitchell, 2015).

Given the international nature of this work there is some variation in how academic units are described and the same label may have a different meaning depending on the context and the size of the institution. In many higher education institutions (HEIs), the top level academic unit would typically be a Faculty or a College, occasionally a School, and the next level down would be a School, Department or Institute. We have endeavoured to remain true to the terms used by each author and where necessary add an explanatory note.

DOI: 10.4324/9781003127413-1

We have used the term 'academic' when referring to academic staff. We have avoided using the North American term 'faculty' to avoid confusion with academic units and have changed it where necessary, for consistency's sake. We use higher education institutions (HEIs) or institutions as inclusive terms that cover the variety of HE providers, both university and college based.

Why this book is necessary

We recognised the need for this book when we each, separately, were undertaking development work in our institutional contexts and found that, although there was an emerging interest and investment in programme leaders and literature problematising the role, a comprehensive, evidence-based guide to developing both programme leaders and programme leadership (including how the role is defined, systematically supported and fits within organisational structures) was wanting.

It seemed programme leader development could easily tumble into a transactional trope, where the responsibility for the programme sits with the PL who can be 'trained' to better manage their portfolio. Note the lack of reference to organisational development, systemic or cultural change or focus on the programme leaders' academic or disciplinary expertise. This is the antithesis to the ethos of our educational development work which positions us as sensitive to the contexts in which colleagues work. We value different expertise, situated knowledge, and we work in consultation with disciplinary academics. Moreover, we believe institutions must harness the privileged perspective of PLs when working on organisational and professional development and grow PLs academic agency – that is their ability to make decisions for the benefit of their programme based on their academic expertise. We recognise that when facilitated to design and contribute to their own development the value is twofold: PLs are validated for their expertise and knowledge of the role and the context, and that expertise is harnessed to aid other PLs' development and to inform the organisational structures they inhabit. PLs involved in building the policies and practices that support the logistics of programme management are those who develop a more assertive, positive role identity, embrace programme leadership as integral to their academic career and will encourage the next generation of academics to take up the role through action and example (Lawrence, 2020b; Scott and Lawrence, 2021, Chapter 6). It is this positive 're-positioning' (Lawrence, 2021) of programme leadership we sought to guide our development work, could not find, and so set out to produce in this edition.

The programme leader in context

The role of the PL in our HEIs is complex and crucial. As HEIs seek to create distinctive programmes that draw on institutional identity and disciplinary strengths to enhance reputation in a competitive global market, the programme is one of the main units subjected to close scrutiny. Data that relate to the student experience on a programme inform university rankings and have become an integral part of student recruitment: academic attainment, retention, graduate success and feedback from programme learning experiences (which includes programme management and administration). The growing canon of Scholarship of Teaching and Learning (SoTL) also has the student experience as its central focus. Therefore, PLs have a high-stake role in their institution's standing, they interpret and lead the curriculum through the design and leadership of a programme which is, in turn, the main locus of a student's experience.

PLs have to manage the consequences of changes in funding and fluctuations in the student population whilst maintaining the integrity of the programme. A change in the regulatory environment in England, for example, took the cap off student numbers which meant some universities increased the numbers on popular programmes, but not always in a planned and well-resourced way. Conversely, if student numbers are reduced, such as is likely to happen as a result of the global pandemic (Mok et al, 2021) staff redundancies may follow. Both of these scenarios can lead to over stretching academic staff which will inevitably change the student experience. This has to be managed by the PL in order to sustain a programme that satisfies students, their university leaders and ensures that graduate-employer requirements and student ambitions for graduate success are met.

This calls for assertive and effective leadership, often from disciplinary experts with little if any leadership experience. PLs have to lead staff through times of change, create a coherent programme identity, whilst ensuring the delivery of a positive student learning experience (Ellis and Nimmo, 2018). We can testify to the crucial role of PLs in our universities' responses to the COVID-19 pandemic (2020–21). They had to affect rapid, successful change, and carry the burden of a programme's staff and students adapting to new ways of doing things (Lawrence, 2021), offering pastoral support to both. All this contributes to the much needed, affirmative 're-imagining' (Robinson-Self, 2020) of the role.

Another aspect of their leadership is the work they need to undertake with the programme stakeholders who stretch across the entire university (Moore, 2018) and disciplinary communities, including quality assurance and enhancement colleagues, registry and administrative officers, library and research officers, student support and careers services, and of course fellow academics and students. Beyond the institution there are professional, scholarly and research bodies, placement providers, employers, and validating bodies (among others identified by Chapleo & Simms, 2010). Programme leaders navigate institutional processes and are the 'linking pin' (Vilkinas and Cartan, 2015, p. 308) as they lead, manage, direct or coordinate the rich mix of colleagues who work on a programme. It is a challenge (Lefoe et al, 2013; Zutshi et al, 2013), though in a world changed by COVID-19 more institutions are beginning to recognise this vital integrative role.

This breadth of responsibility calls for an array of skills: 'administration and trouble-shooting; curriculum design; quality assurance; pastoral care; staff mentoring ... and close collaboration with academic and professional staff across the institution' (Krause et al., 2010, p. 3). Any support must start with a definitive, contextual understanding of the programme leader's complex and multi-dimensional responsibilities (Lawrence and Ellis, 2018). An integrated approach is needed to support such a wide-ranging role, the whole institution must be involved in supporting programme leaders to understand and realise their responsibilities (Moore, 2018).

Leading others, often without direct authority, is a challenge (Murphy and Curtis, 2013) and can be isolating (Cahill et al, 2015), especially for PLs who have a tenuous form of leadership that they often describe as 'responsibility without power'. Bolden et al call this 'informal leadership' (2012). Programme leadership is a unique academic hybrid that attends to the contemporary logistic and academic demands of higher learning. This is not, however, a 'third space' (Mcintosh and Nutt, 2022) or a 'new professional' (Dearing, 1997) academic-related/service career. Programme leadership is anchored firmly within the academic domain, as it typically focuses on the academic practice and administration of teaching and learning in a specific discipline.

However, you will find at least one instance in this book (Hamilton & Donaldson, Chapter 10,) where a different approach is taken; we offer this as an alternative model that may fit better in some contexts. That specific managerial approach acknowledges what we can testify to: that an effective programme manager is a boon to an academic PL. Consistent, coherent and continuing programme support is essential, especially where programme leadership is for a fixed time or where large numbers of parts/courses, students, staff and so on are involved.

The genesis of this book

This book was written at a time during which we have seen an emerging culture of recognition of the PLs' crucial role. In 2017 there was a call on the Staff and Educational Development Association (SEDA) mail list for help in creating continuing professional development (CPD) for PLs. Responses indicated many were already involved in preliminary institutional work, while others had more established approaches. This was reinforced when, in February 2018, we attended the Programme Directors CPD Symposium (called and facilitated by Rowena Senior, then at Aston University, UK). Educational developers from around thirty-five UK HEIs spent the day in discussion about the way we worked with and supported PLs in our institutions.

Interest in this symposium and a SEDA publication (Lawrence and Ellis, 2018) in preparation at the same time made it apparent that this was a significant sector-wide issue, that we had many shared challenges in understanding the scope of the role, how the mechanistic elements of programme leadership work and how PLs bring together these incredibly complex and varied elements of academic and educational leadership. It was clear HEIs (at least in the UK) were collectively increasing their investment in the role, which signalled growing recognition of the role's importance.

Shortly after the symposium the SEDA Special 'Supporting Programme Leaders and Programme Leadership' (Lawrence and Ellis, 2018) was published, in March 2018. This was the first specifically PL focussed publication of its kind and a successful series of events to share the work took place. When we came together to develop the book proposal we hoped to capture work that was underway not just nationally, but internationally. Concurrent work continued elsewhere which we contributed to, for example the Scottish Quality Assurance Agency Enhancement Theme on programme leadership (2019–20) which in 2020 became part of their Resilient Learning Communities work. The Heads of Educational Development Group (HEDG) funded a research study to create a professional development framework for PLs (Petrova, Staddon and Morón-García, in development), SEDA launched a Programme Leader Toolkit (Lawrence, 2020b) and in 2020 Advance HE funded the building of a model for programme leadership (Lawrence and Scott, 2021).

We went on to speak about our work in this field at international conferences, network events, and national development events (for example, Morón-García et al 2018; Lawrence, et al, 2018; Lawrence et al, 2019; Senior et al, 2018; Lawrence, 2020a; Lawrence, 2021a; Lawrence, Morón-García and Senior, 2021). The PL and educational development community continue to tell us that PLs need strategies and tools to enable them to feel less isolated and more valued. Most importantly there is an urgent call to develop the organisational culture of the HEIs they work in to better support and celebrate effective programme leadership.

Structure and content

The structure of the book takes into account the three different lenses through which programme leaders and their professional practice and relationships are generally viewed: the institution, the individual and the team. These make up the three parts of the book. It is worth noting that there are common themes that run through the three parts, for example the importance of the collaborative and socially-mediated spaces through which PLs gain knowledge and strength.

The chapters and case studies take a scholarly approach to PL development across a diversified, international HE sector. They include contributions from teaching- and research-focused HEIs, well-established and modern, college- and university-based providers. Contributing authors are from the northern and southern hemispheres, they are institutional leaders, educational developers and programme leaders. Our aim was that the book should be from the community, for the community. Our approach follows the tradition of 'practical wisdom' in educational development, as exemplified by bell hooks (2010): taking a critical stance to examine our world, aware that 'knowledge cannot be separated from experience' (op cit, p. 185). hooks tells us that:

> practical wisdom shows us that all genuine learning requires of us a constant open approach, a willingness to engage invention and reinvention, so that we might discover those places of radical transparency where knowledge can empower.
>
> (op cit p. 188)

We have worked with the authors to provide evidence-informed, accessible texts that focus on grounded practice which readers can adapt to their own setting. We offer approaches to defining and developing the role, and supporting individual programme leaders in educational and academic leadership. We have solicited practitioner responses for each chapter which offer a cross-cultural perspective, underpinning the global relevance of this international collection. The case studies that sit alongside the chapters in each part, are drawn from those who have programme leader experience and who have grappled with issues that may be familiar to many of our readers; they provide routes through common puzzles and examples to inspire solutions.

We hope that those who read this book will, afterwards, have a better understanding of the different aspects of programme leadership, how it can be enacted, and supported more effectively. Educational developers tend to be those who broker collaborative working between professional, administrative and academic parts of an institution in order to orchestrate coherent action and to inform the necessary development work, so you will find that community well represented, outlining how this can be effectively realised.

The three parts to the book are:

Part 1 'Institutional Development of Programme Leadership and Programme Leaders: Understanding and developing the role' in which we focus on the whole institutional approach needed to support programme leadership.
Part 2 'The Development of Individual Programme Leaders: developing leadership through experience and collaboration' in which we unpack leadership for the individual programme leader, look at how educational developers have supported these individuals and provide examples of how they have helped themselves in different contexts.
Part 3 'The Practice of Programme Leadership: Leading Programme Teams' in which we examine how successful team working has been implemented.

Each part is preceded by a brief introduction from one of the editors indicating who may find that particular part interesting, the themes or topics covered and which chapters or case studies are relevant to specific developmental tasks or activities.

Conclusion

We hope that this book will be seized upon by senior leaders from our institutions as well as educational developers and programme leaders, we have had you all in mind while editing the text and think there will be elements to appeal to you all. We hope that you will learn the importance of creating space for programme leaders to give voice to their experience in the co-creation of educational development activity and collaborative organisational development; growing programme leader academic agency; how programme leadership should be recognised and rewarded; and how important it is to look at the context in which programme leaders work. We want to challenge institutions to enact the 'investing in talent' and 'well-being' policies that so many have and to trust their disciplinary leaders to exercise their academic agency in this crucial role and to establish strategies and cultures necessary to facilitate conversations that educate those working with PLs (both as line managers and as professional and academic colleagues) about the role in order to build sustainable, successful programme leadership.

It is time to recognise programme leadership and leaders as central to the success of higher education and celebrate programme leadership as central to a successful academic career.

References

Bolden, R., et al. (2012) *Academic leadership: changing conceptions, identities and experiences in UK higher education.* London: Leadership Foundation for Higher Education (Now AdvanceHE).

Cahill, J., et al. (2015) 'An exploration of how programme leaders in higher education can be prepared and supported to discharge their roles and responsibilities effectively', *Educational Research*, 57(3), pp. 272–286. doi: /10.1080/00131881.2015.1056640.

Chapleo, C. and Simms, C. (2010) 'Stakeholder analysis in higher education', *Perspectives: Policy and Practice in Higher Education*, 14(1), pp. 12–20. doi: 10.1080/13603100903458034.

Dearing, R. (1997) 'Higher education in the learning society'. London. Available at: http://www.educationengland.org.uk/documents/dearing1997/dearing1997.html. (Accessed: December 2021)

Ellis, S. and Nimmo, A. (2018) 'Opening eyes and changing mind-sets: professional development for programme leaders', in Lawrence, J. & Ellis, S. (eds.) *Supporting programme leaders and programme leadership SEDA Special 39* London: Staff and Educational Development Association, pp. 35–39.

hooks, B. (2010) *Teaching critical thinking: practical wisdom.* New York: Routledge.

Krause, K., et al. (2010) 'Degree programme leader roles and identities in changing times', *Society for Research in Higher Education Annual Research Conference 2010.* Newport, Wales. Available at: http://hdl.handle.net/10072/38879 (Accessed: November 2021).

Lawrence, J. (2020a) 'Meaning and Motivation in a time of change: Towards a competence-based model of programme directorship/leadership', [Presentation]

University of East London, Teaching and Learning Symposium. 17th September 2020. London.

Lawrence, J. (2020b) *Supporting Programme Leaders Toolkit*. London: Staff and Educational Development Association. Available at: https://www.seda.ac.uk/membership/programme-leader-toolkit/ (Accessed November 2021)

Lawrence, J. (2021a) 'Thriving on the winds of change: programme leading across the globe.' QAAS Enhancement Themes Collaborative Cluster on Programme Leadership. [Talk] Online, January 28, 2021.

Lawrence, J. (2021b) 'Thriving on the winds of change: repositioning programme leadership as a career thriller'. QAAS Enhancement Themes Collaborative Cluster on Programme Leadership. Available at: https://www.enhancementthemes.ac.uk/docs/ethemes/resilient-learning-communities/thriving-on-the-winds-of-change.pdf?sfvrsn=57abd681_6 (Accessed: December, 2021)

Lawrence, J., et al. (2018a) '*Supporting Programme Leaders and Programme Leadership*'. [Workshop] University of Hull, 13th September.

Lawrence, J., et al. (2019) '*Supporting Programme Leaders and Programme Leadership*'. [Workshop] University of Birmingham, Birmingham. 10th March.

Lawrence, J. and Ellis, S. (eds). *Supporting Programme Leaders and Programme Leadership*. (London: Staff and Educational Development Association), SEDA Special 39, 11–14.

Lawrence, J. and Moron-Garcia, (2021) Developing sustainable programme leadership for institutional, programme and individual programme leader success. [Workshop] Online. Heads of Educational Development Group, 19th November 2021

Lawrence, J. and Scott, G. (2021) *Competence-based programme leadership*. York: Advance HE.

Lefoe, G. E., et al. (2013) 'A CLASS act: the teaching team approach to subject coordination', *Journal of University Teaching and Learning Practice*, 10(3). Available at: https://ro.uow.edu.au/jutlp/vol10/iss3/8/ (Accessed : December 2021).

Mcintosh, E. and Nutt, D. (eds.) (2021) *The impact of the integrated practitioner in higher education: Studies in third space professionalism* London: Routledge.

Mitchell, R. (2015) 'If there is a job description I don't think I've read one': a case study of programme leadership in a UK pre-1992 university', *Journal of Further and Higher Education*, 39(5), pp. 713–732. doi: 10.1080/0309877X.2014.895302.

Murphy, M. and Curtis, W. (2013). The micro-politics of micro-leadership: exploring the role of programme leader in English universities. *Journal of Higher Education Policy and Management*, 35(1), 34–44. doi: 10.1080/1360080x.2012.727707

Mok, K. H., et al. (2021) 'Impact of COVID-19 pandemic on international higher education and student mobility: Student perspectives from mainland China and Hong Kong', *International Journal of Educational Research*, 105, pp. 101718. Doi: 10.1016/j.ijer.2020.101718.

Moore, S. (2018) 'Beyond isolation: Exploring the relationality and collegiality of the programme leader role.', in Lawrence, J. & Ellis, S. (eds.) *Supporting programme leaders and programme leadership*. London: Staff and Educational Development Association, pp. 29–33.

Morón-García, S., Petrova, P. and Staddon, E. (2018) 'Towards a professional development framework for leaders of degree programmes'. [Presentation] *ISSoTL 2018: Towards a Learning Culture*. Bergen, Norway, 24th–27th October, 2018.

Robinson-Self, P. (2020) 'The practice and politics of programme leadership: between strategy and teaching', in Potter, J. & Devicci, C. (eds.) *Delivering educational change in HE*. UK: Routledge, pp. 116–126.

Scott,G and Lawrence, J. (2022) Harnessing the Potential of Formal Networks and Informal Communities to Support the Holistic Development of Programme Leaders, in Lawrence, J., Morón-García, S. & Senior, R. (eds.) *Supporting course and programme leaders in HE: Practical wisdom for leaders, educational developers and programme leaders.* London: Routledge, pp. 72–83.

Senior, R., et al. (2018) 'Supporting effective programme leadership in Higher Education: a national perspective'. *23rd Annual SEDA Conference 2018: Supporting staff to meet increasing challenges in Higher and Further Education.* Macdonald Burlington Hotel, Birmingham, 15th–16th November 2018.

Vilkinas, T. and Cartan, G. (2015) 'Navigating the turbulent waters of academia: the leadership role of programme managers', *Tertiary Education and Management*, 21(4), pp. 1–10. doi: 10.1080/13583883.2015.1082189

Zutshi, A., et al. (2013) 'Subject coordinator role and responsibility: experiences of Australian academics', *Higher Education Review*, 46(1), pp. 56–80. Available at https://dro.deakin.edu.au/eserv/DU:30060018/zutshi-subjectcoordinator-2013.pdf (Accessed: December 2021)

Part I

Institutional development of programme leadership and programme leaders

Understanding and developing the role

Introduction

Jenny Lawrence, UK

Taking a strategic, whole-institution approach to understanding and then developing the role of programme leader (PL) is crucial to PL and so institutional success. Before PLs can be supported and developed, it is crucial to understand their professional environment, the policies, processes and people they work with. As such, this section explores methods for understanding the nature of programme leadership in specific contexts, organisational development of programme leadership, methods to identify developmental needs and cross-institutional approaches to academic and professional development for PLs. Contributions written by strategic leaders and educational developers working across their institutions or sector offer detailed accounts of their work, successes and lessons learned and spotlight PLs' experience and voices. Here the importance of a comprehensive role descriptor or compendium of activity undertaken by PLs and socially mediated professional development emerge as crucial to PL success.

Institutional development of programme leadership and programme leaders will be of interest to

HE managers, educational developers or programme leaders working at a strategic level across their organisation, faculty or academic unit.

Chapter and case study relevance to specific tasks and activities

1. **Understanding programme leadership across a nation/discipline**
   Chapter 1. A National Approach: Foregrounding programme leadership in Scotland. Martha Caddell, Sam Ellis, Christine Haddow and Kimberly Wilde Davis

2. **Understanding programme leadership in your specific HEI**
   Chapter 2. Understanding and defining programme leadership in a large institution. Rachel Forsyth and Stephen Powell

3. **Defining programme leader responsibilities**
   Chapter 2. Understanding and defining programme leadership in a large institution. Rachel Forsyth and Stephen Powell

DOI: 10.4324/9781003127413-3

4. **Writing a role descriptor**
   Case Study 1. Developing a role statement for programme leadership. Louise Maddock, Samantha Carruthers, Karen van Haeringen, Helen Massa and Christopher Love

5. **Building a programme of development for programme leaders**
   Chapter 2. Understanding and defining programme leadership in a large institution. Rachel Forsyth and Stephen Powell
   Chapter 3. Developing program leadership in an Australian university: An institutional approach to professional learning and development. Louise Maddock, Samantha Carruthers and Karen van Haeringen
   Chapter 4. A collaborative and comprehensive approach to designing an institutional development for programme leaders. Petia Petrova

6. **Principles for design, delivery and update of a cross-institutional development programme**
   Chapter 4. A collaborative and comprehensive approach to designing an institutional development for programme leaders. Petia Petrova

7. **Facilitating a programme leader network**
   Chapter 5. Harnessing the potential of formal networks and informal communities to support the holistic development of programme leaders, Graham Scott and Jenny Lawrence

8. **Supporting PLs understanding of the role and managing their responsibilities**
   Case Study 2. Academic almanac: A practical workshop for programme leaders to plan the academic cycle. Juliet Eve

9. **Growing the esteem of programme leadership and the academic agency of programme leaders**
   Chapter 1. A National Approach: Foregrounding programme leadership in Scotland. Martha Caddell, Sam Ellis, Christine Haddow and Kimberly Wilde Davis
   Chapter 2. Understanding and defining programme leadership in a large institution. Rachel Forsyth and Stephen Powell
   Chapter 3. Developing program leadership in an Australian university: An institutional approach to professional learning and development. Louise Maddock, Samantha Carruthers and Karen van Haeringen
   Chapter 5. Harnessing the potential of formal networks and informal communities to support the holistic development of programme leaders. Graham Scott and Jenny Lawrence

Chapter 1

A national approach

Foregrounding programme leadership in Scotland

Martha Caddell, Sam Ellis, Christine Haddow and Kimberly Wilder-Davis, UK

Introduction

Within the institutional landscape of the university, programme leadership occupies a pivotal position between student learning, academic leadership and strategic decision-making. Yet this critically situated role is often undervalued and under-recognised (Senior, 2018), treated as a repository for the multitude of tasks that simply need to be done. While each may be vital to student support and institutional process, they are often lacking in prestige and institutional recognition (Blackmore and Kandiko, 2011). Programme leaders (PL) experience this as hidden labour, work under recognised and often unrewarded (Murphy and Curtis, 2013), with limited ring-fenced time in an already-complex workload. This labour can be sidelined and masked, particularly in discussions of staff recognition and reward, where 'programme management' may be seen as the poor relation of 'academic leadership', where research is valued over teaching.

We explore in this chapter how collaboration – at national, institutional and individual team levels – can cast a positive light on programme leadership to bring it out from the academic shadowlands. Exploring this in a multi-institutional context, in this case bringing together colleagues from across the nation of Scotland, offers opportunities for greater depth of learning among PLs, a deepening of confidence in individual and institutional decision-making and opportunities for PLs to build networks that enhance both the value and prestige of their leadership position.

This collaborative initiative is built on existing cross-sector enhancement work embedded in the Scottish university landscape – the Quality Assurance Agency Scotland's Enhancement Theme model (www.enhancementthemes.ac.uk). Our chapter explores the formation of a 'Collaborative Cluster' focused on programme leadership to bring together PLs and those responsible for enhancing institutional practice to explore key challenges including leading without authority, role confusion, working with programme-level data and a lack of role-specific opportunities for professional development. Drawing on insights from this work, the chapter highlights the multiple layers of engagement required to bring these key

DOI: 10.4324/9781003127413-4

roles into the institutional and sectoral spotlight and ensure their pivotal position in enhancing the student experience is supported and rewarded.

Specifically, our narrative explores the recognition and value associated with programme leadership, the key role such posts play in relation to the evidence landscape and the action required to enhance practice across multiple layers of intervention – from sector-wide support to the refining and reframing of individual roles. As we do so, we offer opportunities to:

a. Explore specific vignettes of practice from the frontline of programme leadership
b. Consider the importance of collaboration for developing institutional and individual conversation to initiate changed practice
c. Reflect on the value of external, multi-institutional collaboration in offering routes for recognition and reward for those in PL roles

Throughout, we reflect on the challenges associated with developing and sustaining such collaboration and highlight how even modest additional resourcing can boost prestige and practical support for PLs.

Programme leadership: Building an agenda for action in Scotland

As highlighted by Lawrence and Ellis (2018), the centrality of the role runs counter to the (limited) visibility and status it generally affords The PL role remains 'fuzzy' in nature (Mitchell, 2015), the significant variations in the role both between and within institutions, and that day-to-day leadership activities remain 'largely in the shadows' (Murphy and Curtis, 2013). This is surprising, given the linchpin role that PLs occupy in determining the coherence of the student experience and translating university policies into practice (Milburn, 2010).

Exploring the disjuncture between the pivotal institutional position of PLs and their relatively low status and esteem in Scottish institutions was a central concern as we moved forward with the Collaborative Cluster work (c.f. Cunningham and Wilder, 2019; Haddow, 2019). Working across institutions, sharing practice and a common agenda for exploration and change, we sought to identify where practical action was both possible and required. In doing so, we actively sought to reposition these roles often hidden within the institutional landscape, to positions of acknowledged and valued academic leadership.

Framing this work required a multi-layered approach, encompassing four interconnected spheres of enhancement: sectoral, institutional, programme team culture and practice and individual PL support (see Figure 1.1).

Exploring programme leadership through this lens opened space to look at the practical steps to enhance understanding of the programme leadership role, extend its visibility and introduce the everyday changes required to amplify the impact of PLs.

A national approach 17

Figure 1.1 Understanding programme leadership: Spheres of enhancement (adapted from Caddell et al., 2020a)

Colleagues from across the Scottish sector were invited to participate in a collaborative activity on programme leadership under the umbrella of the nation's wider quality enhancement activity. A culture of collaboration is strongly embedded in the Scottish sector, with its 19 universities working together on shared themes, and developing strategic and practical initiatives together with support from the Quality Assurance Agency Scotland [www.enhancementthemes.ac.uk]. This platform provided the springboard into discussion of programme leadership and the development of a shared agenda for action.

Casting light on programme leadership: The *Enhancing Programme Leadership* Collaborative Cluster

From the outset, the *Enhancing Programme Leadership* Collaborative Cluster adopted an action-learning approach, exploring and enhancing individual, institutional and sector practice through collective learning. The Cluster activity sought to create a wide span of involvement, encompassing PLs, educational developers, planners, those with responsibility for learning analytics and other relevant roles. Sharing expertise in this way enabled the group to capture the diversity of approaches taken to programme leadership across institutions, to share experience and practical resources and to identify areas for further learning and development. Its core aims were to provide a greater understanding of what the evidence for enhancement landscape looks like from a PL perspective and to strengthen the culture of sharing practice and experience of programme leadership across Scottish institutions.

Participation was by open invite, as the Cluster sought to initiate a conversation that was meaningful and adapted to the needs of a constituency that had not previously been brought together in pan-sector conversation. Over the course of four in-person workshops, online live meet-ups and the development of a virtual support network, the Cluster collaborated to map out the critical intersection between the enhancement landscape and the programme leadership domain. Three key areas were identified:

PLs and the Data Landscape

PLs identified particular challenges – and support needs – in relation to navigating the complexity of the data landscape of the university. As more data about student learning and institutional practice is produced, there is an increasing need for PLs to have skills in understanding and utilising a range of evidence. Yet programmes are also the source of information and data, a locus for filtering and communicating student voices and performance into the wider institutional structures. As Haddow notes,

> "A key challenge in using data for the purposes of enhancement is posed by the competing priorities in HEIs. PLs arguably have a number of people to appease in this context, including students, module leaders and lecturers, internal and external quality assurance bodies and university business planning teams."
>
> (2019, p. 2)

PLs have to become adept not only at engaging with evidence *for* enhancement but also in producing, negotiating and championing evidence *of* enhancement. The balancing act between institutional requirement, programme-specific insight and the day-to-day reality of skills and time pressures was identified as needing further support if PLs are to be truly enabled to use evidence for enhancement.

Reward and Recognition

A second priority interest was the sharing of insight and practice around individual and institutional perceptions of value in the PL role: where do PLs (following Blackmore and Kandiko, 2011) find motivation, recognition and professional prestige? Over the period of our work, there was evidence of programme leadership being brought 'out of the shadows', with some institutions making direct reference to such roles in promotion pathways, reframing them as part of the academic leadership landscape and even offering performance-related pay based on National Student Survey results. Alongside this sat the perceived importance of extending institutional and sectorial recognition of PLs, through high-profile activity such as the Collaborative Cluster itself.

Supporting PLs

Alongside, the move towards greater visibility is the call for enhanced practical support and guidance for PLs. In some institutions, PLs are taking a 'bottom up' approach and leading their own communities of professional development. Elsewhere, the months on either side of becoming a PL have emerged as of central importance (see also Harkin and Healy, 2013), with the intention of supporting transition in leadership and retaining as much corporate knowledge as possible. Given the mixed experience of support of Cluster participants, this formed a key area of conversation and practice sharing.

Establishing a sector-wide conversation

With a view to bringing together PLs and those responsible for enhancing institutional practice and support, the Collaborative Cluster opened space for the development of a Scotland-wide network and shared schedule of work. The core Cluster activity consisted of a series of four workshops which addressed challenges typically faced by those in the programme leadership role through a range of talks, activities and reflective discussions. The workshops were open to participants from all Higher Education Institutions (HEIs) in Scotland.

A key consideration was the practical challenge of opening space for PLs to attend sessions. Such roles are generally institution/department-facing and exceptionally busy: space and time to attend external events were challenging. As a result, Cluster events were held across the country to encourage broad participation. This enabled a diversity of attendees at each of the workshops and ensured PLs themselves were able to attend sessions at their own institutions alongside their significant on-campus commitments. The sessions were also designed to allow PLs to engage with colleagues and share expertise with collaborators from across the wider UK higher education community, with guest speakers invited to share insight from a range of perspectives.

In addition, a PL panel was convened at each of the workshop sessions. This had a dual purpose: to ensure that a diversity of PL voices informed the work of the Cluster and, critically, that PLs had the recognition of prestige of 'external' presentation and validation of their expertise. The forum consisted of PLs from a range of institutions and disciplines, with membership changing for each roundtable event. It acted as a focal point for the sharing of practice relevant to each roundtable's theme, the development of case studies and the promotion of cross-institutional collaboration. It also sought to ensure that the resources developed as a result of this Cluster's work were of practical use to PLs.

The Cluster format provided a unique opportunity to consider the relationship between planners and PLs, and how we might normalise regular dialogue between these roles. What time and space can be created for such dialogue? To what extent do institutional processes support agile enhancement? In many institutions, an annual report from a PL is considered by a committee, with little scope for feeding into broader initiatives. We therefore explored opportunities for PLs to engage in dialogue that went beyond transactional change with those responsible for enhancement initiatives.

Navigating programme-level data

Initiating a shared conversation across institutions: Focus on practical challenges

Cutting across all four workshops, and in line with the wider QAA Scotland work to which this Cluster connected, was an embedded emphasis on 'Evidence for Enhancement' and the role that PLs played as navigators and brokers of that evidence. Practice-sharing highlighted the instrumental role that PLs had in shaping and framing how student voices were engaged with, through surveys, discussions in student–staff liaison committees, and the everyday programme interactions. Their role is one that is at a critical data interface – able to engage with individual concerns, yet also in the sight of (and able to give insight into) the wider institution and strategic change agendas. The academic programme – and by extension their leaders – are then often the focus for reporting, for intervention – and for demands for change.

As King (2019) notes in her provocative think-piece, there is a risk that institutions allow the process of monitoring metrics, of developing and reporting on action plans, get in the way of authentic programme-level enhancement. Similarly, as Haddow (2019) explored, while PLs welcomed support in engaging with the available data, this was coupled with a concern that the measurement was increasingly the focus rather than the meaningful change. Such questions echoed through much of the work that followed.

> **Programme leader insight: Creating shared space and time for enhancement planning**
>
> PLs identified a practical challenge related to knowing what is expected of them when it comes to annual reporting and planning. Most institutions had regular reporting and pro-forma to be completed at the programme level, yet many felt these were done in a reporting vacuum with limited indication of what was actually required and frequently no feedback on how these reports were then received and acted upon. In addition, PLs undertook this work in isolation, with no sense of what others included in their returns.
>
> One institution highlighted the steps taken to address this through the introduction of an annual PL writing retreat. This two-day event offered PLs the opportunity to meet together, explore reporting requirements collectively. This was welcomed by participants as it offered dedicated, ring-fenced time to explore their own programme data and to write up their enhancement plans for the following year, with peer support and with a clear understanding of how others were approaching the task. Programme planning became visible, and was not an opaque, hidden paper-based exercise.

> Identifying such space in the annual institutional calendar – be that at University School/Faculty level – offers clear recognition of the significance being placed on the programme-level activity. It also opens up an identifiable event for groups across the university to come together (from planning, academic quality and learning enhancement) to actively engage in conversation with the PL community.

Suggestions for practical steps towards enhanced practice focused on supporting PLs to mediate between the diversity of student voices and the institutional data requirements. While there was a perception that such activity required 'superhero-like' abilities (Cunningham and Wilder, 2019), platforms such as student–staff liaison committees offered scope to assist in opening enhanced communication (echoing findings in Nair et al., 2011 and Jones-Devitt and LeBihan, 2018).

Creating cultures of enhancement

Developing data engagement capabilities led the Cluster into a wider discussion of strengthening cultures of enhancement at both programme and institutional levels. This requires consideration of how institutional and programme-generated evidence is utilised by programme teams and how those teams themselves function on an everyday basis. In such a context, the individual skills and capabilities of a PL interplay with the wider team culture (and vice versa), facilitating a move from a 'pseudo team' to a 'real team' that genuinely works together to advance a shared goal (West and Lyubovnikova, 2012; Senior, 2018).

> **Programme leader insight: A business improvement model for marking allocation**
>
> In sharing best practices in embedding enhancement culture within the programme team, one PL reflected on the implementation of a new approach to the equitable allocation of marking for students' research projects.
>
> The team they led worked on a large suite of programmes. The marking of students' final year projects is a significant task, the division of which has the potential to create challenges among the team. A collaborative model of allocation based on a business improvement model was implemented to ensure an equitable and mutually agreed approach. The team developed key principles to guide decision-making in the allocation of marking. They then used a quick heuristic process, involving star ratings, to identify the capacity of each individual team member, to create a practical 'best guess' allocation taking into account other responsibilities among the team.

> As the PL noted, 'Stepping outside my field and working with the University's Business Improvement Team has enhanced my leadership approach in ways I hadn't expected. It has provided me with a new perspective when approaching complex, challenging situations. The "good enough" method we developed achieved much more than a "good enough" result for the team, the programme suite and me'.
>
> Having proved an effective means of approaching marking, the team are now also exploring new collaborative marking practices, including using space creatively and blocking time to mark large pieces of work together.

Practical steps to realising the potential of 'real teams' (West and Lyubovnikova, 2012) centre on the realities of workload and associated challenges of communication, collegiality and institutional expectations in relation to recognition and reward (Wood, 2019). Pressures to demonstrate 'excellence' in specific (often individual) terms mitigated against collegiality in the teaching domain. Indeed, PLs highlighted the challenges of their role centring in practice on the managerial tasks of team time management and institutional reporting, rather than the academic leadership and creative drive that would be more fulfilling professionally and more effective in relation to the enhancement of student experience (Wilder-Davis, 2019).

Enhancing recognition, reward and practical support for programme leadership

The final thematic area explored by the Cluster focused on the formal institutional support offered to PLs. Emergent practice included a focus on defining and articulating the PL position within institutional architectures and identifying the range of tasks and responsibilities associated with the position. One institution produced an extensive checklist of all areas their PLs were expected to engage with (see Caddell et al., 2020b), totalling over 60 entries. While such an approach appeared daunting in terms of the enormity of expectation, it generated institutional appreciation of the breadth of activity and time expectations associated with the role. A further effort to link the checklist of activities to practical training and advice offered a comprehensive 'one-stop shop' to induct new PLs and support those in post to navigate the inevitable changes in university policy and procedure.

The vexed question of recognition and reward generated considerable discussion. Alongside the emergence of more tailored support for those in or considering programme leadership roles, some institutions were accelerating efforts to recognise leadership performance within promotion and recognition criteria. Indeed, one institution highlighted efforts to introduce an additional bonus payment to staff leading programmes demonstrating enhancement evidenced by NSS data, bringing full circle the discussion of data engagement, enhancement activity and appreciation of the pivotal role of the PL.

Valuing sector connections

An unforeseen outcome of our collaborative pan-Scotland approach is that the Cluster work itself has served to elevate the status of the PL role. Creating time and space to discuss the distinct experiences and needs of PLs provided important insights for planners, educational developers and others in similar roles to embed in their ongoing practice beyond the life of the Cluster.

As well as reflecting on the emerging themes, we sought to review the perceived value and impact of the Collaborative Cluster approach itself. Of the 65 participants who joined workshop discussions and contributed to the Cluster conversation, 26 individuals (40%) participated in formal evaluation exercises, through in-workshop activities and an online survey. This offered an additional snapshot into the aspects of the Cluster valued most by participants included learning how various institutions are supporting PLs, hearing directly the perspectives of fellow PLs, and gaining an insight into the national landscape (both Scotland and UK) of programme leadership.

They also reported gaining new insight and knowledge in four key areas. First, participants now better understood the breadth of PL experiences across institutions. The lack of preparedness for the role was shown to be near universal, and across the different institutions (and different *types* of institutions) represented, there was a commonality in the issues faced. One respondent reported that 'as a new PL, the fact that I know nothing [about the role] is actually quite normal'. Second, participants had a clearer understanding (counterintuitively) of the ambiguous and ill-defined nature of the PL role. Respondents had seen how this ambiguity was a feature of the role in many institutions, and how the role could sometimes be defined differently (in practice terms) in different parts of the same institution.

Third, participants had clearly gained much from sharing personal approaches to programme leadership, with these conversations bringing fresh perspectives to their own work, and confirming the need to take care of themselves as well as their programme team. Finally, respondents reported a renewed understanding (or at least confirmation) of the value in having space to engage beyond a single institution, and of the potential for esteem and recognition as a result of being involved with a national network of PLs from a variety of disciplines. Interestingly, around 40% of respondents (13) felt that their institution had supported their participation in the Cluster unequivocally; around 40% (13) felt that their participation had been supported to some extent; 20% (five) felt that their participation had not been supported.

Respondents indicated elements of their learning they had been able to apply in their own contexts. These included ideas around better preparing incoming PLs for the role (both from educational development *and* 'fellow programme leader' perspectives), coherent support and guidance packages, creating informal support networks within institutions and setting goals for programme teams. 40% of respondents (13) reported that they were now much more aware of the emerging scholarship on programme leadership, as a direct result of their engagement with the Cluster.

Finally, we invited respondents to set priorities for the year ahead. Here, responses fell broadly into two areas: data and roles. Participants were newly committed to approaching data more critically, recognising the large volume of available data, but aspiring to interrogate it in a more deliberate way. Many responses related to work on role definition, including balancing work across a team, defining roles and expectations (including across a programme team), reducing unnecessary work and bringing programme leadership 'out of the shadows'.

Moving forward

Emerging from this Cluster activity is a clear challenge: To ensure programme leadership is recognised across the university sector for the key academic enhancement role it fulfils. This requires action across multiple layers, from individual support to senior institutional and sectoral recognition and visibility. Such conversations and actions need to align and interact, ensuring efforts to define and support individuals in a challenging role are aligned with appreciation and reward for excellence in this arena. Similarly, the alignment of programme enhancement activity requires more visible exchange and dialogue with institutional process and strategic agendas: programme action is fundamental to student experience, its leaders deserve institutional and sectorial light to be shone on them.

A change agenda in this area must, we argue, extend beyond support for PLs' 'skills development'. The conversations required centre on reframing how enhancement is understood and a recognition of the multiplicity of layers, and the practical everyday conversations and communications that ensure student voice and staff engagement are acknowledged, supported and resourced. As we highlight below in an extract from our *Guide to Enhancement Conversations*, Figure 1.2, enhancing students' learning experiences requires confident, engaged and valued PLs. Strengthening their position and ensuring they have the voice, space and sense of empowerment to lead change will require a multi-layered focus and cross-institutional collaboration.

As our efforts through the Collaborative Cluster have indicated, sector-wide action can offer a route to re-valuing programme leadership. This collaboration has been facilitated in our particular context, by the history of whole sector enhancement efforts that is central to the Scottish Quality Enhancement Framework. Yet the opportunities for multi-institutional learning will be open and practically realisable in other contexts, through regional or national-level conversation. Exploring programme leadership in a collaborative, multi-institutional context offers openings for greater depth of learning, deepening of confidence in decision making and opportunities for PLs to build networks and platforms that enhance both the value and prestige of their leadership position. And, critically, it shines a spotlight on these often 'invisible superheroes' (Cunningham and Wilder, 2019), ensuring they gain recognition and support from across the wider university community. In doing so we open space to build creative collaboration, share expertise and support a culture that puts academic programmes, and the

THEMES AND QUESTIONS TO GUIDE ENHANCEMENT CONVERSATIONS

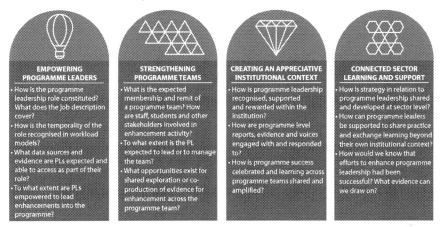

Figure 1.2 Programme leadership: A guide to enhancement conversations (adapted from Caddell et al., 2020a)

diversity of student and staff voices that converge at this level, at the heart of our approach to enhancement.

Acknowledgement

The establishment of the *Enhancing Programme Leadership* Collaborative Cluster was funded by QAA Scotland as part of the *Evidence for Enhancement* Theme that framed Scottish universities enhancement activity from 2017 to 2020. The authors gratefully acknowledge the funding and practical support offered by the QAA Scotland team during the development of this work.

References

Blackmore, P. and Kandiko, C. B. (2011). Motivation in academic life: a prestige economy. *Research in Post-Compulsory Education*, 16(4), pp. 399–411. doi: 10.1080/13596748.2011.626971

Caddell, M., Ellis, S., Haddow, C. and Wilder, K. (2020a). *Programme leadership conversations: Quick start card*. QAA Scotland. Glasgow. Available at: https://www.enhancementthemes.ac.uk/docs/ethemes/evidence-for-enhancement/programme-leadership-in-focus-quick-start-card.docx?sfvrsn=f705c881_4 (Accessed: December 2021)

Caddell, M., Ellis, S., Haddow, C. and Wilder, K. (2020b). *Evidence for enhancement: Programme leadership perspectives. A quick guide to themes and resources*. QAA Scotland. Glasgow. Available at: https://www.enhancementthemes.ac.uk/docs/ethemes/evidence-for-enhancement/a-quick-guide-to-resources.pdf?sfvrsn=3046ce81_4 (Accessed: December 2021)

Cunningham, C. and Wilder, K. (2019). *Programme Leaders as invisible superheroes of learning and teaching*. Available at: https://www.enhancementthemes.ac.uk/docs/ethemes/evidence-for-enhancement/programme-leaders-as-invisible-superheroes-of-learning-and-teaching.pdf?sfvrsn=e862c381_8 (Accessed: December 2021)

Haddow, C. (2019). *Exploring the data landscape from the PLs 'perspective*. Available at: https://www.enhancementthemes.ac.uk/docs/ethemes/evidence-for-enhancement/exploring-the-data-landscape-from-the-programme-leaders-perspective.pdf?sfvrsn=f162c381_6 (Accessed: December 2021)

Harkin, D. G. and Healy, A. H. (2013). Redefining and leading the academic discipline in Australian universities. *Australian Universities Review*, 55(2), pp. 80–92. Available at: https://issuu.com/nteu/docs/aur_55-02 and https://eprints.qut.edu.au/219579/ (Accessed: December 2021)

Jones-Devitt, S. and LeBihan, J. (2018). *Use and abuse of the student voice*. Available at: https://www.advance-he.ac.uk/knowledge-hub/use-and-abuse-student-voice

King, M. (2019). *Student surveys-process to enhancement*. Available at: https://www.enhancementthemes.ac.uk/docs/ethemes/evidence-for-enhancement/student-surveys—process-to-enhancement.pdf?sfvrsn=f062c381_8 (Accessed: December, 2021)

Lawrence, J. and Ellis, S. (eds.) (2018). *Supporting programme leaders and programme leadership*. London: Staff and Educational Development Association, SEDA Special 39.

Milburn, P. C. (2010). The role of programme directors as academic leaders. *Active Learning in Higher Education*, 11(2), pp. 87–95. doi: 10.1177/1469787410365653

Mitchell, R. (2015). 'If there is a job description I don't think I've read one': A case study of programme leadership in a UK pre-1992 university. *Journal of Further and Higher Education*, 39(5), pp. 713–732. doi: 10.1080/0309877x.2014.895302

Murphy, M. and Curtis, W. (2013). The micro-politics of micro-leadership: Exploring the role of programme leader in English universities. *Journal of Higher Education Policy and Management*, 35(1), pp. 34–44. doi: 10.1080/1360080x.2012.727707

Nair, C., Adams, P. and Mertova, P. (2011). Inclusive practice in student feedback systems. In C. S Nair and P. Mertova (eds), *Student feedback: The cornerstone to an effective quality assurance system in higher education*. Oxford: Chandos, pp. 133–142.

Senior, R. (2018). The shape of programme leadership in the contemporary university. In J. Lawrence, and S. Ellis, (eds), *Supporting programme leaders and programme leadership*. London: Staff and Educational Development Association, SEDA Special 39, pp. 11–14.

West, M. A. and Lyubovnikova, J. (2012). Real teams or pseudo teams? The changing landscape needs a better map. *Industrial and Organizational Psychology*, 5, pp. 25–55. doi: 10.1111/j.1754-9434.2011.01397.x

Wilder-Davis, K. (2019) *Creating cultures of enhancement: Programme leader or programme manager?* Available at: https://www.enhancementthemes.ac.uk/docs/ethemes/evidence-for-enhancement/thinkpiece_wilder.pdf?sfvrsn=8347ce81_2 (Accessed: December 2021)

Wood, Phil. (2019). Rethinking time in the workload debate. *Management in Education*, 33(1), pp. 86–90. doi: 10.1177/0892020618823481.

Practitioner response: Considering Canadian programme leadership

Andrea S. Webb, Canada

The leadership initiative to connect and support programme leaders (PLs) at a number of Scottish higher education institutions is particularly interesting because of the engagement with and potential impact of strategic educational leadership.

An educational leader, at the University of British Columbia (UBC), a research-intensive university in Vancouver, Canada, is a faculty member whose employment involves high stakes decisions regarding curricular and pedagogical initiatives at a departmental, faculty, or institutional level (Webb, 2020). These positions are increasingly taken by faculty members on the educational leadership stream. They too are responsible for practice (i.e., teaching), management (i.e., coordinating workloads) and leadership (i.e., curriculum development and innovation), as well as keeping abreast of current developments in their discipline, and in pedagogic practice.

Similarly, the authors characterise PLs as both programme managers and academic leaders; individuals who provide administrative support, curriculum design, quality assurance, mentoring and manage colleagues, often without direct authority. This research supports PLs' desire to devise and lead enhancements in response to data, yet many are missing the strategically aligned support at an institutional or sectorial level.

The needs of both PLs and educational leaders support the increased importance of strategically supported, institution-level educational/academic leadership, especially as these leaders are required to make significant, research-informed and evidence-based decisions around pedagogical, curricular and policy initiatives and/or changes.

Much like the recommendations from this chapter, the recommendations to develop educational leadership are similar:

a. Create institutional cultures that predispose, enable and reinforce educational leadership
b. Provide strategic supports and development programs for educational leaders (Webb, 2019)

DOI: 10.4324/9781003127413-5

Importantly, both these recommendations support building academic leadership over managerial leadership.

We need to heed the call to recognise programme leadership for the educational leadership that it offers within an institution and across the HE landscape. Within an institution, this is vital work for which PLs need to be trained and supported through mentoring, support and guidance. PLs, much like other educational leaders, need to be trusted to make evidence-informed decisions about programme curricula. A regional approach to understand and support programme leadership broadens the scope of recognition of the importance of this work and creates a landscape of practice (Wenger-Trayner et al., 2015) outside of the financial and political whims of any institution. The connection of a collaborative community engaged in sharing their experience is a major move forward in strategic, capacity building and the ongoing implementation of exceptional programmes.

References

Webb, A. S. (2019). Navigating the lows to gain new heights: Constraints to SoTL engagement. *The Canadian Journal for the Scholarship of Teaching and Learning*, 10(2). Available at: https://dx.doi.org/10.5206/cjsotl-rcacea.2019.2.8173 (Accessed: December 2021)

Webb, A.S. (2020). Riding the fourth wave: An introduction to the scholarship of teaching and learning. In R. Plews and M. Amos (Eds.). *Evidence-based faculty development through the scholarship of teaching and learning.* Hershey, PA: IGI Global, pp. 1–19. doi: 10.4018/978-1-7998-2212-7.ch001

Wenger-Trayner, E., Fenton-O'Creevy, M., Hutchinson, S., Kubiak, C. and Wenger-Trayner, B. (Eds.) (2015) *Learning in landscapes of practice: Boundaries, identity, and knowledgeability in practice-based learning.* Oxford: Routledge. pp. 13–30.

Chapter 2

Understanding and defining programme leadership in a large institution

Rachel Forsyth and Stephen Powell, UK

Introduction

Programme leadership is a contested professional space in universities. As Robinson-Self (2020, p. 119) points out, programme leaders (PLs) 'are in a position to be instigators of genuine positive change,' but he also describes the challenges of defining the role and of negotiating the potential tensions of freely adapting a programme and the constraints of institutional organisation. In the UK sector, there is some movement towards recognising such roles in relation to career progression, but it can be difficult to demonstrate success in the role in the same way that might be quantifiable for, say, research output.

As well as inevitable disciplinary differences (Becher & Trowler, 2001), programmes vary in size, complexity, level and number of stakeholders. The experiences of someone leading an undergraduate programme in a business school with 500 new students each year are difficult to compare with those of a colleague in the same role for an MA in Arts Practice with 15 students per year. Neither of these has much in common with a nurse educator assuring academic expectations alongside practice requirements and professional body accreditation. Robinson-Self (2020) also points out that the type and size of the higher education institution may also affect the expectations of the programme leadership role. These variations make it challenging to identify a single effective approach to supporting and developing PLs.

In this chapter, we explain how we have used Soft Systems Methodology (SSM) and Appreciative Inquiry to develop a process for PLs to problematise and so better understand their own situations and develop potential solutions. The work was undertaken over a ten-year period; the use of SSM provides an overarching strategic aim but allows the work to unfold in a way that is responsive to changes in organisational priorities. The overarching aims of this project were to make the role of PL both more impactful on the student experience and also more attractive to take on, providing the opportunity to develop evidence for a promotional pathway for colleagues who put their energies into educational leadership and pedagogic practice. We hope to inspire readers to use this method to understand the issues at play in their own institutions and make improvements for PLs in their given context.

DOI: 10.4324/9781003127413-6

The work was conducted in a modern UK university with around 36,000 students who may study from Foundation Year (pre-degree) to doctorate level, across around 300 programmes; about 70 of these programmes also have external professional body accreditation, with the additional requirements this may bring.

Soft systems methodology

Bringing about change to enhance teaching and learning in Higher Education Institutions (HEIs) is a difficult task, particularly where the initiative is seen as 'top down,' that is led by management (Outram & Parkin, 2020). To be effective, interventions often need to be made at different organisational levels and with very different cultures and working practices that can be found across an institution (Trowler, Fanghanel, & Wareham, 2005). A Soft Systems Methodology (SSM) is particularly well suited to complex and messy problems where there is a variety of views. SSM aims to accommodate different perspectives to identify changes that are desirable and culturally feasible (Checkland, 1985); in practical terms, this means that those concerned across an organisation may co-author and so support with the situation can get behind the proposed changes even if it is not exactly what they would choose. SSM sets out a structured process comprising five learning cycles (Figure 2.1) with supporting tools and techniques to analyse complex situations with multiple stakeholders and perspectives.

The approach illustrated in Figure 2.1 will be broadly recognised by those familiar with action research (AR) or action oriented inquiry paradigms used to bring about improvements to social situations (Guba & Lincoln, 2005; Lewin,

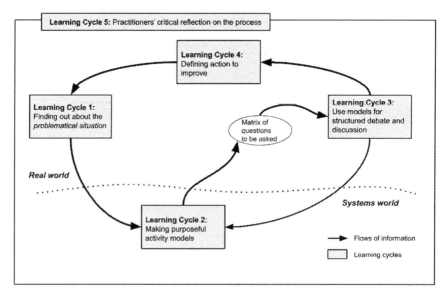

Figure 2.1 SSM cycles (after Checkland & Poulter (2006))

1948). With an AR approach, practitioners identify and find out about an issue; plan an intervention with some evaluation measures; implement the plan; and evaluate the impact through critical reflection, leading to subsequent cycles of action if required. A soft systems thinking paradigm takes this further by offering a specific way of looking at social situations which are problematical. Key elements include:

1. a clear set of distinctions about what the relevant systems are in terms of the problematical situation;
2. an articulation of the purpose of the system and what it is seeking to achieve;
3. the transformation required to achieve the purpose; and
4. indication of how the situation will be evaluated.

Characterising these steps is important, as it keeps a focus on the transformation we are seeking to achieve and the focus of our evaluation to help judge if we have been successful.

Although presented as numbered learning cycles implying a sequential process, in reality SSM practitioner activity in the different cycles will overlap. In the following sections, each learning cycle is unpacked in more detail, but first an overview is presented:

- **Learning cycle one,** it is in this cycle the practitioners find out about the problematical situation and develop a context-specific analysis. This is based on the views of key stakeholders and draws clear distinctions about what is in focus and what is not. It is in this cycle that the contribution of appreciative inquiry will be discussed;
- **Learning cycle two,** it is in this cycle the practitioners develop a 'root definition' that sets out at a high level the desired transformation brought about by the system. This then enables the development of models of purposeful activity for how the system could work in an improved way, including identified evaluation mechanisms;
- **Learning cycle three,** it is in this cycle the activity models are used for structured discussions with stakeholders supported by a matrix of questions. Through an iterative process, a single activity model is developed based on an accommodation of views between the stakeholders;
- **Learning cycle four,** it is in this cycle the actions that need to be taken to improve the situation are selected; and
- **Learning cycle five,** it is in this cycle practitioners' ongoing and conscious critical reflection to refine their thinking around the intervention takes place.

SSM provides an approach that is adaptable to different circumstances and is at its heart inclusive, with its intention to accommodate a wide range of viewpoints in arriving at defining improvement actions. Moreover, as well as an approach used to identify desirable changes at an institution level, at a more granular level it also provides an approach for colleagues seeking to bring about improvements locally in their part of the organisation – that is addressing their own problematical situation in their department or faculty context. For a practical guide to using SSM, we suggest 'Learning for Action: A Short Definitive Account of Soft Systems Methodology' (Checkland & Poulter, 2006) and emphasise that it is an approach to process, rather than a set of instructions to be slavishly followed.

In what follows, we report on research conducted in the context of a significant institutional project to improve the quality of programme data derived from the student records system (attainment and progression of groups of students) and used to support programme enhancements. SSM was used to consider how to involve PLs in the process more effectively.

Learning cycle one: Finding out about the problematical situation

Problematising the role of programme leader

The first stage of the project was to create a report that characterised the situation for PLs in the institution, providing a baseline against which we could review progress. Ethical approval was obtained from the University Research Ethics committee. Using an appreciative inquiry method (Cooperrider & Srivastva, 1987) as part of learning cycle 1, we set up focus groups to collect views of the role from a cross-section of PLs and senior managers, followed by interviews with individual PLs.

From open invitations to around 300 PLs, 28% (83) attended one of the two focus groups. Participating PLs identified a series of common concerns: clarity about expectations, responsibilities and workload allocations, and anxiety about effective prioritisation of the long lists of tasks which were expected of them. These are all issues that can be found in other published literature (Murphy & Curtis, 2013) and we have characterised this as PLs feeling as though they were nailing jelly to the wall: as soon as they felt they had mastered one part of the role, another unexpected task came their way, and whilst they were dealing with that, they lost sight of the first one.

An important outcome from this work was the collation of a list of tasks that PLs undertook across the University, and an action to provide some kind of handbook or guidance in relation to these tasks. This was a relatively straightforward project in itself. However, the persistence in the literature of PL anxiety about the nature and importance of the role despite previous identification of tasks (Johnston & Westwood, 2007) suggested that the practitioners tended to focus on these operational aspects when considering the challenges of the role. Further work was needed to develop different activity models for problematising the situation. Follow up interviews were carried out with five PLs to explore some of the issues in more detail.

As others have reported (Mitchell, 2014), our findings suggested that PLs work without formal descriptions of the role. This lack of clarity caused stress, and made delegation of tasks and succession planning particularly difficult. They often believed that institutional policies and procedures had been formulated without considering the cumulative impact of change, and that the range of stakeholders (heads of department, admissions, library, student support, programme management, assessment management, quality office, professional bodies and so on), and associated institutional processes was very difficult to keep track of.

A parallel focus group for 20 senior managers (Deans, Associate Deans and Professional Services leaders) was attached to a regular briefing session. There was a clear recognition that the role of PL is pivotal in developing a systematic approach to effective programme enhancement, and some frustration that change was slow and difficult. These senior managers were also concerned with the issue of workload allocation for PLs, and wanted clarity about setting targets for programmes, and identifying the links between key performance indicators and actions taken by PLs.

The focus groups and interviews allowed us to summarise the problematic situation using two main headings:

1. **Trying to conform to a perception of generic, normalised expectations of a programme's academic profile, management and administration. Examples of these are:**
   - Working to institutionally set targets and practices which are not contextualised to the programme;
   - University-wide, management-driven practices or policies which do not seem relevant to all programmes;
   - Tensions over targets: for instance, raising English language requirement to ensure students are equipped for their course of study and thus able to progress, which would improve one aspect of programme performance, but may also reduce the number of overseas students, when there is also an institutional target to increase them; or raising institutional entry tariffs may reduce diversity of students; or there might be a university requirement to recruit staff with PhDs when the professional body has a requirement for staff with industry experience;
   - Not enough input into admissions policy: accepting students with the right grade points, but not in the right subjects (for instance, accepting students into accounting courses without a good grade in maths)

   The challenge with this perception of standardisation is that PLs understand that their programme is individual and different, but they sometimes lack the tools and the confidence to produce a strategic plan for their own programme which addresses the expectations in a nuanced way.

2. **Staff dissatisfaction. This applies to both PLs and, as reported by PLs, members of programme teams**
   - Not having management responsibility for staff in the teaching team, which makes change management difficult (illustratively described by a participant as 'having bark, but no bite')

- Finding it difficult to develop team spirit, because not all staff teaching on the programme are available to meet; they may prioritise other activities such as research, or be associate lecturers unavailable outside teaching hours
- Feeling unable to influence academic staff recruitment, competence and capacity development
- Lack of actual career progression related to teaching or quality enhancement, even if the PL role had been promoted as integral to career progression

This problematisation moved us forward from the notion of a list of operational needs that a professional development programme would try to address, and towards a more strategic approach to supporting PLs in developing their practice to address these two areas of expectations and staff satisfaction which we articulated in the subsequent learning cycles.

Learning cycle two: Making purposeful activity models

This learning cycle move from the real world to the one of systems thinking requires the practitioners to develop a 'root definition' which captures the key elements of the activity system in focus, about which there may be different and competing views.

The root definition for this transformation could be expressed as:

Develop programme leader capabilities to manage and lead programmes as they transition into the role, by structured professional development and learning opportunities, to help PLs become more effective, and confident in expressing their teaching and learning contribution.

This definition sets out what the changes processes need to achieve through the subsequent learning cycles.

Learning cycle three: Use models for structured debate and discussion

At this stage, the work moves back into the real world, where the project team and stakeholders interrogate the proposed models and potential ways forward to try and assess which will work. Information is gathered and further analysis undertaken leading to a refinement of activity models.

Responding to the challenges identified above, we aimed to make programme leadership a successful and sought-after role in the institution, embedded within promotion pathways. To do this, we used our findings to model a better approach to supporting PLs across the institution, and to design a series of resources and activities to improve clarity around roles and expectations for programme leadership and to improve understanding among PLs, their line managers and their colleagues in programme teams. We then tested these ideas out with stakeholders before moving to a full implementation.

Learning cycle four: Defining actions to improve

This cycle completes the process of winnowing out of ideas to those which accommodate the different views of stakeholders and are thought to have a good chance of successful adoption. Implementation plans are put in place and follow the practitioners through on using the identified evaluation mechanisms to check and refine actions. These actions were organised around three strands:

1. A database of tasks, PLs might be expected to carry out.

    This provides new PLs with an overview of the operational aspects of the role and is a quick reference point for all PLs, it includes information for completing the given tasks. It is intended to streamline routine activities and in so doing free up time for more strategic work. The use of an appreciative inquiry approach meant that participants were able to describe many aspects of the role which they felt worked well and provide examples of successes; this gave a useful basis for identifying an evidence base of good practice.

    The tasks are presented on an open-access website with different options for viewing. The use of a database approach makes it easy for PLs to select those tasks which are relevant to their programmes, rather than trying to construct a single handbook which attempts to cover all possibilities. These resources are used by colleagues accessing them independently (around 6000 views per year since they were launched) and as a basis for workshop discussions hosted by the academic development unit. The tasks are regularly evaluated and updated by obtaining feedback from PLs and professional services colleagues who manage institutional processes. In a workshop context, discussion invariably turns to the different expectations about the role between different disciplines, academic levels of programmes and the number of enrolled students. These factors determine the staffing of the teaching team and the breadth of the PL role, with larger programmes offering more scope for delegation and specialisation amongst staff. This exploration of leading a programme in different situations is, we believe, an invaluable first step for an individual coming to terms with the role and beginning to take a more strategic approach in their own context. The strategic thinking is then supported by action 2, the production of programme management plans.

2. A system of structured programme management plans

    We created a set of resources to help programme teams to create plans for key aspects of programme management. These were designed to help teams to articulate the core values and to identify tasks and processes which reflect the size, level and characteristics of the programme and to help with workload allocation and delegation of tasks. These plans covered topics such as assessment, personal tutoring, technology enhanced learning and induction. They take the format of a series of questions that are designed to promote reflection on and inquiry into the particular topic as a starting point for the development of improvement plans within a teaching team. Breaking down these key activities into an action plan enables other members of the team to take on designated responsibilities with accountable outcomes, in turn giving them leadership opportunities for their own career planning. These plans are supported by resources which are designed to be tailored to individual programmes. The scope of the activities is wide ranging and requires the breadth of personal capabilities identified in Parkin's (7, p. 31) Leadership Model, that of: champion, organiser, enabler and mentor.

The plans also develop knowledge and understanding of the evidence underpinning interventions around these four core areas, which in turn increases the confidence of PLs to take decisions specific to their context.

3. Making the role more significant: raising the profile and standing of PLs across the institution

   3.1. This has involved rewriting the university's career pathway criteria so that PLs have clear opportunities to show how they have provided educational leadership and what impact this has had. The intention is that this will incentivise PL engagement in the other activities which have been developed, and provides some structure for a narrative of adding value and realising a vision for their programme.

   3.2. In a more strategic way, the Institution's work continues to promote the value of PLs and to recognise their contributions. A key development over recent years has been a step change in the reporting of key programme data and a system of annual review of programmes initiated by the central university management structures as an approach to enhancing accountability at faculty, departmental and programme level. The annual review of data related to the programme, is chaired by a senior member of the university and as part of the process, PLs are asked to develop strategic plans.

   3.3. All of the activity described above is supported by an accredited Programme Leadership module which participants can use as credit for the Postgraduate Certificate in Teaching and Learning in Higher Education or a Masters in Higher Education, or simply attend for non-accredited CPD purposes. There are two parts to the module assessment; one is a reflective account of participants in their leadership role, and the other is an improvement plan on an aspect of their programme that they have identified as requiring attention and informed by an analysis of data and work with the programme team. This work allows PLs to focus on the strategic implications of the enhancements they would like to make and how these fit with other parts of programme operation; the actions identified and evaluation approaches are rigorous in nature and grounded in data.

Learning cycle five: Critical reflection on the process

This cycle identifies a stance that we take throughout the SSM inquiry of being critically reflective, an approach that is central to all forms of action research. Over the lifetime of this project, all three actions described in Learning Cycle Four have been reviewed and updated to reflect institutional key performance indicators in relation to admissions, progression, awards and student satisfaction.

We have used a strategic institutional level theory of change to bring about institutional-wide improvements that in turn support PLs through making appropriate strategic interventions at the programme level. The project was rooted in using institutional data to enhance programmes, as measured by student satisfaction and outcomes. We can see steady improvements in these data, and an increased willingness to undertake the role of PL. For example, over the past 10 years there has been a meaningful improvement in NSS satisfaction scores on assessment and feedback (from below sector average in 2011 to 2.5% above sector average in 2020); this corresponded with a significant amount of work to improve assessment literacy (Forsyth, Cullen, Ringan, & Stubbs, 2015). PLs were at the heart of as part of the programme management planning mentioned above.

A second avenue of evaluation is that Soft Systems Methodology and Action Research/Appreciative Inquiry approaches have an inbuilt requirement to approach problems in an evaluative and reflective way: we are continuously evaluating the effectiveness of the different interventions through their many interactions with academic colleagues through workshops and other meetings. We do this by asking questions about use of the various tools developed and their role in supporting agency and autonomy, and by participating in Education Annual Reviews which look systematically at programme data admissions, progression, awards and student satisfaction. These reviews provide recognition for PLs and the opportunity for a professional dialogue with senior staff (PVC Education and Heads of Department) about the actions taken and their impact. This gives us confidence that the principle of providing PLs with tools designed for an inquiry based approach and a supportive institutional framework is an effective way of making the role of PL a more attractive one as it becomes possible to be successful in the role.

Whilst the issues we were aiming to address may have been particular to the institution, the root definition *to Develop programme leader capabilities to manage and lead programmes as they transition into the role, by structured professional development and learning opportunities, to help PLs become more effective, and confident in expressing their teaching and learning contribution* would be familiar to many. The approach described here could be adopted by PLs working individually or in communities of practice, or academic developers working centrally to address challenges which are specific to their own contexts. A key point about the SSM approach is the idea of arriving at solutions to problematic situations that are constructed by stakeholders to ensure their buy-in to proposed solutions. This is achieved by following the structure outlined in this chapter, with the development of models of how something could work to focus discussions that eventually lead to something that can be implemented, evaluated and further improved.

References

Becher, T., & Trowler, P. R. (2001). *Academic tribes and territories*. Maidenhead, SRHE/OUP.

Checkland, P. (1985). Achieving 'desirable and feasible' change: an application of soft systems methodology. *Journal of the Operational Research Society, 36*(9), 821–831. doi: 10.2307/2582171

Checkland, P., & Poulter, J. (2006). *Learning for action: a short definitive account of soft systems methodology and its use, for practitioners, teachers and students*: Chichester, John Wiley and Sons Ltd.

Cooperrider, D. (2017). The Gift of New Eyes: Personal Reflections after 30 Years of Appreciative Inquiry in Organizational Life. *Research in Organizational Change and Development, 25*, 81–142. doi: 10.1108/S0897-301620170000025003

Cooperrider, D. L., & Srivastva, S. (1987). Appreciative inquiry in organizational life. In Woodman, R. and Pasmore, W. (eds.) *Research in Organizational Change and Development*, pp. 129–169. https://doi.org/10.1108/S1475-9152(2013)0000004001

Forsyth, R., Cullen, R., Ringan, N., & Stubbs, M. (2015). Supporting the development of assessment literacy of staff through institutional process change. *London Review of Education, 13*(3), pp. 34–41. doi: 10.18546/lre.13.3.05

Guba, E., & Lincoln, Y. (2005). Paradigmatic controversies, contradictions, and emerging confluences. In N. Denzin & Y. Lincoln (Eds.), *The Sage handbook of qualitative research*. Thousand Oaks, Sage, pp. 255–286.

Johnston, V., & Westwood, J. (2007). *Academic leadership: developing a framework for the professional development of programme leaders*. London, The Higher Education Academy.

Lewin, K. (1948). *Resolving social conflicts; selected papers on group dynamics*. Oxford, England, Harper.

Mitchell, R. (2014). 'If there is a job description I don't think I've read one': a case study of programme leadership in a UK pre-1992 university. *Journal of Further and Higher Education, 39*(5), pp.1–20. doi: 10.1080/0309877X.2014.895302

Murphy, M., & Curtis, W. (2013). The micro-politics of micro-leadership: exploring the role of programme leader in English universities. *Journal of Higher Education Policy and Management, 35*(1), pp. 34–44. doi:10.1080/1360080X.2012.727707

Outram, S., & Parkin, D. (2020). A tailored undertaking: the challenge of context and culture for developing transformational leadership and change agency. In Potter, J., and Devecchi, C (Eds.) *Delivering Educational Change in Higher Education: A Transformative Approach for Leaders and Practitioners*. London, Routledge, pp. 9–19.

Parkin, D. (2017). *Leading learning and teaching in higher education: the key guide to designing and delivering courses*. London, Taylor & Francis.

Robinson-Self, P. (2020). The practice and politics of programme leadership: between strategy and teaching. In Potter, J., and Devecchi, C (Eds.) *Delivering educational change in higher education: a transformative approach for leaders and practitioners.* London, Routledge.

Trowler, P., Fanghanel, J., & Wareham, T. (2005). Freeing the chi of change: the Higher Education Academy and enhancing teaching and learning in higher education. *Studies in Higher Education*, 30(4), pp. 427–444. doi: 10.1080/03075070500160111

Practitioner response: Understanding and defining programme leadership in a South African context

Nosisana Mkonto, South Africa

In my context, Cape Peninsula University of Technology, a South African University of Technology, PLs are normally appointed without understanding what their roles and responsibilities entail. They are not inducted in the roles nor receive mentorship. They have to find their feet on their own and this causes a lot of stress. Over and above, the programme leader is expected to do the job to the best of their abilities while trying to understand the institutional policies and procedures. The approach presented by Forsyth and Powell's UK work offers a solution attractive to South African Higher Education Providers as it will help the new programme director understand their responsibilities and ability to meet them effectively and almost immediately.

The collation of the list of tasks performed by PLs with the aim of creating a database is most effective aspect of the practice discussed here. The open access database allowed the PLs to choose tasks that are relevant to their programme which will alleviate stress and anxiety for the PLs so that they can focus more on strategic duties. The fact that the database is regularly updated and evaluated based on the feedback from the PLs and other stakeholders in the institution, assists the PLs to understand their role based on their particular context. The feedback provided by the PLs can inform the institutional policies and processes pertaining to the roles and responsibilities of programme leaders, this is something PLs in South African universities would benefit from.

Institutions tend to appoint PLs without preparing them for the role and also not giving them support while they are in the role. Staff earmarked for such roles need to be mentored before assuming the roles to avoid anxiety and stress and to better prepare the PLs for such an important role. The support for PLs can be counted for career progression. The database with tasks related to the programme leader's context is a good example for adapting in my context to make the programme leadership position less stressful. The tasks undertaken and completed by the programme leader can provide evidence in the event the programme leader applies for promotion.

DOI: 10.4324/9781003127413-7

Chapter 3

Developing programme leadership in an Australian university

An institutional approach to professional learning and development

Louise Maddock, Samantha Carruthers and Karen van Haeringen, Australia

Introduction

Academic programme leadership in universities is pivotal in fulfilling the institution's purpose of offering quality educational experiences for students (Stensaker et al, 2018). Our chapter describes the *Building Program Leadership Strategy* designed and enacted at Griffith University during 2014–2018 that aimed to develop programme leadership through facilitating a coordinated, university-wide, systems-based approach to academic professional learning and organisational development. At Griffiths those that lead programmes of study are 'Programme Directors', in keeping with this edition we use the term 'programme leader' (PL) throughout. Initially, we will provide a brief overview of our institutional context, before describing the strategy, focusing particularly on the professional learning approaches and activities developed and facilitated. We will then provide the findings of our participatory action research study, and share key learnings in relation to how the strategy influenced a shift in perceptions and practices of programme leadership by individual PLs and teams, along with the valuing of programme leadership by the wider University system.

Institutional context

Griffith University is a research-intensive, multi-campus university located in South-East Queensland, Australia, and an affiliated member of the Innovative Research Universities network of Australia. Griffith fosters academic research, learning and teaching, and service to the community, through a progressive educational mission to provide contemporary approaches that enable students to make influential and meaningful contributions to society through participatory, ecologically sustainable and socially-inclusive approaches. Learning and teaching is supported by multiple levels of formal leadership roles, including Dean (Learning & Teaching) for each of the four Faculties (Groups), Heads of School/Department and Programme Leaders (responsible for the leadership and management of an academic programme). This role has evolved from a

DOI: 10.4324/9781003127413-8

Programme Convening role recognised in 2001 to that of Programme Director and outlined in Case Study 1, 'Developing a Role Statement for Programme Leadership', which follows this chapter.

Building the programme leader strategy

Building programme leadership strategy: A systems perspective for programme leadership development

A holistic, systems-based approach to building programme leadership initiated across the institution included a new role statement, key academic/educational development roles located centrally and in faculties, a new programme quality dashboard (business intelligence) and a *Framework for Programme Quality and Programme Review* policy. *Learning Futures* (the University's educational development unit) initiated the *Building Programme Leadership (BPL) Strategy*, designed to capitalise on and enhance these organisational development initiatives, recognising that PLs' influence and efficacy are affected by role conception, role clarity, role alignment, role engagement, programme environment, programme context, reward and resources (Lizzio, 2014). Hence, rather than solely focusing on the development of individuals' leadership capabilities, the *BPL Strategy* also sought to build the capacity of the University to support programme-level leadership, resulting in two concurrent aims:

1. For PL to identify themselves as leaders of learning and teaching in their context.
2. For the University Faculties, Schools/Departments and community to recognise, enable and support programme leadership and the role of programme leadership in context and more broadly.

To support these aims, we (the authors), as Senior Consultants (Learning and Teaching) in *Learning Futures*, embarked on generating a research-informed theoretical framework for the strategy and initiated collaborations with Faculty Deans (Learning & Teaching) and PLs from across the University to co-design and develop the *BPL Strategy* and its activities.

Theoretical framework of the building programme leadership strategy

A range of educational leadership literature was used to inform the *BPL Strategy*, including foci on individual leader behaviours (e.g. Bryman, 2007; Vilkinas & Ladyshewsky, 2012), shared leadership approaches (e.g. Harris & Spillane, 2008; Bolden et al, 2009; Jones et al, 2012) and leading or influencing within a complex system (e.g. Gibbs et al, 2008; Marshall et al 2011; Mårtensson et al, 2014). These foundations coupled with programme-level leadership development literature (e.g. Ladyshewsky & Flavell, 2012; Krause et al, 2012; Mårtensson & Roxå, 2016; Zuber-Skerritt & Louw, 2014) and considerations of our institutional context, led to three assumptions:

1. *Programme leadership with a purpose - Enabling context-specific learning.* How do we design a series of professional learning activities that enhance each individual's strengths and cater for diverse programme contexts? Our approach was to help PLs identify their individual, as well as shared purposes as academic leaders (Ramsden & Lizzio, 2003), explore a wide variety of theoretical perspectives on leadership (noted above) and embed practice-based experiences (Scott et al, 2008; Boud & Brew, 2013). This is aimed to enable PLs to conceptualise, describe and apply their leadership practices in their unique contexts.
2. *Developing programme leadership as well as leaders - Building a community of PLs and colleagues with collective efficacy.* How do we bring those people together to form a community who can collectively reflect on, innovate, influence and advocate for programme leadership, programmes and students? We assumed that colleagues from across the organisation, not just PLs, share a vision of transforming the student experience through our programmes. Building on transformational leadership approaches (Bass & Riggio, 2006), this process begins with creating a climate of authentic communication, where trust and collegiality is nurtured, and where new ideas are welcomed and discussed. Playing the long game of transformational change also requires being able to navigate difficult conversations that will occur at times and being comfortable with challenging emotions that some colleagues may express as part of the change process. We aimed for our colleagues to experience a learning organisation, '*where people continually expand their capacity to create the results they truly desire, where new and expansive patterns of thinking are nurtured, where collective aspiration is set free and where people are continually learning how to learn together*' (Senge, 2006, p. 1). We anticipated that these experienced ways of relating would cascade through the PL community.
3. *Programme leaders as agents of change: Creating opportunities for PLs to positively influence the system and advocate for educational transformation.* Universities possess dual hierarchical and distributed operating systems, where innovation and rapid change is best enabled by engaging a network of passionate and committed subject matter experts and advocates (Kotter, 2013). In a system where PLs are responsible for a multitude of complex tasks (including ensuring programme quality) but recognised as lacking formal authority or power (e.g. Cahill et al, 2015), scholars advise universities to support PLs in developing capabilities in 'leading change' (Scott et al, 2008) in relational and collegial ways (Marshall, 2012) to facilitate benefits for students and communities. We decided to infuse transformational change leadership practices into the strategy and chose participatory action research as a methodology to engage colleagues in the process.

The evolution of the 'Building programme leadership' strategy professional learning approaches

Using a bespoke participatory action research methodology (inspired by Kember, 2000; Zuber-Skerritt, 2011; Kemmis et al, 2013), iterative cycles of collaborative action planning, acting, observing and reflecting ensued over a four-year period (2014–2018) to facilitate the *BPL Strategy* professional learning aims and approaches.

We initiated the *BPL Strategy* with an introductory orientation (induction) session for PLs, aiming to orientate new and experienced PLs to the new role statement (Table 3.1).

A small group of motivated PLs accepted an invitation to form an PL interest group, as part of the first steps in the action research process, and in forming the foundation of the *Programme Leaders' Network (PLN)*. Subsequent ongoing collaborations with PLN members led to the co-design of a professional learning ecology (Maddock & Carruthers, 2018) (Figure 3.1) made up of activities,

Table 3.1 Role statement for programme leadership (2015): Five areas of responsibility and indicative tasks

PL Role Statement: Responsibilities	Example indicative tasks
Quality assurance and quality enhancement of programmes	Guiding the programme-level curriculum development and design process (including the relevant Industry Advisory Board) to ensure the relevance of programme design, development of programme learning outcomes, graduate attributes and employability skills of graduates
Leading and facilitating the teaching team	Facilitating collaborative discussion with key stakeholders (Course Convenors, Deans-Learning & Teaching, Deans-Academic, Head/Deputy Head of School/Department, year level advisors, Student Success Advisors, professional staff & students) towards the shared goal of providing an effective and satisfying student learning experience
Engaging with industry & profession	Developing productive relationships with the industry/profession; Managing the preparation of documentation for external accreditation/recognition of the programme by professional bodies
Student administration and progression	Making decisions to admit students to the programme; providing academic advice to students enrolled in the programme; establishing assessment plans and processes with course convenors for managing assessment tasks in first year undergraduate courses in accordance with the Standards for First Year Assessment
Managing the programme	Providing a focal communication link between the academic operation of the programme and Academic Administration, including advising on admission requirements; preparing accurate enrolment and programme information in Admission Guides

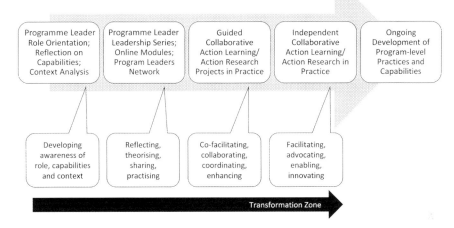

Figure 3.1 Building Programme Leadership Strategy – Professional Learning Ecology

including a *Leadership Series*, the *Network*, the *Orientation* (facilitated workshops for new-to-role or aspiring PLs which aim to explore the role and responsibilities; key policies, processes, resources and support; and where experienced PL mentors share their practice experiences), as well as, co-facilitated programme-oriented *Participatory Action Learning and/or Action Research (PALAR) Projects* with programme teams in discipline-specific sites that focused on areas of particular interest such as programme curriculum development/enhancement, developing shared programme-level resources, programme leadership development and succession planning.

Spotlight: Programme leaders' leadership series

The *Leadership Series* is a professional learning programme of workshops that were designed to support the learning and capability development of PLs and programme team members in relation to programme leadership. Offered initially face-to-face as six workshops across a semester and then alternatively as a two-day retreat experience, the series was forefronted with an introduction to programme leadership with subsequent workshops focussing on one of the five areas of responsibility outlined in a *Role Statement* (Table 3.1). The workshops were intentionally designed to incorporate relational, practice-oriented and experiential learning activities, informed by social-constructivist learning theories (e.g. Vygotsky, 1962), transformative perspectives (Kemmis et al, 2013; Zuber-Skerritt, 2011) and underpinned by relevant theoretical principles. As a result of reflecting in action with the participating PLs, the workshop content and design evolved iteratively in response to co-participant learning needs and context.

Spotlight: Programme leaders' network

The *Programme Leaders' Network* (PLN) aimed to support the development of PLs' leadership capabilities within a community of practice (Wenger, 1998) of 'like-minded' colleagues with similar interests and shared concerns, and willingness to support and encourage each other in approaching challenges and being agents of change, collaboratively and sustainably. We have facilitated monthly one-hour PLN '*Lunchbox Sessions*' in face-to-face and more recently online modes since the network commenced in 2014. Session discussion topics are informed by ideas raised by PLs during PLN workshop discussions or from practice, ensuring that the conversations are practice-based, context-specific and relevant. Depending on the topic, sessions entail opening remarks by the facilitator, followed by PLs or professional colleagues sharing their practice related to the topic, and subsequent questions and answers before closing.

Spotlight: Participatory action learning and action research projects

Participatory action learning and action research projects focusing on programme leadership and/or programme development/innovation were co-designed and facilitated with PLs and teams in their discipline-specific contexts. Key learnings from these projects have been disseminated nationally (Carruthers & Maddock, 2018; Maddock & Carruthers, 2018), and internationally (Delaney et al, 2020).

Evaluation and findings

The *Building Programme Leadership Strategy* underwent a thorough mixed-methods evaluation, collecting and analysing quantitative and qualitative data across four levels of Kirkpatrick's evaluation model (Kirkpatrick, 2006), which informed a contribution analysis (Mayne, 2012) of the underlying assumptions of the programme logic model (forthcoming). Quantitative data was analysed using descriptive statistics methods, whilst inductive thematic analysis was used to analyse qualitative data. This evaluation found that the strategy was highly successful in achieving its aims, and the strategy received an '*Excellence in Enhancing Teaching*' award from the Vice-Chancellor in 2019, based on the evaluation data and recommendations from senior leaders from across the university.

Over the four year period, the *BPL Strategy* engaged many PLs and colleagues across the university. Participation data (2014–2018) indicate there were over 988 attendances at the various professional learning activities including 606 PL attendances and 445 unique individuals engaging overall representing 59 different Schools/Departments/Centres and all four Faculty Groups.

Participants of the *Leadership Series* were invited to participate in reflective focus group discussions and individual online evaluation surveys (composed of quantitative and qualitative questions) at the conclusion of each series. Quantitative data

Table 3.2 Leadership Series evaluation survey quantitative data (2015–2018)

Year*	Number of participants in the series	Number of evaluation survey responses	Q1 Enabled me to orient myself to my learning goals	Q2 Enabled me to gain foundational knowledge of leadership for learning principles and theories	Q3 Enabled me to gain knowledge of the PL role in my current organisational context	Q4 Enabled the development of collegial relationships and networks with other PLs and colleagues
2015	34	22	N/A**	N/A**	96%	100%
2016	22	10	100%	100%	100%	100%
2017	14	7	100%	100%	100%	100%
2018	14	10	100%	100%	90%	100%
Total	84	49	100%	100%	96%	100%

*Note: 2015 & 2016 (Semester 1) facilitated as 6 individual 3-hour workshops; 2016 (Semester 2)-2018 facilitated as 2-day intensive retreat
**Note: Questions 1 and 2 were not part of the earlier version of the evaluation survey.

collected from the completed online surveys (N = 84) indicated that a very high proportion of respondents (>95%) agreed that as a result of their participation they gained a greater understanding of their PL role within the broader context (96%); gained knowledge about leadership theories and principles (100%); were able to identify their learning goals related to leadership development (100%); and were able to develop collegial relationships and networks with other PLs and colleagues (100%) (Table 3.2).

Analysis of the qualitative survey data revealed that PLs perceived a developing self-awareness and confidence with respect to understanding and enacting their leadership role, particularly related to facilitating team conversations about programme development/innovation, along with generating/optimising opportunities to influence change within their specific programme contexts and the wider university system:

> *The Leadership Series was instrumental in the ongoing development of my confidence, my capability and my identity as Program Director. This excellent grounding stood me in good stead to progress my leadership capacity in successive learning and teaching leadership roles.*
> (Dean, Learning & Teaching – former Program Leader 2016)

> *I gained some valuable insight into how I might manage and lead staff members ... I now have new strategies to use and I have a better understanding of my strengths and weaknesses in my own ability to cope with and lead change and innovation within my discipline and program.*
> (Program Leader 2015)

> *As part of my guiding coalition, I'm meeting with the Deputy Head of School, Student Success Advisors, First Year Coordinators and Honours Program Director and Program Directors of other Schools to achieve [program development emphasising career pathways for students].*
>
> (Program Leader 2015)

Key learnings

Individual and collective critical reflections (informed by Argyris & Schön, 1978; Kemmis et al, 2013; Mezirow, 1997) on the qualitative and quantitative data gathered from multiple sources throughout the enactment of the *BPL Strategy* were used to inform the iterative design, development and evaluation of the professional learning activities and experiences. It is from these reflections that we share our learnings.

On the surface, it was evident from formal and informal data gathered throughout the strategy that participant PLs gained a deeper understanding of contemporary leadership perspectives and practices and experienced a growing sense of becoming leaders of learning and teaching capable of facilitating changes or innovations within their specific context, thus meeting the broad aims of the *BPL Strategy*. Key to this evolution, were opportunities for PLs to engage in meaningful discussions and debates about leadership in higher education, sharing their experiences of programme leadership and the challenges of their circumstances, as well as, observing facilitators modelling leadership practices and practising newly acquired micro-skills with colleagues within a supportive learning environment. We have noticed that within our context that the transfer of learning related to 'programme leader as an agent of change' has taken time to become enacted in practice, however, has been assisted with a strengthening *Program Leaders' Network* and collaborative projects supported by University scholarship funding. We also observed that participant PLs would encourage fellow colleagues within their School/Department to engage with the activities, resulting in clusters of PLs who were discussing programme leadership and development.

> *I loved how the facilitators kept bringing us back to our moral purpose: students! It affirmed for me that I was on the right track, keeping student needs as my focus.*
>
> (Program Leader 2017)

In diving deeper and reflecting on the process of developing the BPL Strategy professional learning approaches, our overarching participatory action research methodology has proven to be successful in enabling the collaborative design, development and facilitation of the various professional learning activities. Through this iterative process, collegial professional relationships amongst PLs themselves and with other colleagues across the university have been established and have persisted over time through the involvement with the ongoing *Program Leaders' Network*. We found that initially these relational approaches require a great deal of guided facilitation, however, can be successfully scaffolded toward co-facilitation and then independent facilitation over time. As the process was driven by the needs and concerns of the PLs, the activities were intentionally co-designed to suit our collective and particular university context, and our role became one of supporting the PL to have influence within this system. We would recommend the use of participatory action research methodologies by others in order to support the development of context-specific professional learning activities suited to the characteristics and needs of the PL and colleagues in the site, and would encourage the inclusion of students as co-participants in this process, as was modelled in one action research project.

> *Having attended a number of activities in the suite, as well as mentoring [PL] staff, it is clear the activities have fostered a shared understanding of leadership and I have observed staff enacting leadership and feeling confident about this, which has had positive effects on staff culture. The network of support that has been generated now means that staff are able to better reflect on their leadership practice and become proactive and mindful.*
> (Head of School, former Program Leader)

In the depths, we consider why it matters that we engage in these participatory approaches with PLs. As participant observers and educators ourselves, we know the significant influence that leadership can have on learning and teaching practices, and thus, how important it becomes to recognise and support the critical leadership role that our PLs play. Over time we have had the privilege of supporting many PLs progressing towards becoming capable 'agents of change' who are 'leading with purpose' and actively 'developing their leadership practices' within their specific context and sites. We are often encouraged by their passion, enthusiasm and advocacy for creating and developing high-quality programmes that provide their students and graduates with valuable learning experiences. We are also inspired by their intentions to 'make a difference' to the lives of their students, their colleagues and the community at large, despite the many challenges they face every day. Consequently, adopting approaches that value the experiences and contributions of individual PLs, that foster inclusive and participatory collaborative processes, and that encourage connections across the university, is a worthy pursuit.

Conclusion

This chapter has presented a holistic, systems-based approach to developing programme leadership at an Australian university. Underpinned by a multi-layered theoretical framework and enacted through a participatory action research methodology, the *Building Program Leadership Strategy* has effectively enabled the creation of a professional learning ecology that supports individual PLs in developing their identities and capabilities as leaders of learning and teaching, as well as, augmenting University systems and processes that support programme leadership and PLs in their roles within discipline-specific sites and more broadly across the University. Further qualitative research inquiring into the long-term influence of PLs' engagement within professional learning ecologies on their leadership experiences and leading practices in specific sites is recommended.

Acknowledgements

We would like to kindly thank our colleague Ms Karen van Haeringen, Principal Advisor (Strategy and Innovation) of Student Life Executive at Griffith University, for providing information and documents related to the history and development of the initial Programme Convenor role statement at Griffith University.

References

Argyris, C. and Schön, D. A. (1978) *A theory of action perspective*. Reading, MA: Addison-Wesley Publishing Company.

Bass, B. M. and Riggio, R. E. (2006) *Transformational leadership*. London: Psychology Press.

Bolden, R., Petrov, G., and Gosling, J. (2009) Distributed leadership in higher education: Rhetoric and reality. *Educational Management Administration & Leadership*, 37(2), pp. 257–277. doi: 10.1177/1741143208100301

Boud, D. and Brew, A. (2013) Reconceptualising academic work as professional practice: Implications for academic development. *International Journal for Academic Development*, 18(3), pp. 208–221. doi: 10.1080/1360144X.2012.671771

Bryman, A. (2007) Effective leadership in higher education: A literature review. *Studies in Higher Education*, 32(6), pp. 693–710. doi: 10.1080/03075070701685114

Cahill, J., Bowyer, J., Rendell, C., Hammond, A., and Korek, S. (2015) An exploration of how programme leaders in higher education can be prepared and supported to discharge their roles and responsibilities effectively. *Educational Research*, 57(3), pp. 272–286. doi: 10.1080/00131881.2015.1056640

Carruthers, S. and Maddock, L. (2018) *Trees falling in forests: Evidencing leadership of learning and teaching within a system of distributed leadership*. [Roundtable discussion and presentation] Council of Australasian University Leaders in Learning and Teaching (CAULLT), Learning Leaders in Higher Education Conference.

Delaney, D., Stewart, H., Cameron, R., Cardell, E., Carruthers, S., Love, A., Pearson, A., and Calleja, P. (2020) Supporting the development of program leaders in higher education: An action research case study. *Australian Journal of Career Development*, 29(3), pp. 205–217. doi: 10.1177/1038416220927796

Gibbs, G., Knapper, C., and Piccinin, S. (2008) Disciplinary and contextually appropriate approaches to leadership of teaching in research-intensive academic departments in higher education. *Higher Education Quarterly*, 62(4), pp. 416–436, doi: 10.1111/j.1468-2273.2008.00402.x

Harris, A. and Spillane, J. (2008) Distributed leadership through the looking glass. *Management in Education*, 22(1), pp. 31–34. doi: 10.1177/0892020607085623

Jones, S., Lefoe, G., Harvey, M., and Ryland, K. (2012) Distributed leadership: A collaborative framework for academics, executives and professionals in higher education. *Journal of Higher Education Policy and Management*, 34(1), pp.67–78. doi: 10.1080/1360080x.2012.642334

Kemmis, S., McTaggart, R., and Nixon, R. (2013) *The action research planner: Doing critical participatory action research.* London: Springer Science & Business Media.

Kember, D., (2000) *Action learning and action research: Improving the quality of teaching and learning.* London: Psychology Press.

Kirkpatrick, D. L. (2006) Seven keys to unlock the four levels of evaluation. *Performance Improvement*, 45(7), pp. 5–8. doi: 10.1002/pfi.2006.4930450702

Kotter, J. P. (2013). Accelerate! (new management systems to replace traditional hierarchies and managerial processes in companies). *Human Resource Management International Digest*, 21(2), pp. 45–56. doi: 10.1108/hrmid.2013.04421baa.006

Krause, K. L., Scott, G., Campbell, S., Lizzio, A., Spencer, D., Bath, D., Fyffe, J., and Clark, J. (2012) *Developing program leader networks and resources to enhance learning and teaching in multi-campus universities.* ALTC. Available at : https://ltr.edu.au/resources/LE8_810_Krause_Report_2012.pdf (Accessed: December 2021)

Ladyshewsky, R. K. and Flavell, H. (2012) Transfer of training in an academic leadership development program for program coordinators. *Educational Management Administration & Leadership*, 40(1), pp. 127–147. doi: 10.1177/1741143211420615

Lizzio, A. (2014) *Program leadership: Yes you can! Yes you are! Yes you must!* [Presentation] Program Leaders' Network, Griffith University.

Maddock, L. and Carruthers, S. (2018) *Leading learning & teaching at the program-level: Developing practice-informed approaches for continuing professional learning.* [Paper presentation] Higher Education Services' Learning Leaders Conference, Melbourne.

Marshall, S. G. (2012) Educational middle change leadership in New Zealand: The meat in the sandwich. *International Journal of Educational Management*, 26(6), pp. 502–528. doi: 10.1108/09513541211251361

Marshall, S. J., Orrell, J., Cameron, A., Bosanquet, A., and Thomas, S. (2011) Leading and managing learning and teaching in higher education. *Higher Education Research & Development*, 30(2), pp. 87–103. doi: 10.1080/07294360.2010.512631

Mårtensson, K. and Roxå, T. (2016) Leadership at a local level–Enhancing educational development. *Educational Management Administration & Leadership*, 44(2), pp. 247–262. doi: 10.1177/1741143214549977

Mårtensson, K., Roxå, T., and Stensaker, B. (2014) From quality assurance to quality practices: An investigation of strong microcultures in teaching and learning. *Studies in Higher Education*, 39(4), pp. 534–545. doi: 10.1080/03075079.2012.709493

Mayne, J. (2012) Contribution analysis: Coming of age? *Evaluation*, 18(3), pp. 270–280. doi:/10.1177/1356389012451663

Mezirow, J. (1997) Transformative learning: Theory to practice. *New Directions for Adult and Continuing Education*, 1997(74), pp. 5–12. doi: 10.1002/ace.7401

Ramsden, P. and Lizzio, A. (2003). Learning to lead: Personal development as an academic leader. In Ramsden, P (Ed.), *Learning to lead in higher education*, London:Routledge, pp. 237–262.

Scott, G., Coates, H., and Anderson, M. (2008) *Learning leaders in times of change: Academic leadership capabilities for Australian higher education.* University of Western Sydney and Australian Council for Educational Research.

Senge, P. M. (2006) *The fifth discipline: The art and practice of the learning organization.* London: Random House.

Stensaker, B., Frolich, N., and Aamodt, P. O. (2018) Policy, perceptions, and practice: A study of educational leadership and their balancing of expectations and interests at micro-level. *Higher Education Policy,* 33, pp. 1–18. doi: 10.1057/s41307-018-0115-7

Vilkinas, T. and Ladyshewsky, R. K. (2012) Leadership behaviour and effectiveness of academic program directors in Australian universities. *Educational Management Administration & Leadership,* 40(1), pp. 109–126. doi: 10.1177/1741143211420613

Vygotsky, L. S. (1962) *Thought and language.* Cambridge: MIT press.

Wenger, E. (1998) *Communities of practice: Learning, meaning, and identity.* Cambridge: Cambridge University Press.

Zuber-Skerritt, O. (2011) *Action leadership: Towards a participatory paradigm* (Vol. 6). The Netherlands: Springer Science & Business Media.

Zuber-Skerritt, O. and Louw, I. (2014) Academic leadership development programs: A model for sustained institutional change. *Journal of Organizational Change Management,* 27(6), pp. 1008–1024. doi: 10.1108/JOCM-11-2013-0224

Practitioner response: Reviewing the programme leadership strategy in an Australian university: Could it be adapted in the Greek context?

Marianthi Karatsiori, Greece

This chapter is particularly interesting for academia in Greece, since universities in Greece do not integrate a coordinated, university-wide, systems-based approach to academic professional learning or organisational development. Though, there are synergies between different departments within a university and across universities both in Greece and in Europe (mostly via funded projects), this knowledge is not disseminated in an organised and cohesive manner to all members of the institution; the notion of a leadership strategy within and across universities is absent. Thus, this chapter offers insights about a leadership strategy that universities could implement in order to build a network of leaders that would share expertise and reflect on professional learning practices.

The *Building Program Leadership (BPL) Strategy* enacted at Griffith University during 2014–2018 resulted in re-writing the PL *Role Statement*. This new role statement became a central focus for building a strategy to support programme leadership development across the university in five distinct areas, namely, 1. quality assurance and quality enhancement, 2. leading and facilitating the teaching team, 3. engaging with industry and profession, 4. student administration and progression and 5. managing the programme. The *BPL Strategy* supported PLs and the university faculties, schools/departments to embrace their role as leaders of learning and teaching in a broader context. As a result, PLs engaged in meaningful discussions and debates about leadership in higher education, sharing their experiences of programme leadership and the challenges of their circumstances, as well as, observing facilitators modelling leadership practices and practising newly acquired micro-skills with colleagues within a supportive learning environment. In addition, the *Network* initiated expansive ways of thinking and co-facilitation practices that enabled context-specific learning and resulted in building a community of colleagues with collective efficacy.

Universities in countries that have not yet articulated a comprehensive leadership strategy could adopt the BPL strategy as it is or some parts of it. In Greece, one of the primary actions to integrate leadership with a purpose across university departments within an institution would be to lead and facilitate the teaching team. As the second area of the *Program Director Role Statement* mentions, some indicative tasks could be to facilitate collaborative discussions with key stakeholders (Course Convenors, Head of School/Department, academic staff and other professional staff and students) towards the shared goal of providing an effective and satisfying student learning experience. The other areas are implemented in Greek Universities to a certain degree. The development of a *Program Leaders' Network* within Greek Universities could also strengthen leadership skills by building a community of trust where successful professional practices, challenges and expertise could be shared. An idea would be for this Network to take place online (3–4 times per year) and be attended by all members of the Institution. During these online meetings, the new research and academic programmes could be presented, the milestones of colleagues, schools and departments could be shared, along with the challenges they may be facing.

Case study 1

Developing a role statement for programme leadership

Louise Maddock, Samantha Carruthers, Karen van Haeringen, Helen Massa and Christopher Love, Australia

With the establishment of the Australian Universities Quality Agency (AUQA) in July 2001, Griffith University reviewed its self-accrediting processes, including programme planning, approval and review. This led to the adoption of a university-wide approach to programme management, with new policies and processes endorsed by the Academic Committee in 2001. The roles and responsibilities for academic management were attributed to the Course Convenor and Programme Convenor (in the interests of clarity and to chart the evolution of the role we are here true to the titles given to the role of programme leadership at Griffith). In 2002, following consultation with the University's Teaching and Learning Excellence Committee (TLEC), Faculty Boards and Office of Human Resource Management (OHRM), Student Life staff created the *Role Statement Program Convenor*, which was approved by the Academic Committee. The 'Programme Convenor' was conceptualised as a quality assurance management role. However, in the years that followed, those undertaking the role reported a lack of specificity and representation of their leadership responsibilities, as they explain:

> *The [initial] role statement didn't necessarily capture the extent of administrative tasks and procedures required to ensure quality teaching. Program Convenors had responsibility but not necessarily the authority or administrative support. As a result, many academics viewed the Program Convenor role as additional administration workload rather than an aspirational leadership role.*
>
> **Christopher Love**

> *The [original] role statement did not reflect the multiplicity of tasks and responsibilities performed… and I believed the [University's] review [of the role statement] was the opportunity to gain recognition of the leadership role being undertake but frequently undervalued by many.*
>
> **Helen Massa**

The 2010 work of the University *Program Leaders Network* and *Reference Group* generated the establishment of a *Program Leader Task Force* (PLTF) in 2011, with two specific goals: (a) To inform the review of the 'Programme Convenor'

DOI: 10.4324/9781003127413-10

role statement and make recommendations to the Deputy Vice-Chancellor (Academic) regarding changes to the statement and associated work profiles; and (b) To provide advice on strategies for those undertaking the role to engage strategically with the requirements of the five-yearly programme review process. The Task Force included Convenors representing faculties, staff from OHRM, Centre for Learning Futures and Student Life. They revised and renamed the role statement to reflect and support current academic priorities and local needs following a comprehensive consultation process with the wider university community. The new title for those leading programmes, '*Program Director*', recognised the significant leadership orientation of the role. The launch of the new role statement was a catalyst for a long-term transformational change initiative (see Chapter 3), which aided in shifting the role in practice from being administrative, managerial and transactional to more transformational, strategic and leadership-oriented. Such role clarity and perceived organisational support emboldened those leading programmes to become more influential as leaders of learning and teaching. The University developed systematic support, such as role-based professional learning, a new role-based learning and teaching capabilities framework and defined career path and succession planning processes. These interventions were successful because of the readiness created by the collaborative consultation process. The *Role Statement Program Director* has since enabled the use of consistent language across the role's lifecycle in recruiting, creating work plans, professional learning and development, and describing the role to others.

> *I welcomed the opportunity to contribute to the Program Leaders' Task Force, ... The open and frank views expressed during PLTF discussions were a rarity, a collaborative shared and trusting environment for active and vigorous debate of differing experiences and views ... the final role statement reflected the consensus.*
>
> **Helen Massa**

> *Being invited to be part of the University Program Leaders' Network and Reference Group and Program Leader Task Force provided an opportunity to be involved in the transformation of the Program Convenor role to one of status and viewed as genuine leadership by the wider university community, and the change of name to Program Director immediately signified status.*
>
> **Christopher Love**

The most recent major review of the role statement occurred in 2018 in response to an external review of student and academic administration in the Academic Faculties. The intent of the revisions was to provide clear policy advice on the appointment process, position, responsibilities and key inter-relationships with adjunct positions directly involved in the effective delivery and quality assurance and enhancement of programs to enrich the student experience at Griffith University. This process included initial consultations with the Group Pro Vice-Chancellors, Deans (Academic) and Deans (Learning and Teaching). Changes included additions to capture the elevation of status for the position, including a stronger emphasis on the leadership dimension of the role being pivotal to driving programme innovation, student retention and graduate success.

> *The subsequent reviews and changes of the Role Statement for Program Directors reflects the ever-evolving nature of universities, with more emphasis on student success and retention, while continuing to ensure quality teaching and an excellent student experience.*
>
> Christopher Love

> *The ongoing evolution of the Program Directorship role will be strongly influenced by changing employability requirements for graduates... Further clarification and improved recognition of the actual work-loads that necessarily scaffold the essential work responsibilities and tasks performed by academic and professional staff is an increasing focus to ensure sustainability of the staff and university commitment to quality and student employability success.*
>
> Helen Massa

The current *Role Statement Program Director*, co-designed and developed over a decade with those leading programmes across the university, now forefronts the critical leadership role of these pivotal educational leaders.

Role Statement Program Director Excerpt: Broad Role

BROAD ROLE

The Program Director has a critical leadership role in learning and teaching innovation within the University. The Program Director is responsible for assuring the quality of the University's programs and in achieving the University's strategic performance expectations for learning and teaching...

 The Program Director demonstrates leadership through:

- *Designing, delivering and reviewing the program*
- *Promoting the inclusion of innovative, student-centred pedagogy*
- *Ensuring quality assurance and quality enhancement of the program, and ensuring alignment with University Learning and Teaching frameworks*
- *Facilitating and leading the program's teaching team and Program Support Team*
- *Managing the program and engaging with Group and School/Department learning and teaching professional and support services*
- *Engaging with the Industry/Profession*
- *Making decisions on student admission and progression*
- *Monitoring student engagement, retention and graduate outcomes and addressing any identified deficiencies or issues*

The role statement document also provides context-setting introductory sections (scope, definitions, appointment), identifies four role responsibilities (leading the program; quality assurance and quality enhancement; engaging with industry/profession; student administration and progression) and associated practice-based and action-oriented activities, as illustrated below.

Role Statement Program Director Excerpt: Detailed Responsibilities

DETAILED RESPONSIBILITIES (SECTION 6)

The Program Director, is a critical leadership role, which, under the direction of the Head of School or their delegate, has responsibility for the following:

6.1. *Leading the Program*
- *Seeking insights into the performance of the programme and overseeing its quality and management*
- *Guiding student support and the management of students within the programme or the programme cluster through engagement with the Programme Support Team*
- *Being the focal communication link between the academic operation for the programme and Student Life …*

6.2. *Quality Assurance and Quality Enhancement of Programs*
- *Programme Development:*
  - *Guiding the program-level curriculum development and design process, including student assessment, learning and teaching approaches, in collaboration with the Programme Support Team*
  - *Producing a New Programme Proposal which is the curriculum design document, described in the Programme Approval and Review policy in collaboration with the Programme Support Team*
  - *Aligning the programme development with Griffith University's strategic priorities …*

Consequently, the role statement has not only provided guidance for everyday programme leadership practice, it has also served as a common reference point for critical discussions about programme leadership within the University community, its importance and value, and how to intentionally best support and resource the role to facilitate sustainable educational practices that beneficently influence student learning and graduate outcomes. Programme leaders explain:

> *The success of the redevelopment is the clarity of the requirements of the Program Director role and the need to adapt to the various program contexts across the university. Leadership and transformative change are central tenets of the role and recognition of the critical importance of Program Directors in monitoring, designing and actioning program change to meet community, employer and professional accreditation.*
>
> **Helen Massa**

> *My personal view is that the role of Program Directors is now viewed by academics and University executives as a significant leadership role, with a high-level of status and responsibility.*
>
> **Christopher Love**

Chapter 4

A collaborative and comprehensive approach to designing a cross-institutional development programme for programme leaders

Petia Petrova, UK

Introduction

HE today is in an age of constant change (Barnett, 2000), and the Programme Leader (PL) role is key in absorbing this change 'often at short notice and with severe impact, and unpredictable emergent outcomes' (Vilkinas and Cartan, 2015, p. 213). The PL role is pivotal for ensuring high-quality student experience in this environment (Cahill et al., 2015, Murphy and Curtis, 2013), working at the intersection between institutional functions and departments (Cahill et al., 2015; Milburn 2010; Vilkinas and Cartan; 2015). Recognising this, HE institutions have begun to focus on how best to support PLs in their roles (Senior, 2018), with PL staff development programmes becoming more common across the sector (Senior et al., 2018).

This chapter argues that staff development for PLs need to respond to the complexity of the role and should be comprehensive, as the PL role is increasingly wide-reaching. This chapter outlines a cross-institutional Programme Leader Development Programme (henceforth, PLDP), the ethos and approach to the development of this programme and the design principles adopted in creating PL-centred workshops. Participant evaluations are embedded throughout, demonstrating how the ethos of the programme and the workshop design principles are reflected in the experiences of the programme participants.

Context

The University of the West of England – Bristol (UWE) is a large institution with over 30,000 students. It has 4,000 staff employed across four faculties and fifteen professional services departments (UWE, 2020).

In 2018, UWE PLs had access to support opportunities offered by faculties (in the form of regular PL away days and meetings between PLs and key faculty/department academic leads). Staff development opportunities were also offered to all staff by the institutional Learning Development Centre. Additionally, many professional services departments offered bespoke workshops and support,

DOI: 10.4324/9781003127413-11

delivered to PLs locally, within faculties and departments. In 2018, UWE adopted an Enhancement Framework (EF) for academic programmes and practice. EF workshops were also delivered, bespoke to programme teams, to develop relevant expertise around curriculum design.

It became apparent that PLs would benefit from an integrated professional development programme, embedded as part of the academic development portfolio of the institution and drawing on existing practices. The programme was developed over the 2018–19 academic year, launched in the spring of 2019 and is now an established institutional offer. This chapter shares insights from the approach taken to design this programme. The collaborative and integrative ethos underpinning the programme, together with key design principles of its constituent PL workshops, are fundamental to the success of the programme.

Designing an institutional Programme Leader Development Programme

The UWE PLDP is comprehensive – in breadth as well as depth. The PLDP design recognized the need for high-quality support for PLs (Senior, 2018), reflecting the boundary-spanning nature of the role (Mitchell, 2015) that requires developing expertise in a number of areas of practice (Lawrence and Ellis, 2018). It recognizes the importance of offering leadership development (Milburn 2010; Mitchell, 2015; Murphy and Curtis, 2013;Vilkinas and Cartan, 2015), environment scanning (Vilkinas and Cartan, 2015) and change management skills (Milburn, 2010). The programme design recognizes the role confusion and bureaucratic burdens experienced by PLs (Murphy and Curtis, 2013), the need for PLs to balance administration, management and leadership duties (Mitchell 2015). And, as much of the role includes curriculum design and management (Milburn, 2010; Mitchell, 2015, O'Neill, 2015, Senior 2018), PLDP is designed to offer relevant support in these areas. PLs often come to know their role informally, therefore articulating institutional expectations is important (Mitchell, 2015). The UWE PLDP was designed to introduce PLs more formally to their role and reduce the uncertainty about the role often experienced by PLs (Vilkinas and Cartan, 2015). PLDP includes the following groups of workshops:

Essential workshops for PL:

- Introduction to the PL Role
- Effective Curriculum Design
- Inclusivity, Widening Participation and Awarding Gap
- Promoting Student Well-Being
- Academic Leadership for PLs
- PL Data – what do you need to know?

Workshops for enhancing programmes and modules (also open to Module Leaders [MLs]):

- Professional Development and Employability
- Designing Effective Assessment and Feedback Strategies
- Creating Meaningful Learning Outcomes

The PLDP recognizes the complexity of the role and that expertise is required in a number of key areas, offering a range of relevant workshops as 'formalised CPD' (King, 2004). The Programme draws on examples from across the sector. Many of these focus on specific aspects of the role. These include the work of Ellis and Nimmo (2018) on the topic of leadership and personal effectiveness; Whitfield and Hartley (2018) on assessment challenges; Quinlan and Gantogtokh (2018) on lessons learned from designing new interdisciplinary programmes, highlighting the leading role of PLs in programme design, developing module learning outcomes, assessment and feedback. Additionally, the design of the PLDP was informed by a parallel longitudinal research study by Morón-García et al. (2018).

PLDP sees expertise as a continuous process of learning and development that begins early in taking up a role, but can also extend into one's career (King, 2019). Hence, the programme was designed for early career PLs, about to become a PL, still learning about the role and more experienced PLs who may wish to update their expertise or enhance their programmes of study.

The PLDP recognizes the boundary-spanning nature of the PL role, and is boundary spanning itself. The design and delivery of the programme brings together key UWE experts from faculties and professional services. Thus, institutional expertise is shared and collective institutional expertise built.

To create this boundary-spanning, collaborative programme, a series of institutional consultative workshops and meetings with PLs and key stakeholders were held. These included heads of department, faculty academic leaders and those already involved in supporting PLs from the faculties and professional services. This process also helped identify key institutional experts to lead workshops or contribute to the programme. Workshop leads have responsibility for a workshop, whereas each workshop may include a number of contributors who offer expertise to relevant segments of a workshop (henceforth, both workshop leads and contributors are referred to as contributors). In total, there were 25 members of staff who contributed to the design and delivery of PLDP workshops. To ensure a shared ethos, vision and approach, a set of design principles were drawn which all contributing to the programme adhered to. These principles are useful for those devising or delivering a cross-institutional development programme for PLs and are outlined in this chapter.

Continuous enhancement

The constantly changing institutional practices in the HE context, together with new published research (on workshop topics), required a continuous process of updating the PLDP. To ensure any development programme remains relevant, continuous evaluation is also required (Ramsden, 2003). Evaluation surveys are sent to workshop participants and contributors, ensuring that reflections from all members of the workshop community are captured, considered and addressed.

> I have gained confidence to deliver the workshop more effectively as it has been revised after each run. (contributor)

The workshops are designed to allow for learning that can be easily transferred and applied to practice. The evaluation surveys capture perceptions of usefulness (via a five-point scale) and open questions on (1) what participants have gained from a workshop, (2) what are they going to do next, (3) what can be commended, (4) improved and (5) if any further topics should be offered.

The programme encourages participants to be 'co-creators' (Bovill, 2017). For example, during the first COVID-19 lockdown (in the spring of 2020), participants requested an in-depth conversation about remote teaching design. This was to help with their own teaching, but also allowed us to reflect further on the remote delivery of the PLDP.

Programme in numbers

In the pilot year (2018–19), the PLDP registered 175 workshop attendances, and in 2019–20 there were 1. Reflecting the high pressure on staff time posed by the challenges of COVID-19 and the move to remote teaching, over the 2020–21 period, there were 58 attendances (until February 2021) and further 76 bookings to date for forthcoming workshops (February to June 2021). All 2020–21 workshops were delivered remotely. Overall evaluation score has held consistent at around 80% of participants rating the workshops either 'very' or 'extremely useful'.

In 2020, the PLDP was expanded to offer workshops to MLs. Two essential workshops were introduced in 2019/20 academic year: 'Introduction to the ML Role' and 'Effective Curriculum Design for MLs'. A further one, 'Inclusivity, Widening Participation and Awarding Gap for MLs', was introduced in 2020/21. These workshops are excluded from the numbers presented here.

Workshop design principles

The PLDP offers 'learning processes at or near the workplace' (Eraut, 2009). It encourages and supports 'learning activities located within work/learning processes' (Eraut, 2009), such as asking questions, getting information. Workshops offer opportunities for peer review, feedback and input as well as guidance and affirmation from workshop contributors. Workshops use 'mediating artefacts' (Eraut, 2009), such as a programme/module specification forms, and offer opportunities for 'self-evaluation', encouraging PLs disposition to learn and improve practice (Eraut, 2009). The workshops are formalized CPD opportunities, structured to create spaces for less formalized CPD activities such as professional interactions, networking, consulting experts and learning by doing (for discussion of the formalized and less formalized aspects of PD see King, 2004).

> Useful examples that spoke to our experience as PLs, plus time and care given to discussion and feedback in the room. (PL, 1–3 years in role, feedback on Promoting Student Well-Being workshop)

The principles that underpin the programme's successful workshop design are outlined below:

1. **Make workshops relevant to individuals**
   A dynamic learning space responds to participant needs (Ramsden, 2003). The PLDP recognizes that PLs have a vast array of backgrounds and experiences, and thus their learning needs may vary. Upon booking, PLs are asked to describe what they hope to gain from attending and years of experience in role. Contributors review the answers and consider how they may best respond to the needs of those attending.

   > Good range of activities and light touch approach. Pitched appropriately for Programme Leaders, so that we were able to focus on development, rather than being told things we already know (and do). (PL, 1–3 years in role, feedback on Promoting Student Well-Being workshop)

   This places the needs of PLs at the heart of the workshop and supports PLs to learn what is appropriate to them (a key benefit from student-centred approaches to learning – see Edwards, 2001):

   > I was particularly impressed by how the workshop leaders 'rolled with' the shared learning experience of the participants. As the workshop progressed it had a structure but was allowed to deviate from this to cater with questions and shared experiences. When we discussed around subjects workshop leaders scaffolded and supported participants, and we found ourselves organically covering content of the workshop along the way though dialogic exchange. (PL, less than one year in role, feedback to Designing Effective Assessment and Feedback Strategies workshop)

   Workshops create space for discussions that surface PLs values and priorities. These often 'motivate academics, to engage, or turn away' (Åkerlind and McAlpine, 2010, p. 161) and influence how academics choose to employ their responsibilities, skills and knowledge (Åkerlind and McAlpine, 2010). Thus, supporting PLs to recognize their own values is important to maintain their motivation and engagement with the role.

   > Renewed enthusiasm. Better understanding of the importance of some aspects of the role. (PL, over three years in role, feedback to Academic Leadership for PLs workshop)

Workshops surface PLs key objectives, what they hoped to achieve in the role and their own 'principled personal projects' (Clegg, 2008, p. 343). Academics have agency through the act of prioritising (Billot, 2010), and that only through surfacing their aspirations for the role, prioritising can take place and hence motivation for sustained engagement with the role:

> I think I have a clearer understanding of the scope of the role, so this should have an impact on how I may manage my time in the future. (PL, less than one year in role, feedback to Introduction to the PL Role workshop)

2. **Design workshops as spaces for professional reflection**
   To facilitate learning from experience, time needs to be set aside for reflection on experiences and for learning from each other (Eraut, 2009). Recognising the importance of reflection to professional development (Eraut, 2009; Schön, 1983) and in the learning process (Dewey, 1916), the workshops provide time and space to reflect. Activities encourage PLs reflect upon their own practice, sharing issues to be resolved with the group:

> Space to reflect. Seeing the leadership role as potential. (PL, over three years in role, feedback to Academic Leadership for PLs workshop)

The workshops facilitate consideration of how learning can impact PLs' practice (a learning process in itself, according to Eraut, 2009). This allows participants to think explicitly about their next practical steps:

> As a very new program leader I am keen to build in a roadmap for myself and my wider team with regular updates and actions. (PL, less than one year in role, feedback to Inclusivity, Widening Participation and Awarding Gap workshop)

3. **Create opportunities for experiences to be shared**
   For some, becoming a PL can be part of the transformation from early career to an experienced academic (Åkerlind and McAlpine, 2010). It requires the development of new knowledge, skills and values (Gardner and Willey, 2016). PLs work in a 'turbulent environment' (Williams, 2014) that may result in past expertise losing currency and may demand new expertise. In some cases, the most important thing a workshop may achieve maybe allowing space for PLs to re-conceptualize their own role and responsibility and to reflect with others in similar roles on their experiences.

   The interactivity of the workshops facilitates learning and application 'within the context of the workplace' (Eraut, 2009): asking questions is encouraged and so is listening, observing and learning from the mistakes and wisdom of others. The workshops are spaces for frank exchange of ideas, experiences and practices, and of learning though, and with each other (see Eraut, 2009):

> The opportunity to meet other PL's and discuss challenges and best practice. (PL, less than one year in role, feedback to Introduction to the PL Role workshop)

PLs need to and benefit from having time and space to share experience with colleagues (Cahill et al., 2015; Ellis and Nimmo, 2018), and peer support activities help PLs 'to reflect on, and clarify their role, share practices' (Mitchell 2015, p. 731):

> Better understanding of the PL role. Time to reflect on some of the responsibilities it entails. (PL, more than three years in role, feedback to Academic Leadership for PLs workshop)

PLDP workshops create CPD opportunities that allow 'for interactions between academics within departments, between different disciplines (.) and between all those who teach and support learning' (King, 2004, p. 5). Developing an understanding of local context and working practices is key to developing a professional's occupational capacity (Winch, 2015). Workshops invite PLs to share practices and experiences across teams, departments and faculties while clearly highlighting what is considered good practice (by the sector or the institution).

4. **Ensure everyone's expertise is welcomed**

Learning in a community of practice (Lave and Wenger, 1991) is identified by Eraut (2009) as one of the key learning trajectories for early career professionals in the workplace. Workshops adopt a dialogic approach and embed 'peer teaching' (Ramsden, 2003). Drawing on ideas from Moore (2018), PLDP workshops offer spaces for learning from all experts, be it workshop contributors or participants. Workshops are designed to create an open scholarly community (Brew, 2006), where it is acknowledged that all have something to contribute and each workshop is enriched by its participants. The workshops' design creates space to surface and draw on participant expertise (i.e. cognate research area, past involvement in relevant educational enhancement projects). It is recognised that engaging in 'supportive dialogue, collaborating and questioning' (Moore, 2018, p. 29) is beneficial and can create conditions for sharing expertise and developing a sense of collective ownership (ibid). In doing so, workshops become spaces for building a community of practice of PLs:

> It was good to learn from other Programme Leaders. (PL, less than one year in role, feedback to Promoting Student Well-Being workshop)

5. **Focus on what is most important**

A PL role is characterised by its complexity (Cahill et al., 2015; Murphy and Curtis, 2013; Senior 2018). PLs often experience uncertainty about the role (Vilkinas and Cartan, 2015). PLDP workshops are designed to demystify the role, what is expected of PLs and what on the vast array of relevant literature and scholarship to focus on. Contributors consider what is key – what *all* PLs need to be aware of, able to do, know about. Contributors ensure that there is clarity about the topic, key literature that underpins it and the institutional practices related to it:

> A good overview of the services available and how to access them. (PL, 1–3 years in role, feedback to Promoting Student Well-Being workshop)

Workshops establish a shared understanding and appreciation; they offer synthesis, coherency and comprehensiveness in relation to the workshop topic. Then focus on what would help PLs engage with the topic further and transform learning to practice: signpost to further training, institutional guidance/regulations, academic literature, good practice guides and empowering PLs to pursue areas they have identified as important to them and their programmes:

> Really useful signposting to tools and information that will be useful. (PL, less than one year in role, feedback to PL Data workshop)

6. **Be grounded in scholarship**
Learning from publications is a source of key professional knowledge (Eraut, 2009). Workshops offer opportunity to engage with relevant literature: key academic concepts, theories and theorists that underpin assumptions and practice around the workshop topic. Some of this is shared in advance of the session as pre-reading and some are signposted as further reading.

Systematic, professional knowledge based in the literature underpins and empowers professional judgement (Winch, 2015). Workshops orient PLs to key scholarship and ideas that can inform their practice or further engagement with scholarship as a result of the workshops:

> The theoretical background was really helpful, again to help me structure my thinking. (PL, more than three years in role, feedback to Academic Leadership for PLs workshop)

7. **Influence institutional practice**
Asking questions and getting information from their superiors are key areas of practice early career professionals need to develop (Eraut, 2009). Workshop contributors are often key institutional stakeholders and experts representing departments that lead the work on well-being, inclusivity and data, among others. Contributors include senior managers (Deputy Vice Chancellor, Head of Student and Academic Services) and faculty leaders (such as faculty Academic Directors). The involvement of such colleagues, importantly, demonstrates institutional acknowledgement of the importance and value of the PL role:

> Access to members of senior management who take the time to attend. (PL, less than one year in role, feedback to Introduction to the PL Role workshop)

Workshops are specifically designed as spaces where PLs can share experiences, ask questions and pose problems directly relevant to their role and the roles of the workshop contributors. Workshop design thus allows for some of the many obstacles PLs experience as a result of institutional practices (Murphy and Curtis, 2013) to be surfaced and brought directly to the attention of key stakeholders. This, in turn, helps contributors develop a fuller awareness of the PL's lived experiences and work challenges:

> opened my eyes to their reality and helped me 'walk in their shoes' in order to then adapt/inform [our department's] approaches to their challenges. I appreciated the opportunity to get closer to the academic staff/student-facing experiences [of this work].
>
> (Contributor)

Conclusion

This chapter outlined the PLDP ethos and PLDP workshops' design principles. It offers an approach to designing a PLDP that can be considered and adopted by other HEIs. Interspersed throughout the chapter were quotes from workshop participants and contributors showcasing how the design principles are reflected in their experiences and learning from these workshops. It is argued that although focussed development initiatives on key aspects of the PL role can be beneficial for PLs, the complexity of the PL role requires a collaborative and comprehensive approach to designing development for PLs that brings the whole institution together. Only then can the workshops support the need for clarity in the role and the development of the wide-ranging expertise that the role requires.

References

Åkerlind, G. S., and McAlpine, L. (2010) Rethinking preparation for academic careers. In L. McAlpine and G. S. Åkerlind (eds), *Becoming an Academic: International Perspectives*. Basingstoke, Hampshire: Palgrave Macmillen.

Barnett, R. (2000) University knowledge in an age of supercomplexity. *Higher Education*, 40, pp. 409–422. doi: 10.1023/A:1004159513741

Billot, J. (2010) The imagined and the real: identifying the tensions for academic identity. *Higher Education Research and Development*, 29(6), pp. 709–721. doi: 10.1080/07294360.2010.487201

Bovill, C. (2017) A framework to explore roles within student-staff partnerships in Higher Education: which students are partners, when, and in what ways? *International Journal for Students as Partners*, 1(1), pp. 1–5. Available at:https://mulpress.mcmaster.ca/ijsap/article/download/3062/2770 (Accessed: December 2021)

Brew, A. (2006) *Research and Teaching: Beyond the Divide*. New York: Palgrave Macmillan.

Cahill, J., Bowyer, J., Rendell, C., Hammond, A., and Korek, S. (2015) An exploration of how programme leaders in higher education can be prepared and supported to discharge their roles and responsibilities effectively. *Educational Research*, 57(3), pp. 272–286. doi: 10.1080/00131881.2015.1056640

Clegg, S. (2008) Academic identities under threat? *British Educational Research Journal*, 34(3), pp. 329–345. doi: 10.1080/01411920701532269

Dewey, J. (1916) *Democracy and Education*. New York: The Macmillan Company.

Edwards, R. (2001) Meeting individual learner needs: power, subject, subjection. In Paechter, C., Preedy, M., Scott, D., and Soler, J. (eds), *Knowledge, Power and Learning*. London: SAGE.

Ellis, S. and Nimmo, A. (2018) Opening eyes and changing mind-sets: professional development for programme leaders. In Lawrence, J. and Ellis, S. (eds), *Supporting Programme Leaders and Programme Leadership*. London: Staff and Educational Development Association, SEDA Special 39, pp. 35–39.

Eraut, M. (2009) How Professionals Learn Through Work. In: Jackson, N., ed., *Learning to be Professional through a Higher Education*. Surrey: University of Surrey, SCEPTrE, pp. 28. Available at: http://learningtobeprofessional.pbworks.com/w/page/15914952/How%20professionals%20learn%20through%20work (Accessed: December 2021).

Gardner, A. and Willey, K. (2016) Academic identity reconstruction: the transition of engineering academics to engineering education researchers, *Studies in Higher Education*. 43(2), pp. 234–250. doi: 10.1080/03075079.2016.1162779

King, H. (2004) Continuing Professional Development in Higher Education: what do academics do? *Educational Developments: The Magazine of Staff and Educational Development Association Ltd (SEDA)*, 5(4), pp. 1–5. Available at: https://www.seda.ac.uk/seda-publishing/educational-developments/past-issues-2000-onwards/educational-developments-issue-5-4-2004/ (Accessed: December 2021)

King, H. (2019) *Continuing Professional Development: What do award-winning academics do? Educational Developments: The Magazine of Staff and Educational Development Association Ltd (SEDA)*, 20(2), pp. 1–5. Available at: https://www.seda.ac.uk/seda-publishing/educational-developments/past-issues-2000-onwards/educational-developments-issue-20-2-2019/ (Accessed: December 2021)

Lawrence, J. and Ellis, S. (eds), (2018) *Supporting Programme Leaders and Programme Leadership*, SEDA Special 39. London: Staff and Educational Development Association.

Lave, J. and Wenger, E. (1991) *Situated Learning: Legitimate Peripheral Participation*. Cambridge: Cambridge University.

Milburn, P. C. (2010) The role of programme directors as academic leaders. *Active Learning in Higher Education*, 11(2), pp. 87–95. doi: 10.1177/1469787410365653

Mitchell, R. (2015) 'Is there a job description I don't think I've read one': a case study of programme leadership in a UK pre-1992 university. *Journal of Further and Higher Education*, 39(5), pp. 713–732. doi: 10.1080/0309877X.2014.895302

Moore, S. (2018) Beyond isolation: Exploring the relationality and collegiality of the programme leader role. In Lawrence, J. and Ellis, S. (eds), *Supporting Programme Leaders and Programme Leadership*. London: Staff and Educational Development Association, SEDA Special 39, 29–34.

Morón-García, S., Petrova, P., and Staddon, E. (2018) Towards a professional development framework for leaders of degree programmes. [*Paper presentation*] *ISSoTL 2018: Towards a Learning Culture*, 24th–27th October, 2018, Bergen, Norway.

Murphy, M. and Curtis, W. (2013) The micro-politics of micro-leadership: exploring the role of programme leader in English universities. *Journal of Higher Education Policy and Management*, 35(1), pp. 34–44. doi: 10.1080/1360080X.2012.727707

O'Neill, G. (2015) *Curriculum Design in Higher Education: Theory to Practice*. Dublin: University College Dublin. Teaching and Learning. Available at: http://hdl.handle.net/10197/7137 (Accessed: December 2021)

Quinlan, K.M. and Gantogtokh, O. (2018) Lessons in programme leadership from two cases of designing new interdisciplinary master's programmes. In Lawrence, J. and Ellis, S. (eds), *Supporting Programme Leaders and Programme Leadership*. London: Staff and Educational Development Association, SEDA Special 39, pp. 29–34.

Ramsden, P. (2003) *Learning to Teach in Higher Education*, 2nd ed., London: Routledge Falmer.

Schön, D. A. (1983) *The Reflective Practitioner: How Professionals Think in Action*. London: Ashgate Publishing Ltd.

Senior, R (2018) The shape of programme leadership in the contemporary university. In Lawrence, J. and Ellis S., eds), *Supporting Programme Leaders and Programme Leadership*, Staff and Educational Development Association, SEDA Special 39, pp. 11–14.

Senior, R., Bowen-Jones, W., Eve, J., Forsyth, R., Morón-García, S. and Powell, S. (2018) *Supporting effective programme leadership in Higher Education: a National perspective*. [Paper presentations] 23rd Annual SEDA Conference 2018 Supporting staff to meet increasing challenges in Higher and Further Education 15th–16th November 2018, Macdonald Burlington Hotel, Birmingham.

UWE (2020) Student and Staff Numbers. Available at: https://www.uwe.ac.uk/about/demographic-data/student-and-staff-numbers#a96fa7113-3b62-4ce7-af88-874fcd28c105 (Accessed: December 2021)

Vilkinas, T. and Cartan, G. (2015) Navigating the turbulent waters of academic: the leadership role of programme managers. *Tertiary Education and Management*, 21(4), pp. 306–315. doi: 10.1080/13583883.2015.1082189

Whitfield, R. and Hartley, P. (2018) Assessment challenges for programme leaders: Making the move to programme-focussed assessment. In Lawrence, J. and Ellis, S. (eds), *Supporting Programme Leaders and Programme Leadership* London: Staff and Educational Development Association, SEDA Special, 39, pp. 21–26.

Williams, J. (2014) A critical exploration of changing definitions of public good in relation to higher education. *Studies in Higher Education*, 41(4), pp. 619–630. doi: 10.1080/03075079.2014.942270

Winch, C. (2015) Towards a framework for professional curriculum design. *Journal of Education and Work*, 28(2), pp. 165–186. doi: 10.1080/13639080.2014.1001335

Practitioner response: Considering co-constructing a Programme Leadership Development Programme in a research-intensive HEI

Deanne Gannaway, Australia

I work as an academic developer within the Institute for Teaching and Learning Innovation, The University of Queensland, a large research-intensive university in Australia with over 50,000 students and 300 award programmes. Traditionally, curriculum design focus has been on semester-long courses, with teaching academics having autonomy over content, learning activities, assessment design and learning outcomes. Rather than a recognised leadership role, programme oversight has tended to be restricted to accreditation and quality assurance. This situation, however, is changing.

This chapter's opening statements about the challenges of working in the ever-changing and complex higher education sector resonates. For a variety of reasons, including government requirements and funding changing to meet public and industry needs and expectations, the view of curriculum design is shifting to a whole-of-programme focus. Classes are larger – it's common for first year students at my institution to be in a class of over 1,000 students. These large classes increase the size of teaching teams and the need to use digital learning approaches and systems; in turn, intensifying the need to assure intended curricula outcomes are met (Allais, 2014). Someone needs to take on that role – a role that is far removed from the quiet solitude of highly individualised research through a PhD – still the entry point to an academic career for most teachers (Probert, 2014).

Despite this transformation in practice, at my institution, programme leaders develop their capabilities through experience – basically via trial and error. This chapter's description of the development of a programme co-constructed with existing practitioners and refined in an ongoing fashion by programme participants shows that induction to programme leadership does not have to be a baptism of fire.

I have been recently charged with developing a similar programme at my institution, so the principles to guide the development are of particular use. I can see our programme adopting most of these principles, although I believe we will

DOI: 10.4324/9781003127413-12

need to adopt a similar process of co-creation to translate this programme and these principles into our context.

One of the questions that remains for me is whether the workshop-based and formal CDP approach adopted by the programme does result in the kinds of long-term, systemic change that Gibbs argues is needed when he advocates a move away from the CDP approach (Gibbs, 2013) towards a more project-based and need/outcomes orientation that is particular to the participant. This is something that I am sure will surface as we go through our own programme development.

References

Allais, S. (2014) A critical perspective on large class teaching: The political economy of massification and the sociology of knowledge. *Higher Education*, 67(6), pp. 721–734. Available at: http://www.jstor.org/stable/43648686 (Accessed: December 2021)

Gibbs, G. (2013) Reflections on the changing nature of educational development. *International Journal for Academic Development*, 18(1), pp. 4–14. doi:10.1080/1360144X.2013.751691

Probert, B. (2014) *Becoming a University Teacher: The Role of the PhD: Discussion Paper*. Sydney: Australian Commonwealth Government. Available at: https://ltr.edu.au/resources/Probert_Becoming_uni_teacher_%20discussion%20paper3.pdf (Accessed: December 2021)

Chapter 5

Harnessing the potential of formal networks and informal communities to support the holistic development of programme leaders

Graham Scott and Jenny Lawrence, UK

Introduction

This chapter compares two Programme Director Networks at a UK research-focussed, pre-1992 University. Although we use the term 'directors' at the University of Hull, we will refer to programme leaders (PLs) hereafter. The first is a cross-University central-formal network led by an educational development unit, the Teaching Excellence Academy. The second is a local-informal network led by PLs in an academic department. Both offer personally constructed, socially mediated and inherently situated development, recognised as effective in growing educational leadership (e.g. Hubball et al., 2013; Hubball et al., 2017). However, interrogation of the networks suggests they have different implications for members' understanding of the opportunities afforded by the role and the development of their practice of programme leadership. We offer useful intelligence for HE leaders, educational developers and PLs looking for a holistic approach to building PL capability and information useful in motivating engagement with these models of development by making explicit the professional and personal benefits of academic development (Lawrence and Herrick, 2019).

The activities of PLs are wide-ranging (Lawrence and Ellis, 2018) and specific activities vary depending on local contexts; as Moore (2018) suggests, 'each PL is in a unique position: operating within a specific organisational context in relation to particular individuals, structures and systems' (Moore, 2018, p. 29). In contrast, however, professional development for PLs tends to be delivered by academic developers who may have no personal PL experience working from the 'centre' of the university rather than by experienced peers or near-peers 'at the chalk face' within academic departments (Moore, 2018). This is potentially problematic if centrally delivered support is designed under the misapprehension that all PLs are equally motivated to undertake their role, and similarly experienced and supported in their academic departments. Whilst some PLs hold their role for a significant period of time, for others it is a temporary arrangement (Irving, 2015); and whilst some PLs are 'accepted', others have difficulty negotiating the peer/leader space (Marchiando et al., 2015) – all issues unique to PL that potentially only other PLs can understand.

Cahill et al. (2015) suggest that PLs (and other academic leaders) should be provided with opportunities to share experiences in a non-threatening environment. In the UK, PLs learn their craft through personal experience and the relationships that they develop with peers (Ellis & Nimmo, 2018; Mitchell, 2015). Moore (2018) suggests that the difficulties inherent in centrally provided professional development might be overcome if activities for PLs are complemented by transdisciplinary support networks and structures to foster effective communication with stakeholders. Similarly, Sharpe (2017) recognises that whilst PLs work most commonly at the interface of strategy and operations, they are most effective where an emphasis is placed upon the social/human dimension of practice. Ellis and Nimmo (2018) demonstrated that most PLs value mentorship by experienced colleagues and opportunities to develop personal effectiveness through social practice, particularly self-facilitated developmental activities like action learning sets. It is apparent that the locally situated support of colleagues in a social network is a potentially effective basis for a PL professional development strategy. Through research conducted with PLs active in two such networks, a central-formal and a local/disciplinary-informal, this chapter will outline their specific strengths and personal benefits to PLs and conclude with guidance on how such networks can be effectively organised.

Method

The project was grounded in a constructivist/interpretive epistemology (Cresswell, 2003; Cleaver, Lintern & McLinden, 2018). A qualitative survey was made available to PLs for two months, starting during the second month of the first COVID-19 lockdown period (May 2020). Of the 175 names on the Teaching Excellence Academy PL mailing list, 29 (17%) PLs responded. Although this response is one of the lowest in recent years consulting with PLs (73 of 120 responded in 2018 and 50 of 160 in 2019), given the context we were working in this response rate is understandable. The survey gathered the following information: individual characteristics, years working in HE, type of academic contract (research or scholarship and teaching) and years in post as PL; how they were assigned PL; what attracted them to the role; what activities integral to the role make them feel energised/effective; what they value most about their role as PL; the qualities they think makes them a good PL; and what would help them be more effective in the role.

Findings were used to scaffold the second phase of data collection: an Appreciative Inquiry (AI) involving members of the networks that represent our two case studies. The pervasive culture in HE is often one that problematises enhancement and as a result training and development activities tend to be framed, at least initially, as strategies to overcome a deficiency. Without due consideration, it is possible that by adopting a deficit model of PL development, PLs themselves become disengaged (Ellis *pers comm* with Graham, 21 June

2019). Given the local context (a time of institutional change and the start of the first UK COVID-19 lockdown), it was important to us that participation in the project provided PLs with agency and reinforced their personal effectiveness. Because we aim to better understand and enable improved working practices by focusing upon the ways teams work together well rather than attempting to identify and solve problems in isolation (Cooperrider 2017, in Cockell & McArthur-Blair, 2012), AI is an appropriate methodology in the context of our research project. Ethical approval was granted through the University's Research Ethics Committee system and all participants gave informed consent for their contribution to be included in academic outputs.

The AI followed the standard four-stage model carried out in two discrete phases (the first phase of which is the focus of this chapter). We followed Collington and Fook's (2016) and Kung et al.'s (2013) two-stage approach, where *Discover* and *Envisioning* phases generate data that when analysed became the basis of the development of an action plan through the *Engaging* and *Innovating* phase. Our ultimate aim was the co-development of a model for institutional PL support that simultaneously enables participants to be heard, to be change agents and to have a sense of ownership of their professional development. Here, our focus is the first phase of the AI (*Discover, Envision*), which elucidates the positive benefits of the PL role in the context of membership of a PL community or network, intelligence that might be harnessed by educational developers and HE leaders to shape PL support processes within other institutional contexts.

Each network attended separate workshops, where participants reflected upon the survey responses (the *Discovery stage*) and were then guided through an *Envisioning* discussion where a consensus view on the positive value of the PL role and the activities it involves was developed. The second workshop brought the two networks together.

Survey responses, transcripts of the workshops and notes were subjected to an iterative thematic coding to identify emergent themes following a Grounded Theory approach (Atkins & Wallace, 2012; Glaser & Strauss, 1999). The following case studies outline the networks' history, formulation and function in supporting the effective practice in programme leadership and make explicit the personal benefits of those networks to PLs. This leads to an understanding of the strengths of both models of socially mediated professional development useful to those investing in PLs at their institution.

Case study: Central-Formal network

In 2017, the central educational development unit established a Programme Directors Network. Membership included PLs across all four faculties identified by Faculty Academic Managers. Biannual all-day events focused on the management of a programme quality processes or administrative leadership (Parkin, 2017, p.52). Attendance was low, and many abandoned events early citing the top-down transmission of process information unappealing.

In 2018, with the aim of better understanding PLs developmental needs and preferences and increasing engagement, PLs were invited to take part in a brief survey (73 of 120 PLs participated) and focus groups (up to 10 in 3 focus groups) (April 2018). A recognition that effective and preferred support mechanisms for PLs is sharing experience with others in similar roles (Ellis and Nimmo 2018; Moore, 2018) and research findings informed the revision of the Network. We aimed for regular discussion fora, with time for networking where PLs could build mutually supportive and informative professional relationships with PL peers.

A centrally organised calendar of events was scheduled in September for the 2018/19 academic year. Monthly, 90-minute facilitated discussions covered topics identified by PLs as pressing. The scholarship of teaching and learning-led programme fell broadly into Parkin's (2017) 'educational' (designing, delivering and creating a vision for a programme of study) and, to a lesser degree, 'academic' leadership (linking teaching, research and scholarship, knowledge exchange). This regularly brought PLs together to knowledge-share and keep abreast of cross-University initiatives. Fifty of the now 160 members responded to evaluation, and five PLs attended a consultation to plan network activity for the coming academic year (2019/20). PLs appreciated keeping abreast of new initiatives and found the brief regular meetings (same time, place and date each month) easy to recall and plan for. Participants expressed a strong desire to better understand the rational driving strategic initiatives and requested that decision makers attend.

In response, over the following academic year, members of the University Leadership Team, chairs of committees or working groups and directors spoke to PLs at Network events. Sector leaders were also invited to discuss pedagogic practice aligned to our Education Strategy. In this way, the 2019/20 programme added 'intellectual' (conceptualising innovation, HE's impact and responsibility to students and the wider world; Parkin, 2017, p. 52) to educational and academic leadership. This led to conversations between PLs and senior leaders about the national, often global, HE sector. Through these discussions, several PLs contributed to university-wide working groups. On PLs' request, invitations to the monthly meetings were now pushed into diaries and forthcoming network speakers were listed in a regular PL bulletin, which also included links to information/activity specifically relevant to them.

Attendance grew between September 2018 and September 2020. When a PL steps down, they connect us with the new incumbent and advise them to attend. Attendees at the network are most usually early career academic staff new to programme leadership or the institution. Numbers vary between 10 and 50, depending on the topic or time of year.

Of the 175 members, 16 responded to the survey conducted for the research presented here. Six attended the first 'Discovering and Envisioning' workshop, where the guided discussion established a common understanding of the developmental and personal benefits of the PL role in the context of membership of the central-university network.

Professional development benefits of the Central-Formal Network

- Strategic thinking/planning
- Understanding of institutionally specific strategic decisions/new initiatives and application to a programme
- Understanding of national and international trends in HE and integration with a programme
- Educational and academic leadership

Personal benefits of the Central-Formal Network for the programme leader

- Contributes to a positive professional identity 'PL'
- Establishes commitment to programme success
- Raises individual profiles with decision makers
- Confidence in leading teaching teams
- Inspires individual ambition

Case study: Disciplinary, local-informal community of practice

At the same time as the central-formal university network was being developed, a discipline-specific, localised-informal community of practice (CoP) of PLs emerged in the biological sciences department of the Faculty of Science and Engineering. This community was developed and is led by the PLs themselves and its membership is fluid. Although most members of the group are current PLs, some have been PLs in the past and have either taken on other responsibilities within the department or used their PL experience to move into Faculty/University-level roles related to teaching and learning. There is a core membership of five current PLs and a wider membership of up to six ex-PLs and other role holders, who join the group when they feel motivated to do so or when they are invited to contribute their experience. Experienced ex-PLs who have moved into Faculty/University-level roles are particularly valued for their ability to share institutional practices and priorities through a disciplinary lens. Recently, the community instigated a new role of deputy PL that is unique to the department and is a means by which succession planning and an effective handover of responsibilities can be managed. The network is an example therefore of a CoP (Lave & Wenger, 1991) membership of which affords opportunities for situated learning related to their individual development as PLs.

CoP meetings are informal and take place as and when required rather than following a predetermined schedule. It might therefore be described as a network of necessity and one having the benefit of agility. It has been particularly active during times of institutional reorganisation and curriculum change, most recently to negotiate the COVID-19 crisis. When it meets, the group discusses and responds to a broad range of programme-relevant topics such as the experience of their students, recruitment to their programmes, programme-level responses to internal and external surveys (such as the UK National Student Survey) and key programme performance measures. Group meetings always begin with a purposeful informal 'chit-chat' that is an opportunity to share mutual frustrations in a safe space. This purposeful informality establishes the non-threatening environment considered by Cahill et al. (2015) to be a prerequisite for the development of PL practice. Group members value their community as a locus of mutual support and mentorship, particularly around personal and career development.

Between meetings, members of the CoP do communicate via the university email system, but they find particular value in being members of an active digital community facilitated through the use of Slack, a mobile phone application that facilitates group discussion and file sharing. Through their Slack channel, members of the group can share ideas and information, ask questions and receive trusted responses quickly. This rapid response is important – the community shares its expertise/experience and responds to immediate operational and administrative queries: where to find information/who to speak to/what to do. This informal network supports 'administrative leadership' (Parkin, 2017, p. 52) enabling a programme team to complete the necessary reporting, evaluating and governance of the programme.

Four members of the group attended the first 'Discovery' workshop. The guided discussion that took place during that workshop established a common understanding of the developmental and personal benefits of the PL role in the context of membership of the local-informal CoP:

Professional development benefits of the disciplinary local-informal community of practice

- How to navigate the institution's specific policy, practice and political terrain
- Understanding of PL responsibilities
- Where to find faculty/institutional/disciplinary sources of information, advice and guidance
- Administrative and Academic Leadership and collegiality

Personal benefits of the disciplinary local-informal community of practice for the programme leader

- Contributes to positive disciplinary identity 'Biologist', intersects with 'PL'
- Moral support from peers and a practical steer
- Career development support from peers
- Flexible, often immediate, response to operational queries
- Confidence in assuring programme and student success

The success of socially mediated support

The network and community develop quite distinct professional capabilities and bring differing, if related, personal benefits to PLs. The focus on strategy in the central-formal network develops for PLs an understanding of University-specific and sector-wide policy drivers. This is a seat of confidence that underpins their educational and academic leadership. In the CoP, access to experienced PLs in the same discipline to guide the governance of the programme, point to appropriate services (student support or professional) and direct to disciplinary-specific information builds educational and administrative leadership capabilities. In both instances, the ability to assertively direct, design and ensure the rigour and currency of the programme and evidencing the success of an improved programme through, for example, NSS uplift and student attainment/retention, affords PLs a sense of empowerment and personal pride, as noted by Blackmore and Kandiko (2011).

For PLs at the University of Hull, this contributes to an esteemed professional identity 'PL'. Central-formal network PLs claim that the title 'PL' speaks of advanced responsibility and reflects high levels of pedagogic expertise, leadership ability and professional standing in the immediate and wider learning community. For example, when first stepping up to PL Respondent 04 'change my email signature to director of XX programmes, I mean there was a nice warm feeling inside of me...', Respondent 06 acknowledged that having PL in their email signature instigated swifter responses from colleagues, and Respondent 02 'sat a little bit taller' in light of their advanced status and responsibilities. The issue of academic identity is important when investing in programme leadership (Robinson-Self, 2020). In HE, the professional identity of academic staff is often based on disciplinary expertise coded by a recognised role (senior lecturer, reader etc.). The PL role must be positively framed as credible academic work integral to and dependent on a high level of disciplinary expertise to be esteemed and aspired to by disciplinarians.

Although the CoP participants did not speak of how they felt esteemed in the university, some members recognised how PL supported career progression. Early career academic staff (up to 10 years working in HE) participating in this research (in the survey and both networks) conceive of PL as integral to career progression, more so than more experienced colleagues (10 years + working in HE). Ambition is, however, inspired quite differently in the two groups. Members of the central-formal network's access to and engagement with senior leaders affords a 'voice' (Respondent 05) and 'place at the table' (Respondent 02) of university leadership and presents opportunity to work on pan-university projects. This widens academic horizons beyond a department or discipline and raises aspirations beyond PL, with the added value of involvement in strategic work contributing to (successful) bids for reward (promotion) and recognition (Senior Fellowship HEA). For members of the CoP, moral support from peers and community-alumni who have progressed to more senior leadership roles encourages members to strive for progression, seeing the role as having value 'in terms of your career development and taking your career in different directions' (Respondent 06). Peer support enables effective programme management, evidence of which contributed to one PL being promoted 'PL of XX programme led directly to Director of Student Experience and both of those things were integral in making Senior Lecturer' (Respondent 07). Hull makes an assertive leap beyond Robinson-Self's suggestion that 'giving such roles to junior staff ... presents opportunities and, for some, may keep the wolf from the door' (2020, p. 120). Hull's recently developed academic career framework recognises three distinct academic domains – research, education and knowledge exchange – and ensures that staff can progress through the ranks by evidencing academic citizenship and achievement in a variety of ways. For PLs, this is transformative, and those aligned to the education domain focusing on teaching and scholarship who participated in our research have evidenced their service to students, colleagues and programmes and have been rightly rewarded with promotion. However, those members of the CoP aligned to the research domain and who had been in-service for a longer period were less optimistic in relating PL to career progression: 'I have never seen it as something that was strategic for career development, because I did it for so long and didn't get promotion because of it' (Respondent 08). Although they did acknowledge that the times are changing, 'now it seems that it is a much more valued role in this institution' (Respondent 09) and 'we have got a reworked academic framework, so it allows you to climb that ladder through teaching and scholarship [the Education domain], that wasn't there before' (Respondent 08).

How institutions can support the holistic development of PLs

Within HEIs, disciplinary communities sit within an institutional environment of organisational priorities and structures (Hubball & Pearson, 2010). This institutional context and culture may conflict with the positive understanding of developing PLs derived from our AI. In essence, HE leaders, educational developers and PLs wishing to adopt a network and community-based approach to developing PLs should read our work against a confident understanding of their specific institutional context, culture and contractual arrangements for PLs.

The central-network and local-CoP approach together offer the transdisciplinary support network complemented with an effective communication system for sharing crucial operational intelligence (what to do), stakeholders (who to approach) and why (policy and strategy) advocated by Moore (2018). They are a successful means of developing PLs so they are able to confidently balance what Burt and Hubball (2016) describe as the art, science and (institutional) politics of programme leadership. The developmental and personal benefits to PLs of engaging with the central-formal network and local/disciplinary-informal CoP 'outweigh the threats' (Senior, 2018, p. 12) programme leadership has been said to pose to an academic career. For participants in this research, programme leadership is recognised as integral to the PL's standing in the academic community, career progression and ultimately professional satisfaction. This is a stark contrast to the perceived wisdom, which claims PL is an isolating (Ellis and Nimmo, 2018) 'career killer' (Cahill et al, 2015), fraught with frustration (Senior 2018) and corroborates Robinson-Self's notion that acknowledgement of the roles 'worth' (Robinson-Self, 2020, p. 121) within an institution through career advancement is key to the reimagining of programme leadership.

The implication of the findings of this research for HE Leaders, educational developers and PLs are clear: institutions must acknowledge programme leadership is inherently situated within disciplinary contexts (Wenger et al., 2002; Shulman, 2005) and embrace both central and localised/disciplinary-specific approaches to professional development. As Robinson-Self reflects, any developmental support for PLs must be 'tailored to institutional *and* departmental contexts' (2020, p. 112, emphasis ours). Together the network and local-informal community offer holistic development of PLs, where academic, educational and administrative leadership development is realised through Sharpe (2017) and Moore's (2018) relational side of professional practice: peer support, positive professional relationships with senior leaders and institutional reward and recognition for their efforts. All of which may underpin PL confidence and pride in the professional identity 'PL'.

Six-point guide to developing a Central-Formal Network and local-informal PL community of practice

Central-Formal Network

1. Facilitated by a central Educational/Staff Development Unit
2. Members identified by Faculty admin, update at least annually
3. Mailing list, VLE, push dates into calendars
4. Two × trimester/term bulletins (need to know, i click to intel/booking)
5. Monthly 90-minute fora (F2F/online) with decision makers
6. Cover topics identified by Programme Leaders and new initiatives

NB: Be prepared to flex the schedule and build in time for unstructured networking.

Local-Informal community of practice

1. Facilitated by a school/department's programme directors
2. Members identified by programme leaders, includes 'PL alumni'
3. Informal, regular communication stream
4. Regular informal, often ad hoc, gathering (e.g. coffee face to face or remote)
5. Frank exploration of individual challenges
6. Ad hoc invitations to institutional experts

NB: Connect with central network to ensure knowledge of practice/policy/structure is current.

References

Atkins, L. & Wallace, S. (2012) *Qualitative Research in Education*. London: BERA, SAGE.

Blackmore, P. & Kandiko, C.B. (2011). "Motivation in academic life: a prestige economy." *Research in Post-Compulsory Education.* 16(4), pp. 399–411. doi: 10.1080/13596748.2011.626971

Burt, H.M. & Hubball, H. (2016) A strategic approach to the scholarship of curriculum leadership in a research-intensive university context: the art, science and politics of implementation. *International Journal for University Teaching and Faculty Development.* 5(4), pp. 203–218.

Cahill, J., Bowyer, J., Rendell, C., Hammond, A. & Korek, S. (2015) An exploration of how programme leaders in higher education can be prepared for and supported to discharge their roles and responsibilities effectively. *Educational Research.* 57(3), pp. 272–286. doi: 10.1080/00131881.2015.1056640

Cleaver, E., Lintern, M. & McLinden, M. (Eds) (2018) *Teaching and learning in higher education: disciplinary approaches to educational enquiry*. 2nd Edition. London: SAGE.

Cockell, J. & McArthur-Blair, J. (2012) *Appreciative inquiry in higher education: a transformative force*. San Franscisco CA.: Jossey-Bass, Wiley.

Collington, V. & Fook, J. (2016) Instigating change through appreciative inquiry: a case study. *International Journal of Higher Education Management.* 3(1), pp. 1–13. Available at: https://ijhem.com/details&cid=37 (Accessed: December 2021)

Cresswell, J.W. (2003) *Research design: qualitative, quantitative and mixed methods approaches*. California: SAGE.

Ellis, S. & Nimmo, A. (2018) Opening eyes and changing mind-sets: professional development for programme leaders. In Lawrence, J. and Ellis, S. (eds), *Supporting programme leaders and programme leadership*, SEDA Special 39. London: Staff and Educational Development Association, pp. 35–39.

Glaser, B.J. & Strauss, A.L. (1999) *The discovery of grounded theory*. Chicago IL: Aldine Transactions.

Hubball, H.T., Clarke, A. & Pearson, M. (2016) Strategic leadership development in research-intensive higher education contexts: the scholarship of educational leadership. In P. Tripathi and S. Mukerji (eds), *Handbook of research on administration, policy and leadership in higher education*. PA: IGI Global.

Hubball, H., Clarke, C. & Pratt, D.D. (2013) Fostering scholarly approaches to peer review of teaching in a research-intensive university. In D. Salter (ed) *Cases on quality teaching practices in higher education*. Hershey, USA: IGI Global.

Hubball, H. & Pearson, M.L. (2010) Grappling with the complexity of undergraduate degree programme reform: critical barriers and emergent strategies. *Transformative Dialogues: Teaching and Learning Journal.* 3(3), pp. 1–17. Available at: https://journals.kpu.ca/index.php/td/article/download/1079/543/ (Accessed: December 2021)

Irving, K. (2015) Leading learning and teaching: an exploration of 'local' leadership in academic departments in the UK. *Tertiary Education and Management.* 21(3), pp. 1–14. doi: 10.1080/13583883.2015.1033452

Kung, S., Giles, D. & Hagan, B. (2013) Applying an Appreciative Inquiry Process to a Course Evaluation in Higher Education. *International Journal of Teaching and*

Learning in Higher Education, 25(1), pp. 29–37. Available at: https://files.eric. ed.gov/fulltext/EJ1016417.pdf (Accessed: December 2021)

Lawrence, J. & Ellis, S. (eds) (2018) *Supporting programme leaders and programme leadership*. SEDA Special 39. London: Staff and Educational Development Association.

Lave, J. & Wenger, E. (1991). *Situated learning: legitimate peripheral participation*. Cambridge: Cambridge University.

Lawrence, J. & Herrick, T. (2019) Supporting wellbeing in HE through the scholarship of teaching and learning. *Journal of Applied Research in Higher Education*. 12(5), pp. 871–881. doi:10.1108/JARHE-05-2019-0111

Marchiando, L., Myers, C. & Kopelman, S. (2015) The relational nature of leadership identity construction: how and when it influences perceived leadership and decision-making. *Leadership Quarterly*. 26(5), pp. 892–908. doi: 10.1016/j. leaqua.2015.06.006

Mitchell, R. (2015) If there is a job description I don't think I've read one: a case study of programme leadership in a UK pre-1992 university. *Journal of Further and Higher Education* 39(5), pp. 713–732. doi: 10.1080/0309877x.2014.895302

Moore S (2018) *Beyond isolation: exploring the relationality and collegiality of the programme leader role*. In J. Lawrence and S. Ellis. (eds) (2018) *Supporting programme leaders and programme leadership*. London: Staff and Educational Development Association. pp. 29–33.

Parkin, D. (2017). *Leading learning and teaching in higher education: the key guide to designing and delivering courses*. Abingdon: Routledge.

Robinson-Self, P. (2020) The practice and politics of programme leadership: between strategy and teaching. In Potter, J. and Devicci, C. (eds) (2020) *Delivering Educational Change in HE*. UK: Routledge.

Senior, R. (2018) The shape of programme leadership in the contemporary university. In J. Lawrence and S. Ellis. (eds), *Supporting programme leaders and programme leadership*. London: Staff and Educational Development Association. pp. 1–14.

Sharpe, R. (2017) SWEET strategies for developers working in the third space. *Educational Developments*. 18(1), pp. 1–5. Available at: https://www.seda. ac.uk/seda-publishing/educational-developments/past-issues-2000-onwards/ educational-developments-issue-18-1-2017/ (Accessed: December 2021)

Shulman, L.S. (2005) Signature pedagogies in the professions. *Daedelus*. 134(3), pp. 52–59. doi: 10.1162/0011526054622015

Wenger, E., McDermott, R.A. & Snyder, W.M. (2002) *Cultivating communities of practice: A guide to managing knowledge*. Boston, MA: Harvard Business School Press.

Practitioner response: It's a good start: Reflections through indigenous eyes on a holistic approach to supporting course and programme leadership

Piki Diamond, Aotearoa New Zealand

Below the surface of Scott and Lawrence's chapter are two issues crucial to the success of programme leader (PL) support. These two issues are the importance of building mutually beneficial relationships and the role of a shared cultural understanding. The latter can be too dangerously assumed within higher education.

Relationships are crucial to the success demonstrated in Scott and Lawrence's focus on Networks and CoPs (Buissink et al., 2017; Lester & Costley, 2010; O'Carroll, 2013; Rawlings, 2013). Their chapter demonstrates a co-ordinating of roles between formal networking from the centre and the informal communities of practice within schools and discipline. Their six-point guides are practical, outlining the responsibilities and therefore accountability that this relationship has in providing support to PLs.

The relational aspect cannot be underestimated and the six-point guides should be seen as such: as guides, but not absolutes. As Scott and Lawrence have stated, flex is required. It is required for the success of the programmes, it is finding that fine balance of meeting the needs of the community that establishes shared understanding of expectations of good practice for PLs whilst also ensuring that it is sustainable from the institution perspective.

Moving beyond mutually beneficial relationships is the engagement in ethical relationships. The need to identify and recognise the differing cultures of these individuals, that is, staff personal values and beliefs within the communities and institutions, is also crucial to growing the success of these programmes. Values, beliefs, behaviours and language can cause resistance between central units, as agents of the university, and local disciplines, at the coalface of student education. Each culture gives power to motivations, needs and emotions; so, when different cultures come together, these values, beliefs, behaviours and language require ethical and careful negotiation and the common cause of mutual grounds must be defined (Blackstock, 2011; Freire, 2005; Loesel, 2006; Maddox, 2009; UNESCO, 2020).

DOI: 10.4324/9781003127413-14

My attention to values and culture rose in the modest detail 'NB: Connect with central network to ensure knowledge of practice/policy/structure is current' (Scott and Lawrence, this volume, p. 81). A critical conscious caution could be added here: practice/policy/structure are mechanisms of cultural resilience for the Eurocentric bureaucracy, formalising and instilling preferred behaviour/values/culture. This caution challenges the above mechanisms of effectiveness to care and humanity.

Attention to ethical and mutually beneficial relationships and the critical consciousness of our academics, and in this case PLs, their communities, disciplines and institutions, will support the evolution of the work Scott and Lawrence have begun here. They have a fundamental starting point in the focus on relationships, yet as academics we do not have the luxury of resting too long on our laurels; and in this time of COVID-19 we are required to make character-defining choices that will reveal our valuing of humanity.

References

Blackstock, C. (2011). The emergence of the breath of life theory. *Journal of Social Work Values & Ethics*, 8(1). Available at: https://jswve.org/download/2011-1/spr11-blackstock-Emergence-breath-of-life-theory.pdf (Accessed: December 2021).

Buissink, N., Diamond, P., Hallas, J., Swann, J., & Sciascia, A. D. (2017). Challenging a measured university from an indigenous perspective: Placing 'manaaki' at the heart of our professional development programme. *Higher Education Research & Development*, 36(3), pp. 569–582. doi: 10.1080/07294360.2017.1288706

Freire, P. (2005). *Teachers as cultural workers: letter to those who dare teach* (D. Macedo, D. Koike, & A. Oliveira, Trans.). Boulder, Colorado, USA: Westview Press.

Lester, S., & Costley, C. (2010). Work-based learning at higher education level: Value, practice and critique. *Studies in Higher Education*, 35(5), pp. 561–575. doi: 10.1080/03075070903216635

Loesel, I. (2006). *Returning to the void: Papa Joe, Māori healing and sacred teachings.* New York: iUniverse Inc.

Maddox, M. (2009). Cultural Justice. *UNESCO Encyclopedia of Life Support Systems*, 1, 6.

O'Carroll, A. D. (2013). Virtual Whanaungatanga: Māori utilizing social networking sites to attain and maintain relationships. *AlterNative: An International Journal of Indigenous Peoples*, 9(3), pp. 230–245. doi: 10.1177/117718011300900304

Rawlings, C. (2013). *Tuakana-Teina: E-Belonging* (p. 31) [Ako Aotearoa]. Open Polytechnic. Available at: https://ako.ac.nz/knowledge-centre/maori-distance-students-tuakana-teina-e-belonging/ (Accessed: December 2021).

UNESCO. (2020). *Key recommendations from the Art-Lab review:* 'Art-Lab # 4- *The imperative of cultural justice: Arts for inclusion, equity and human rights*' (Art Lab) Available at: https://unesdoc.unesco.org/ark:/48223/pf0000375117 (Accessed: December 2021).

Case study 2

Academic almanac
A practical workshop for programme leaders to plan the academic yearly cycle

Juliet Eve, UK

Introduction

This case study focuses on the practical element of running an introductory workshop which addresses a recognised *'desire for a calendar so that* [programme leaders] *know what to prepare for'* (Murphy & Curtis, 2013, p. 42).

The aim of the session is to support the creation of an almanac of activity, detailing programme leader's (PL's) responsibilities, encompassing educational, administrative and academic duties as well as noting the student lifecycle. Colleagues from across the University are brought together, to enable personalised planning within a broader discussion of programme leadership and to facilitate the sharing of practice (Moore 2018). Drawing on metaphors for teaching (Mortiboys 2012, p. 17), I use the term 'gardeners' calendar' to encourage colleagues to consider their wider environment (seasonal, institutional and sectoral rhythms and 'winds of change') in conjunction with their specific, local 'microclimate' (school or department and disciplinary context).

Session outline

We start by creating a collective calendar on a whiteboard or shared document, using this structure.

Component 1: PL activity

The group records the range of PL activities month by month, starting in the month before the start of the academic year. In the UK this is August so they list items such as planning induction, open days, exam boards and report writing. This activities enables colleagues to identify when key activities take place during a typical academic year, and facilitates the sharing of good practice, as well as identifying the different patterns of activity integral to the running of an HE programme.

Component 2: Student lifecycle and activity

Underpinned by relevant literature, e.g. on retention (Wilcox & Winn, 2015), a second component is added to the calendar: the student journey (arrival and induction, first assessments, final projects). This identifies where there may be increased demand for pastoral care which the PL can accommodate – for example, promoting personal tutor or academic advisor support around assessment deadlines and planning cross-programme activities to support student belonging during 'wobble week' (usually week five of the first term of an undergraduate programme, when students can experience uncertainty about remaining on the course).

Component 3: Institutional processes and HE-wide activity

This component is the University calendar; being aware of institutional activity, such as curriculum change deadlines, policy updates, and when national student survey data is published, enables a broader contextual understanding, important for newer staff (Cahill et al 2015, p.281) and alerts colleagues to institutional and sector drivers.

With this richly detailed cross-university calendar created, individual PLs next develop their own calendar using a blank template (on paper or editable Word document), consulting relevant course documents they bring to the session, and mindful of the elements of their specific programmes.

Programme Leaders leave with the beginnings of a personalised calendar and a better understanding of responsibilities, with the added value of developing connections with a community of colleagues.

Impact

Around 150 staff members have attended these workshops since they were introduced in 2011, the practical nature of the planning exercise is regularly commended in evaluation:

> *an overview of what usually happens when is extremely helpful. It meant I could plan my time ahead of deadlines to work on larger pieces of work. I found it helpful to consider when student activities or periods of stress might be happening in the year and then consider the impact of this alongside tasks/activities that I may have scheduled.*

The institutional workshop runs annually, and has also been delivered to groups of colleagues within schools, to facilitate targeted, team-based approaches to planning:

> *The session helped us think more objectively about our roles and how they could be developed to enhance communication and create a more collegiate culture. The yearly planning exercise was particularly useful and helped us to devise a scaffold to take us into and through the year. The session felt supportive but also purposeful.*

88 Juliet Eve

	August	September	October	November	December	January	February	March	April	May	June	July
	Clearing Processing A level results Marking referral work NSS scores Having a holiday!	(Preparing for) induction week Exam boards	Teaching starts	Academic Health report		Applications	Exam boards Open Days ↑ NSS	Open Days		Marking	Exam boards	Graduation Academic Health report
	Stressing about A level results Going into clearing Getting ready to go to Uni Accessing new student pages on VLE	Induction week – being bombarded with info Transition to Uni	Acclimatising to new context	First assessment due Wondering whether to stay or not	Christmas 'wobble' – home students; international students	Exams/end of semester assessments	↑ NSS			Dissertations due in (final year students) Exams	Exams	Graduation
		Freshers' fair	Open Days	Re-freshers week; University academic health day	HESA returns		Graduation					Graduation

Staff Focus

Student Focus

Institutional Focus

Figure CS2.1 Example calenda

I have offered the session at other institutions, and the approach has been disseminated across the sector via SEDA, various conferences, and the sharing of resources with other educational developers. One PL, responding to evaluation of the Workshop at another institution, noted 'this has significantly improved my working life'.

Acknowledgement

I would like to thank my colleague, Pauline Ridley, for coining the term 'gardener's calendar' and for her involvement in the workshops.

References

Cahill J. et al. (2015) An exploration of how programme leaders in higher education can be prepared and supported to discharge their roles and responsibilities effectively, *Educational Research*, 57(3), pp. 272–286. doi: 10.1080/00131881.2015.1056640.

Murphy, M. & Curtis, W. (2013) The micro-politics of micro-leadership: exploring the role of the programme leader in English universities. *Journal of Higher Education Policy and Management*, 35(1), pp. 34–44. doi: 10.1080/1360080x.2012.727707.

Moore, S. (2018) Beyond isolation: exploring the relationality and collegiality of the programme leader role, in Lawrence, J. & Ellis, S. (eds.) *Supporting Programme Leaders and Programme Leadership* London: Staff and Educational Development Association SEDA Special 39 pp. 29–33.

Mortiboys, A. (2012) *Teaching with Emotional Intelligence*. 2nd ed. London: Routledge.

Wilcox P. & Winn, S. (2005) It was nothing to do with the university, it was just the people: the role of social support in the first year experience in higher education. *Studies in Higher Education*, 30(6), pp. 707–722. doi: 10.1080/03075070500340036.

Part 2

Individual programme leaders

The development of leadership through experience and collaboration

Introduction

Sue Morón-García, UK

Becoming an effective programme leader

This section uses personal experience (of colleagues either working with or as programme leaders (PLs)) and knowledge (gleaned from research studies) to discuss the complexities of this pivotal leadership position. The PL sits at the centre of a web woven from the learner's need, their own and other academics' expertise, the institution's status and employer demands. They orchestrate developments and coordinate complex processes that allow others to succeed, but often feel underappreciated and frequently overwhelmed. We asked:

- How do they become an effective academic and educational leader?
- What should they bear in mind?
- Where and who do they get help and support from?

Individual programme leaders: The development of leadership through experience and collaboration will be of interest to ...

... individual PLs who seek to develop their understanding of the leadership role they are asked to undertake and to those, such as academic or educational developers who work closely with PLs to create a supportive environment and facilitate development. It highlights the power of collaborative and consultative learning, the benefits that come from expressing vulnerability, from valuing your own expertise, and the ways in which colleagues can be included and consulted so that, crucially, they share responsibility for the programme and potentially become the future PL. Between them these chapters and case studies unpack what it is to be and become a PL. They identify things that should be borne in mind, how to navigate institutional culture by developing your relationships, identifying allies and sources of support and how to marshal the evidence for desired change.

The opening chapter sets the scene. In it Parkin identifies the different dimensions of leadership that a PL should consider, the ways in which they can

DOI: 10.4324/9781003127413-17

develop their style and the impact of the institutional context. One of the tricky issues that PLs often report is the need to lead through influence rather than positional authority so subsequent chapters and case studies discuss the relational and affective aspects of individual programme leadership and the way that collaborations and connections can be formed and harnessed to support the effectiveness of individual PLs.

Chapter and case study relevance to specific tasks and activities

1. **Learning about leadership: Dimensions, approaches and styles**
   Chapter 6. Programme leaders as educational and academic leaders: A question of influence — relationships, behaviour and commitment. Doug Parkin

2. **Learning in a shared space: Building confidence and connections**
   Chapter 7. 'It can be a lonely job sometimes': The use of collaborative space and social network theory in support of programme leaders. Maeve O'Dwyer & Rebecca Sanderson
   Chapter 8. Empowering programme leaders: Developing relational academic leadership. Sarah Moore

3. **Working with educational developers: critical friendship and collaboration**
   Case Study 3. Honesty and the power of open approaches that foster trust. Jessie Johnson and Frances Kalu
   Case Study 4. Reflecting on the transition from traditional to blended programmes: 6 critical messages to manage change. Emma O'Brien, Carol O'Sullivan and Gwen Moore
   Chapter 7. 'It can be a lonely job sometimes': The use of collaborative space and social network theory in support of programme leaders. Maeve O'Dwyer and Rebecca Sanderson
   Chapter 8. Empowering programme leaders: Developing relational academic leadership. Sarah Moore

4. **Taking a strategic approach: Programme and process development**
   Case Study 5. Leading joint and combined honours programmes: Amplified complexity. Dawne Irving-Bell and Sue Morón-García
   Case Study 6. Taking the lead: Creating an undergraduate environmental science programme to meet the benchmarks and expectations. Bethan L. Wood

Chapter 6

Programme leaders as educational and academic leaders

A question of influence – relationships, behaviour and commitment

Doug Parkin, UK

I have previously described programme leadership as 'an underestimated undertaking' (Parkin, 2017, p. 18), and that observation still holds true today. A significant mismatch exists between the low level of recognition, development and support provided and the pivotal role that good programme leadership plays in institutional performance. It is time to recognise the depth and complexity of the programme leadership role and address the leadership support needs.

I will begin by outlining the complexity of academic leadership and then go on to explore educational leadership and programme leadership within the context of higher or tertiary education. I will look in detail at programme leadership practices and institutional enablers relating to the four dimensions of programme leadership: relational, embodied, enabling and administrative.

Understanding academic leadership

> Academic leadership includes 'headship, linking teaching research and scholarship, direction of academic activity, influence and eminence, and preserving the academic environment'.
>
> (Parkin, 2017, p. 52)

Influence combined with a focus on social identity and sense-making are key aspects of academic leadership, and the approach is fundamentally relational: 'leadership works when relationships work—and fails when they don't' (Bolman and Gallos, 2011, p. 46). Academic environments require a high level of self-leadership (Bolden et al., 2012) and this is often characterised by driven individuals and independent thinkers with their own goals. An agenda flowing from one individual is, therefore, a far less persuasive proposition than shared leadership (Bolden et al., 2015), engaging through dialogue the collective commitment of a dynamic community.

Academic leadership has multiple dimensions, a range of 'leadership territories' with 'associated areas of focus and possible accountability' (Parkin, 2017, p. 52 and Figure 6.1). These dimensions could be regarded as a composite or operating separately as requiring different skills or drawing upon a combined set of leadership values

DOI: 10.4324/9781003127413-18

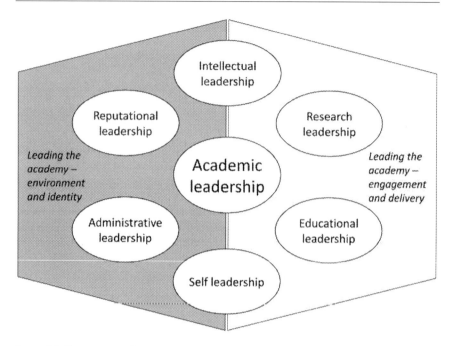

Figure 6.1 Dimensions of Academic Leadership

and approaches, but in any event it would be unusual to come across an academic leadership role that did not have several of the dimensions overlapping. Within these dimensions can be seen the many hats that academic leaders wear or, if you prefer, the different plates they spin. Opportunities to develop necessary skills and competencies across these dimensions are important if programme leaders (PLs) are to be fully effective.

In the literature, different approaches, aspirations or theoretical standpoints are often denoted by the addition of a word or short phrase before either 'leadership' or 'leader'. An awareness of key leadership models or perspectives relating to these can help empower PLs to develop their own leadership style. Those most often applied to the academic context come from either the altruistic family of leadership ideas, consciously concerned with supporting not just achievement but also the emotional state and well-being of colleagues, or they express a philosophy in which leadership is enacted within the group/community based on the fluid dynamic of relationships, roles and responsibilities. Examples include servant leadership, emotionally intelligent leadership, authentic leadership, engaging leadership, shared leadership, inclusive leadership, collective leadership (also used in relation to enabling patient-centred care in UK health service settings (West et al., 2014)), collaborative leadership and distributed (Bolden et al., 2009) or dispersed leadership.

There is a prestige economy (Blackmore and Kandiko, 2011) at work within higher education. PLs are both part of this and need to understand the subtleties associated with engaging with academic colleagues who are highly attuned to valuing themselves and others within a system of recognition that is both local and worldwide. Credibility and trust are crucial elements, alongside the potential ambassadorial role any academic leader plays across institutions, within communities and in wider society.

Finally, it is particularly key to consider the notion of social identity (Haslam et al., 2011). What are the manifestations of 'we' that people ascribe to? That is the crucial question of identity in all contexts, but the multifaceted environment of academia with a complex intersection of self-driven, group-driven and organisation-driven agendas makes the question of 'we' so much more challenging and important. Resolving this is not about imposing an uncomfortably alien business paradigm, achieving conformity or looking to bring about some kind of homogenous monoculture. Far from it! Freedom and autonomy thrive in heterogeneous, multicultural environments in which difference and conflict strengthen creativity, ideation and relationships. However, appreciating social identity does involve leaders being closely attentive to the sense of 'we' that exists within a group, between group members and indeed across groups. And a key question that has to be negotiated or reconciled at all times is whether the leader is part of the group or apart from it.

Educational and programme leadership

Reflecting on findings from a range of accounts exploring the distinctive nature of school leadership, Moos (2012, p. 26) observes that:

> They point to the fact that in the practice of schools there is not only one leader; leadership needs to be distributed and therefore people need to be developed and empowered so they can accept and carry out leadership functions at different levels.

This returns to the theme of leadership as a distributed and shared sense of agency running through the organisation. Sharing leadership needs to become a reflex for PLs, so that colleagues are inspired and trusted to innovate their practice routinely, deliver teaching inclusively and provide feedback for learning conscientiously. The question is: how to inspire this sense of trust and engagement?

In the same way that motivation is a 'fire from within' (Covey, 2013, p. 98), inspiration comes from the soul of the individual. However, there are environments that encourage this inspiration to be expressed in purposeful and useful ways – ways that bring learning to life and encourage critical dialogue – and environments which inhibit its expression. The academic environment is profoundly influenced by leadership, whether appointed leadership with authority or emergent leadership derived from actions taken or values displayed. Fullan

(2001, p. 7) describes this environment as a constellation consisting of 'energy-enthusiasm-hopefulness'.

For PLs, specifically there are four essential ways in which to define and develop their approach to influence through trust and engagement. The four dimensions of programme leadership are:

- Relational leadership – *the mentor*
- Embodied leadership (which includes ethical leadership) – *the champion*
- Enabling leadership – *the enabler*
- Administrative leadership – *the organiser*

For further information on the use of the terms mentor, champion, enabler and organiser, see the Programme Leadership Model (Parkin, 2017, pp. 29–31). This is not a direct mapping.

Relational leadership

> Relational leadership puts the quality of relationships on an equal footing with all other practical outcomes. I believe that *how* we do something together matters as much as *what* we are doing. When we collaborate in ways that are mutual, voluntary, and connected, we increase the likelihood we will want to collaborate again… A relational leader envisions a future for their relationships that goes beyond near-term goals and plans. Through fair-play and respect, a relational leader fosters trust, loyalty, and camaraderie.
>
> (Porcelli, 2019)

Relational leadership as it is emerging in the literature has many parallels with key factors identified in authentic leadership, particularly self-awareness, relational transparency and having an internalised moral perspective (Walumbwa et al., 2008). As regards programme leadership, the following practices and institutional enablers have a strong relational basis:

Programme leadership practices	Institutional enablers
Investing in relationships and developing networks for both delivery and support. 'Having a network of peers can be a helpful source of advice and support' (Malone, 2019). Within these networks, PLs may also mentor the development of others, including for progression / succession.	Enable support networks of PLs within and across departments and even beyond the institution, recognising that this will enrich performance. Enabling includes providing time and resources.

Developing spheres of influence that go beyond positional or expert authority. An individual PL may interact with a range of groups based on interests, common goals or shared needs. These groups may be loosely associated and informal, but may hold the key to 'getting things done' in ways that formal structures sometimes struggle to achieve.

Covey (1992, p. 83) distinguishes what he terms a proactive focus where positive energy, working on the 'things they can do something about', causes the person's circle of influence to increase. The opposite is a reactive focus in which negative energy is focused on 'the weakness of other people, the problems in the environment, and circumstances over which that have no control'. PLs can lose a lot of energy and momentum by reactively focusing on things that may be of concern but over which they realistically have very little immediate control or influence (e.g. suboptimal IT infrastructure or even fluctuating student numbers). Amongst many competing priorities, far better to build relationships around the things that matter and grow the sphere of influence based on positive impact and effectiveness.

Establishing a legitimacy base that is grown from relationships of mutual respect, honesty, compassion and connectedness. Rather than a 'power base' made up of position, expert knowledge, the control of rewards and consequences and even social dependence, the relational leader influences through collaboration around a shared vision, deep connections linked to core values, trust and the desire to serve others. This attunement or deep influence better enables a PL to translate goals, targets and external drivers in a way that whilst not always palatable, at least has resonance for the core mission of the group (e.g. student engagement and success).

Cultivate a culture that profitably combines formal structures (the hierarchy) with more fluid and informal groupings, networks and associations. Empower these to develop agendas and take action based on both 'in the moment' imperatives and emergent change.

John Kotter (2013, p. 21) puts forward the powerful notion of what he describes as a dual operating system in which work that 'demands innovation, agility, difficult change and big strategic initiatives executed quickly' are 'shifted over to the network part' of the organisation leaving the hierarchy 'less encumbered and better able to perform what it is designed for: doing today's job well'.

It is hard to foster a collaborative community within an institutional environment that is not itself collaborative. If the values of the organisation clearly express a commitment to progress on the basis of openness, respect and collaboration and if those qualities are shown and even exemplified by senior leaders across the organisation even when faced by rapidly evolving policy or market forces, then that will enable PLs and others to relationally engage with colleagues on a similar basis. There is often a 'political' dimension to legitimacy and working with the cultural grain of an organisation or in a way that is 'congruent with present assumptions' (Schein, 1984, p. 14) is likely to be more relationally successful.

Embodied leadership (including ethical leadership)

> Leadership research has entered a new phase where the focus is to produce sustainable leaders through authenticity and compassion... Several factors that contribute to the characteristics of embodied leadership have been identified...[among which are]:
>
> - Being non-judgmental,
> - Listening actively,
> - Embracing uncertainty and
> - Reflective practice
>
> (Koya et al., 2017, p. 3028 and p. 3031)

If there is one word that encapsulates modern leadership, it is congruence. This is a three-way congruence between what the leader says (thinking), what the leader does (doing) and the fundamental way the leader is (being). And the last of these, *being*, has the potential to bring with it integrity, a sense of the standards to which the group aspires and a template for how colleagues should interact. This ontological core also sets, in many ways, the emotional tone of the work environment. For the leadership of learning and teaching, there is also the further congruence involved in embodying the values of a learning leader (the four factors identified in the definition above exemplify this). As regards programme leadership, there are three key practices that relate to the notion of embodied leadership or behavioural modelling and corresponding institutional enablers:

Programme leadership practices	Institutional enablers
Visibility – being visible both generally and when it matters most. Generally, a leader's presence in terms of modelling standards, being positive and demonstrating accountability, is key to the focus and cohesion of the group. For programme leadership, embodying 'how we are with students' in terms of relationship and support is, perhaps, the very essence of quality enhancement. And this needs to be consistent over time, taking in both the good days and the bad. There are then key moments when how the leader responds can be the pivot point between a programme team progressing or starting to dysfunction. Unforecast change that initially seems unhelpfully challenging is a key example of this. If the leader responds by authentically showing concern, listening carefully to others and then in a balanced way starting to identify opportunities, it can significantly influence the climate of the team in a positive way. At these moments, the visibility of the leader is absolutely key.	How the institution constructs, communicates and celebrates the role of PLs is central to enabling positive visibility. PLs generally have 'a strong sense of responsibility and accountability for the programme' (Moore, 2018, p. 32) or programmes which they lead. To build a constructive environment around this natural sense of accountability a well-defined role that is clearly and convincingly communicated is essential. It should not be left entirely to individuals to 'sell' their role as PLs to others, the institution should broadcast the importance of the role, how it is supported and celebrate achievements and points of innovation. The modelling of good practice by PLs should be prized as exemplary. They have a role in championing both the programme and the institution, and need support in developing the skills to negotiate effectively.

Be the change you want to see and build collective commitment around the behaviours needed for both growth and success. Mahatma Gandhi (1869–1948) is credited by some with having said 'be the change you want to see in the world', and this is really a call for both humble and committed leadership. Humble because rather than directing people to act or behave in particular ways, the mindset of the leader is to perform alongside colleagues and be an active part of the evolution of practice. This is a critical aspect of effective programme leadership, balancing practitioner excellence with colleague engagement. It is also key for the social identity of the group, as mentioned above, shifting the focus in leadership from 'me' to 'we'.

Doing the right things for the right reasons is the strategic dimension of programme leadership based on the educational philosophy that drives the curriculum. One of the drawbacks with a number of the current curriculum review and development methodologies is that they do not emphasise sufficiently the importance of capturing and expressing the educational philosophy of a course. This should be an ever-present aspect of programme leadership, a clear ethical dimension, guiding practice and decision-making and acting as the very basis of student engagement. It is the PL's role to embody this ethos and through sustained collaborative engagement to make it clear to others. Being truly purpose-driven as a leader is a key part of this, as is staying true to core values in the face of external pressures.

With regard to all aspects of transformational change, but perhaps particularly in relation to pedagogic change which is charged with maintaining or enhancing engagement, senior leadership needs to acknowledge two things. Firstly, complex change cannot be entirely driven – aspects of it will be iterative, emergent and rooted in the practitioner community. Secondly, notwithstanding distinctive disciplinary cultures, for PLs to model change effectively and sympathetically in their own areas, there must be a reasonably robust alignment with the vision and values that guide the institution overall. The values must be 'lived values' and resonate across the curriculum portfolio, not just in parcels or pockets.

The American comedian Groucho Marx (1890 to 1977) said, 'those are my principles, and if you don't like them... well, I have others'. The neoliberal forces that have emerged around higher education such as marketisation, deregulation and even privatisation have created a tension in the system (sometimes quite a profound tension) between what might be termed ancient and modern values. This is increasingly a challenge for higher education leadership, upholding deeply rooted and fundamental principles such as autonomy and academic freedom at the same time as responding to contemporary forces such as competitive market pressure and policy-driven regulation. Despite these challenges, PLs need to be empowered to uphold and evolve the distinctive character of their course offerings and the educational philosophy that underpins them, working to a 'long arc' rather than reactively reshaping pedagogic practice in response to constantly changing circumstances, the 'short arc' of events. Worse still is a flip-flopping of pedagogic direction and priorities as external pressures swell and fluctuate.

Enabling leadership

> Isn't enabling leadership just the sort of progressive, collective approach that has the best chance of meeting the competitive challenge by getting the whole organization involved and committed?... Leaders are responsible for tapping into the strength and capabilities of other people. This is an indirect form of leadership, perhaps less visible but in fact no less useful and necessary than the obvious 'I am in charge' type.
>
> (Kaplan, 1996, p. 6)

> *Enabler* – this is the most facilitative and collaborative of the four leadership attributes. It is about bringing people together: staff, students and other stakeholders, where appropriate. It is about creating transformative spaces for collaborative engagement, co-creation and collective learning... The enabler has a strong belief in human potential and looks to work with people in teams to pursue innovation and develop a sense of energy and collective commitment about the way ahead.
>
> (Parkin, 2017, p. 30)

The essence of enabling leadership is facilitating the environment, convening the group and promoting high-quality conversations through collaborative engagement. The skill is to facilitate engagement so that programme design, delivery and assessment has a sense of cohesion and purpose rather than being a series of disparate threads, loosely brought together by a curriculum structure. There are three core practices that relate to the notion of enabling leadership or social facilitation and corresponding institutional enablers:

Programme leadership practices	Institutional enablers
Fostering connections across the team so that colleagues have, firstly, a good level of awareness of other contributions; secondly, an appreciation of the organisational landscape around the programme; and thirdly, a sense of pride about what is being achieved collectively at a team level. These connections need to be thought of expansively taking in the work and expertise of professional colleagues, the role of 'visiting' contributors, critical partnerships with accreditors and the quality of relationship with a wide range of stakeholders. Rather than the PL being the midpoint or the 'pressed middle' in all these relationships with individuals and	For any community to thrive, it needs time, space, support and encouragement to meet, spend time together and build bonds through conversations, creativity and productive conflict. Enabling and legitimising this is a key aspect of institutional support. Making programme meetings an expected part of the institutional routine (not just in the form of programme reviews), bringing together not just the academic contributors but also professional colleagues and other stakeholders, is both practically and culturally valuable. Such meetings or extended workshop-type sessions should be encouraged to include creative elements in addition to administrative considerations and planning. On an

subgroups lobbying regarding their needs and concerns, the way forward is to bring colleagues together in purposeful ways to collaborate on issues of mutual interest. Working collaboratively on one issue, if well facilitated, can foster the connections needed to have positive interactions about a range of other challenges. So, don't be a go-between leader, be a go-together facilitator.

- **Using creative approaches** to enable colleagues to think differently, challenge assumptions, appreciate diversity and find new solutions for innovative teaching design and quality enhancement. Very often, the problem is not so much that 'we go on having the same conversations' but that we go on having them in the same way. There is no creative spark to shift thinking and help colleagues to see things differently. It can feel odd and unusual to bring a creative spark to a conversation or to use a creative process, but actually this is often what we are trying to encourage our students to do and the same principles apply to us as a staff community when it comes to learning, thinking differently and developing insight. It may take both courage and persistence but using creative approaches can unlock a huge amount of untapped potential in a programme team.
- **Developing collective commitment about the way ahead** and supporting others to develop and grow. A good course or programme never stands still, it is constantly growing and evolving, and the human system that surrounds the course is growing, too. But growth takes inspiration, particularly during busy and pressurised times. Writing about the challenge of inspiring collective

occasional basis, more senior stakeholders can have an involvement to support PLs and make links with wider institutional developments.

Whilst fostering connections is important, it should also be recognised that when programme leadership changes, those connections can be very quickly lost. Having development support in place to manage these transitions and ensuring the investment in course knowledge and relationships passed across makes strong organisational sense as 'the months either side of becoming a programme leader have emerged as of central importance' (Ellis, 2019, p. 3).

The points on time, space and support above apply equally to encouraging PLs to use creative approaches. This is also a leadership development challenge. Equipping PLs with the confidence and skills to use creativity as part of their leadership role is a key institutional responsibility. There is so much to be gained if creative leadership can be brought to transformational change processes around education, assessment and student support and engagement. And it is not an easy thing to do alone or in isolation, as creative confidence can be a fragile thing: 'the creative impulses of most people can be suffocated by negative criticism, cynical putdowns or dismissive remarks' (Robinson, 2017, p. 200). Developing PLs (and others) in this way should be seen as an important piece of institutional investment.

Collective commitment is inextricably linked to purpose. Who we are, what we stand for and what we are here to achieve – these are the three ingredients of purpose. Agreed and set at an institutional level, this clarity of purpose should cascade its way through the organisation influencing the character and direction of programmes with regard to education, and projects and partnerships as regards research. This should also be the big commitment in universities, Gentle and Forman (2014, p. 3) highlight six central propositions:

1. Participatory decision-making
2. Collective learning
3. Leadership at all levels
4. Personal authenticity
5. High-quality discussions
6. A sustainable legacy

Some of these have been touched on in the practices identified so far in relation to relational and embodied leadership, but are nevertheless well worth highlighting again here. Levels of participation in decision-making can be a gauge to both community and individual growth. Where participation is high, growth is likely to follow. Similarly, leaders who pay 'attention to creating a lasting, sustainable legacy', as Gentle and Forman describe it, not for themselves but for the collaborative working culture they have been striving to promote, will prioritise the growth and development of others.

ongoing conversation in any educational establishment, and for higher education 'purpose' should be central to the proposition which attracts students and those who support them.

Translating purpose into the overarching programme narrative and rationale is then the key strategic role of the PL, made possible (or not) by the institutional clarity which surrounds them.

The other part of this is vision. Based on that clear purpose, what is our vision for achievement and impact over the next three/five years? If an organisation can capture purpose and vision together in a way that is honest, authentic and compelling, then that is the strongest possible basis for inspiring collective commitment.

Leadership requires two things: a vision of the world that does not yet exist and the ability to communicate it.

(Sinek, 2009, p. 227)

Administrative leadership

Writing about early childhood leadership, Abel (2016) gives us two clear and powerful words, 'orchestrating tasks'. He goes on to add that 'successful administrative leaders are able to establish systems that protect and sustain essential operational functions'.

Organiser – for a dream to succeed, it must become a plan – something executable that can be managed, monitored and controlled. The leadership of learning and teaching involves very close planning and management. Educational programmes that lead to recognised qualifications linked to standards, national frameworks and other forms of recognition do not happen by accident. A plan essentially links activities, resources and time (the ART of planning) and uses the logic of goals, sequencing and priorities to map what should happen, when and where, and who should be involved.

(Parkin, 2017, p 30)

The following are some of the interests and activities that PLs pursue that could be seen as administrative leadership:

- Orchestrating tasks
- Ensuring the smooth interaction of people and tasks by planning and organising

- Agreeing on goals and outcomes
- Aligning activities (vertically and horizontally)
- Creating sympathetic and supportive systems that people can trust
- Removing obstacles and troubleshooting
- Interfacing productively with the wider organisation
- Empowering others to discover new approaches and efficiencies
- Emphasising the importance of key deadlines
- Helping colleagues to manage time and balance urgent and important tasks
- Meeting/committee management and arrangements
- External relations and supporting course promotion
- Aspects of quality assurance

There can also be a complex interaction around some of these activities with the roles, responsibilities and talents of professional colleagues. From the functioning of committees through to the accessing and maintaining of student records and from course marketing through to other aspects of student support, the quality of relationships and behaviours and the need for a shared sense of commitment will make all the difference to well-functioning systems. Once again, the key institutional enabler here is to facilitate, resource and carefully align these interactions.

By its nature, administrative leadership does not stand on its own, it is enmeshed with other aspects and dimensions of leadership such as relational, embodied and enabling leadership, as discussed here. But without this clear administrative capacity, creating the conditions for leadership and the scaffolding for performance, the other dimensions will struggle to gain traction. A study of 176 PLs in three multi-campus Australian universities identified that they perceived their academic leadership role as involving 'a complex skill set including: administration and trouble-shooting; curriculum design; quality assurance; pastoral care; staff mentoring; external relations with industry partners and professional bodies; and close collaboration with academic and professional staff across the institution' (Krause et al., 2010, p. 3). This list highlights the interplay in the PL role between administrative leadership and leading with influence to achieve trust and engagement. It is this interplay which is the essential art of effective and transformational leadership.

Conclusion

There is a complex sophistication to any leadership role that is fundamentally about leading through influence rather than overt authority, and that is certainly the case with programme leadership in higher education:

> True leadership cannot be awarded, appointed, or assigned. It comes only from influence, and that cannot be mandated. It must be earned.
> (Maxwell, 2007, p. 13)

Components of academic and educational leadership are clearly part of the role. Programme leadership involves many of the same nuances experienced in research leadership, interacting with important values associated with independence, autonomy, prestige and self-leadership. It also operates within a distributed ethos similar to that which might be found in many schools, colleges and other educational settings: an environment which thrives on shared leadership. Facilitating the environment and attending selflessly to the social identity of the group is also key, notwithstanding the increasing marketised pressures of targets, performance goals and multiple internal and external metrics. An educational environment consisting of 'energy-enthusiasm-hopefulness' (Fullan, 2001, p. 7) captures the positivity needed for learning, teaching and student engagement to thrive.

More so than perhaps any other leadership role in higher education, programme leadership working with a rich and diverse spectrum of colleagues, an intellect community, on goals and challenges that are often 'wickedly' complex, from the humanistic depths of adult learning through to the detailed intricacy of criterion-based assessment, is multifaceted. It is profoundly relational, it needs to be visible and congruently embody values and high standards, and to build collective commitment through collaboration it also involves high-level enabling skills: relational, embodied and enabling leadership. The metaphors of swapping hats and spinning plates mentioned previously apply. The following programme leadership practices with corresponding institutional enablers were discussed in this chapter:

Relational leadership:

- Investing in relationships and developing networks
- Developing spheres of influence
- Establishing a legitimacy base

Embodied leadership:

- Visibility – being visible both generally and when it matters most
- Be the change you want to see
- Doing the right things for the right reasons

Enabling leadership:

- Fostering connections across the team
- Using creative approaches
- Developing collective commitment about the way ahead

Administrative leadership, which includes:

- Orchestrating tasks
- Aligning activities

- Creating sympathetic and supportive systems
- Removing obstacles and troubleshooting

Successful programme leadership really is a question of influence and investing in relationships, modelling behaviour and inspiring collective commitment around the things that matter. As part of sustained organisational performance and to continuously transform and evolve learning and teaching, institutions large and small should review their investment in recognising, developing and supporting the individuals who undertake the programme leadership role. With evermore diverse and demanding student cohorts and educational goals, the importance and sophistication of this role will continue to grow.

References

Abel, M. (2016) *Deconstructing Whole Leadership*. McCormick Center for Early Childhood Leadership at National Louis University Available at: https://mccormickcenter.nl.edu/library/deconstructing-whole-leadership/ (Accessed: October 2020).

Blackmore, P. and Kandiko, C. B. (2011) 'Motivation in academic life: a prestige economy', *Research in Post-Compulsory Education*, 16(4), pp. 399–411. doi: 10.1080/13596748.2011.626971.

Bolden, R., et al. (2012) *Academic Leadership: Changing Conceptions, Identities and Experiences in UK Higher Education*. London: Leadership Foundation for Higher Education (Now AdvanceHE).

Bolden, R., et al. (2015) *Developing and Sustaining Shared Leadership in Higher Education*. London: Leadership Foundation for Higher Education (now Advance HE).

Bolden, R., Petrov, G. and Gosling, J. (2009) 'Distributed leadership in higher education: Rhetoric and reality', *Educational Management Administration & Leadership*, 37, pp. 257–277. doi: 10.1177/1741143208100301.

Bolman, L. G. and Gallos, J. V. (2011) *Reframing Academic Leadership*. San Francisco: Jossey-Bass.

Covey, S. R. (1992) *The Seven Habits of Highly Effective People: Powerful Lessons in Personal Change*. London: Simon & Schuster.

Covey, S. R. (2013) *The Wisdom and Teachings of Stephen R. Covey*. London: Simon & Schuster.

Ellis, S. (2019) 'Programme Leadership: A Review of Evidence and an Agenda for Action'. Available at: https://www.enhancementthemes.ac.uk/docs/ethemes/evidence-for-enhancement/programme-leadership—a-review-of-evidence.pdf?sfvrsn=97f4c381_6 (Accessed: October 2020).

Fullan, M. (2001) *Leading in a Culture of Change*. San Francisco: Jossey-Bass.

Gentle, P. and Forman, D. (2014) *Engaging Leaders, the Challenge of Inspiring Collective Commitment in Universities*. Oxon and New York: Routledge.

Haslam, S. A., Reicher, S. D. and Platow, M. J. (2011) *The New Psychology of Leadership: Identity, Influence and Power*. Hove and New York: Psychology Press.

Kaplan, R. E. (1996) *Forceful Leadership and Enabling Leadership*. Greensboro, NC: Center for Creative Leadership.

Kotter, J. (2013) 'Accelerate! New management systems to replace traditional hierarchies and managerial processes in companies', *Human Resource Management International Digest*, 21(2). doi:10.1108/hrmid.2013.04421baa.006.

Koya, K., Anderson, J. and Sice, P. (2017) 'The Embodied Nurse: Interdisciplinary knowledge exchange between compassionate nursing and recent developments in embodied leadership studies', *Journal of Advanced Nursing*, 73(12), pp. 3028–3040. doi: 10.1111/jan.13363.

Krause, K., *et al.* (2010) 'Degree Programme Leader roles and identities in changing times', *Society for Research in Higher Education Annual Research Conference 2010*. Newport, Wales. Available at: http://hdl.handle.net/10072/38879 (Accessed: November 2021).

Malone, E. (2019) 'Top Tips for Programme Leaders'. Available at: https://www.enhancementthemes.ac.uk/docs/ethemes/evidence-for-enhancement/top-tips-for-programme-leaders.pdf?sfvrsn=fb92c781_8 (Accessed: October 2020).

Maxwell, J. C. (2007) *Irrefutable Laws of Leadership: Follow Them and People Will Follow You*. 10th anniversary edn. Nashville: Thomas Nelson.

Moore, S. (2018) 'Beyond isolation: Exploring the relationality and collegiality of the programme leader role', in Lawrence, J. & Ellis, S. (eds.) *Supporting programme leaders and programme leadership*. London: Staff and Educational Development Association, pp. 29–33.

Moos, L. (2012) 'From Successful School Leadership Towards Distributed Leadership', in Preedy, M., Bennett, N. & Wise, C. (eds.) *Educational Leadership: Context, Strategy and Collaboration*. Milton Keynes: The Open University (Sage Publications), pp. 101–123.

Parkin, D. (2017) *Leading Learning and Teaching in Higher Education: The Key Guide to Designing and Delivering Courses (Key Guides for Effective Teaching in Higher Education)*. Abingdon: Routledge.

Porcelli, M. (2019) 6 *Qualities of Relational Leaders: Welcome to the Relational Dimension of Leadership*. The StartUp Available at: https://medium.com/swlh/6-qualities-of-relational-leaders-94b60ee964d7#:~:text=A%20relational%20leader%20envisions%20a,leader%20plays%20the%20infinite%20game (Accessed: October 2020).

Robinson, K. (2017) *Out of Our Minds: The Power of Being Creative*. 3 edn. Chichester: John Wiley & Sons.

Schein, E. H. (1984) Coming to a New Awareness of Organizational Culture, *Sloan Management Review*, 25(2), pp. 3–16. Available at https://sloanreview.mit.edu/article/coming-to-a-new-awareness-of-organizational-culture/ (Accessed October 2020)

Sinek, S. (2009) *Start With Why: How Great Leaders Inspire Everyone to Take Action*. London: Penguin Books Ltd.

Walumbwa, F. O., *et al.* (2008) 'Authentic leadership: Development and validation of a theory-based measure', *Journal of Management*, 34(1), pp. 89–126. doi: 10.1177/0149206307308913.

West, M., *et al.* (2014) *Developing Collective Leadership for Health Care*. London: The King's Fund.

Practitioner response: A sympathetic approach and practical strategies

Svitlana Kalashnikova and Olena Orzhel, Ukraine

The chapter 'Programme Leaders as Educational and Academic Leaders: A question of influence – relationships, behaviour and commitment' by Doug Parkin is dedicated to PLs and programme leadership – an important topic and undervalued issue in the academic leadership discourse. Its author draws attention to the underestimated role that PLs play at different stages of programme development, delivery, review and evaluation and pay tribute to their numerous and often unrewarded endeavours in academic life.

In the first part of this chapter, different perspectives on academic leadership are provided and insightful observations regarding programme leadership are made. Parkin mentions the undertaking and responsibility of PLs to 'wear many hats' simultaneously: build trust and engagement, maintain dialogue and inspiration, safeguard freedom and autonomy, take care of colleagues' well-being and so on.

The text is filled with sympathy towards PLs. While listing the numerous virtues that PLs are to possess in order to function effectively, Parkin remarks on their specific identity: being part of the programme team, PLs should simultaneously stand beyond and/or above the team in order to assess, judge, manage, propose changes and lead the team to excellence. Another interesting insight within the chapter is the reference to numerous agendas that PLs have to consider while leading the programme team: remaining oneself, being a member of the team, part of the faculty, member of the institution, considering the demands of the local community or competing with peers globally.

Considering responsibilities and challenges that PLs meet on a regular basis, the author emphasises the need to recognise, reward and support them in everyday accomplishments as well as stressing the necessity to consistently develop their leadership competencies and capacities.

In the second part of the chapter, the author illustrates how four different styles of leadership – 'the mentor', 'the champion', 'the enabler', 'the organiser' (generated and scrutinised in his previous book; Parkin, 2017) – can combine in programme leadership. Typical, for a certain leadership style, practices are listed with explanations regarding how, for example, 'investing in relationship and developing networks' under relational leadership; or 'ensuring the smooth

DOI: 10.4324/9781003127413-19

interaction of people and tasks by planning and organising' under administrative leadership; or 'developing collective commitment' under enabling leadership, contribute to better performance, developing and empowering staff and/or strengthening programme promotion. Key enablers identified include removing obstacles, cultivating desired cultures, boosting creativity or motivation and championing the programme and the institution.

This chapter winds up with the prognosis that the need for successful PLs will grow under global and competitive markets for educational services instigating institutions to support, develop and invest further in programme leadership.

The text contains some practical recommendations that can be straightforwardly applied in the Ukrainian higher education context. Particularly useful is the linking of programme leadership practices like 'investing in relationship', 'developing networks', 'using creative approaches', 'developing collective commitment' and so on, with 'institutional enablers' in the form of tools, techniques and resources that facilitate the successful realisation of those specific practices. For instance, for 'fostering connections across the team' PLs and their colleagues will need institutional backing to create and carve out the time and space needed to meet and have high-quality conversations. They will also need appropriate support and encouragement from the institution to actively build bonds, discuss and debate, challenge or support each other's ideas and work together productively on issues and challenges.

In addition, several insights from the author hold great promise for helping the Ukrainian higher education community to advance in academic leadership. Specific examples that are of key value are (a) closely connecting educational, programme and research leadership, (b) leading through influence rooted in relationship, behaviour and commitment and (c) establishing an appropriate educational environment based on a culture of energy, enthusiasm and hopefulness.

Chapter 7

'It can be a lonely job sometimes'

The use of collaborative space and social network theory in support of programme leaders

Maeve O'Dwyer and Rebecca Sanderson, UK

Introduction

For Wheatley and Kellner-Rogers, organisations have become too wedded to rigid and mechanistic conceptions of human behaviour:

> when individuals fail to experiment or when the system refuses their offers of new ideas, then the system becomes moribund. Without constant, interior change, it sinks into the death grip of equilibrium....
>
> (1996, p. 33)

Life wants to self-organise, they argue, to create webs of relationships which provide stability and support, and in so doing, provide the conditions for creative responses to the inevitable, continuous flux which characterises the world in which we live. This approach to leadership development, which prioritises building relationships and creating safe spaces for critique and the incubation of new ideas, has particular resonance for academic leadership, which has been positioned as a distinct type in the taxonomy of leadership (Anthony & Antony, 2017). Characterised by 'disciplinary tribes' (ibid., p. 631), networks of relationships and working together towards common goals (Kohtamäki, 2019), it has been described as a form of 'distributed leadership', where multiple staff contribute through a network of diverse expertise (Laing & Laing, 2011). According to Burke:

> If [traditional] leadership defines itself as the singular influence of an individual over a group in order to achieve an end, then distributed leadership is the collective influence of the group.
>
> (2010, p. 52)

At the University of Lincoln in the UK, we were interested in using these ideas on the importance of relationship-building to influence and inform support for programme leaders (PLs). This chapter is a reflective account of the authors' experience of trialling a forum-based approach to supporting PLs, and includes an account of our rationale for and the delivery of our approach. We anticipate that our learning from trialling this approach will be of use to educational developers in particular, while the importance of social network theory will become apparent to any reader, especially given the current challenges in creating connections and networks through virtual means.

As educational developers at the University of Lincoln, a teaching-focused university in the UK, we implemented a forum as part of a wider effort to diversify support for PLs from across the institution. This support targeted over 200 PLs of undergraduate, postgraduate and foundation year courses, hoping to provide an opportunity to ensure their engagement with the community of colleagues in a similar role, provide practical support for their work through network-building and in particular enable them to maintain communication with educational developers and with senior management across the institution. Within this chapter, we include a case report, sharing an example of a forum meeting designed and delivered by an individual PL, evidencing how this opportunity was initiated and developed through the forum-based approach.

Throughout this chapter we will use the term 'forum', but colleagues interested in the impact of this approach can understand this to mean any collaborative and flexible space for discussion and relationship-building. Inspired by social network theory, but moving beyond the hierarchical connotations of social networks, we aimed to create an equitable and inclusive place focussed on seeking solutions to common challenges affecting the PL community. This non-hierarchical approach was particularly important in our context, where PLs could be early career or senior academics facing similar issues regardless of experience, position or discipline.

Social network theory and relationship-building can be nebulous concepts to detangle in terms of formal evaluation of the impact of the forum. Our process of evaluation comprised a variety of methods, including online polls at and following fora, online surveys and in particular ongoing conversations with PLs regarding their development. The authors are grateful to members of the PL community for giving permission to reproduce their anonymous comments here.

Designing a forum-based approach

The formal concept of communities of practice (Lave & Wenger, 1991; Wenger, 1998) has been used for many years. However, communities of practice can be difficult to initiate and sustain (Roberts, 2006; Kerno, 2008). They rely on active participation and sustained commitment from PLs, which, in turn, require a commitment of time and resource that may be difficult to sustain given the complex nature of the role and demands upon their time. The concept of professional fora as learning space has been utilised in various sectors, including health care settings (Hutcheon et al., 2010) and online fora for academic development have been discussed in the literature (Hammond, 1997; Price et al., 2015). The concept of a physical space for meeting, sharing, discussing and networking is less well explored, though social network theory provides a useful starting point. Social network theory and analysis are a long-established sociological approach to understanding organisations, class structures and social mobility. According to Scott:

> Individuals are, as it were, tied to one another by invisible bonds which are knitted together into a criss-cross mesh of connections, much as a fishing net or a length of cloth is made from intertwined fabrics.
>
> (1998, p. 109)

Within this conception, in which individuals are often described as 'nodes' and the relationships between them as 'ties', social network theory provides both a theoretical framework for understanding and a means of analysis of a situation (Mujis et al., 2011). Applying the principles of social network theory within our own institution, it was clear that for PLs, the 'ties' between them were clustered around disciplinary areas and not strongly linked to other PLs across the institution. This lack of regular opportunities to share practice or 'silo-ed approach' had resulted in each PL developing in isolation their own subset of skills to manage the role over time. Events aimed at breaking down silos, such as teaching and learning conferences, were useful, but were not targeted at the PL role, which at our university requires a unique combination of leadership, management, administrative and academic skills.

The forum-based approach was therefore conceived in response to the way these isolated working practices had left PLs feeling unsupported and underappreciated, despite undertaking one of the most difficult strategic roles in a university where teaching excellence and student experience underpin the institution's focus and identity. During conversations with individual PLs, started by the Organisational Development team within Human Resources, later in partnership with educational developers from the Lincoln Academy of Learning and Teaching Engagement team, PLs expressed concern about their lack of meaningful engagement or 'ties' with colleagues and a lack of agency to influence institutional policies and practices that impacted on their role. This was further compounded by the fact that in some cases, the academic in question may not have actively volunteered for the role of PL (some had inherited it or felt otherwise obliged to take it on), they may be new to the institution or they may be attempting to fulfil the role for the first time. In addition, new programme formats constantly arise in response to emerging learning needs; so, for example, PLs for degree apprenticeships or foundation years were particularly disadvantaged by a lack of opportunities to share practice with colleagues in a similar role within the institution.

As educational developers, we wanted to provide flexible opportunities for shared communication in order to enable good practice to be disseminated across the cohort of around 200 PLs. From an academic perspective, we envisaged that this approach would improve the quality of the work environment and provide efficient, targeted development opportunities for time-poor PLs. The approach was supported by feedback from PLs, who through a formal evaluation of available support quickly identified that a significant benefit from meeting colleagues was the possibility of sharing practice and learning from their similar experiences:

> ... the conversations and talking to different people, and then suddenly realising that there is someone else that you've never seen in your life before because they work on the other side of campus, but they are dealing with a programme that has similar issues and then you end up picking things up.
> (Pepper et al., 2018, p. 11)

By adopting a forum-based approach, we aimed to support and realise the full potential of the non-disciplinary aspects of PL experience and expertise, and increase both the number and quality of the ties between PLs across the various Schools and Departments of the institution. The anticipated outcomes of this included:

- Knowledge exchange across disciplines and professional hierarchies with regard to pedagogy and leadership.
- Development of a professional identity as PLs and as part of a community of PLs.
- PLs feeling more supported to carry out their role and empowered to challenge institutional practice.

Implementation of the forum-based approach

A key benefit of the proposed design of the forum-based approach was that it allowed us to respond to individual PL needs without a substantial increase in workload for the educational development team. The main workload, once the approach had been agreed, was the logistical implications of attempting to create an opportunity for communication despite busy diaries, different timetables and three campuses. We focussed on face-to-face communication in the first instance, so our first challenge was to choose an appropriate time and space for the forum to suit the majority of PLs.

We worked with colleagues in Human Resources to maintain an up-to-date list of PLs, and found that diary invitations sent to the whole community were the most effective means of communication. This was in recognition of anecdotal reports from PLs that they received a high volume of emails and this, along with their challenging and an uneven workload, lessened the impact of 'pull' marketing strategies (that is trying to generate interest and engagement through information emails and advertisements) since it was easy for these communications to be missed or forgotten.

In advance of each term or semester, we would reach out to PLs requesting hosts for upcoming fora, or making suggestions on areas for development or sharing of practice to take place during the forum. Through this approach, we felt we could harness some of the strengths of a community of practice, driven by educational developers with minimal resources and delivering tangible benefits to the PL community without requiring a significant commitment of their time. The forum took place regularly, usually every six to eight weeks for one hour, depending on termly requests from the PL community.

In order to break down silos and help support a sense of community, we aimed to create a socially relaxed space, located on the main campus, in spacious rooms with lunch provided. This attempted to emulate the spontaneous social bonding which occurs through conversation and consultation of fellow academics over lunch in our main cafeteria. Throughout the implementation of the forum, we found that the most effective approach occurred through aligning the delivery to the personal and professional needs of the PLs. One small way in which this was achieved came from reflecting on Maslow's hierarchy of needs (1943) by:

- Providing physiological comfort in the form of a warm, light space with food and refreshments – no need to worry about food
- Creating a sense of safety through ensuring individual contributions to discussions are kept confidential through mutual agreement of the 'Chatham House rule' – no judgements on needs expressed and confidentiality observed
- Facilitating development of a sense of belonging through a focus on PL concerns and avoiding preoccupation with professional hierarchies – privileging their needs and their agendas, making sure they are at the centre of discussions
- Promoting esteem by continued recognition of the importance of PLs, their expertise and contribution; proactively seeking the community's views and sharing these with senior leaders – valuing and building a sense of recognition for an important role being undertaken
- Offering a space in which achievements, particularly innovative, creative practices, can be identified and shared – showcasing and disseminating effective practice and breaking down silos

This visible consideration of PL needs was well received. By offering a space exclusively for PLs to foster new ideas and acting as a means of feeding back their views to senior leaders through reporting on discussions or through surveys, the forum allowed members to feel a greater sense of empowerment and recognition from the wider institution – they were both seen and heard.

PLs possess expertise and insight into wider institutional challenges with respect to pedagogy and the student experience more broadly; there is potential for educational developers to realise institutional benefits in making use of that tacit knowledge. In return, open dialogue in a collaborative space allows PLs the opportunity to address any frustrations or concerns they experience. Discussion often touched on the fact that they felt a surfeit of responsibility yet a deficit of power. By creating the forum as a space to allow this community to form, discuss and debate, the key needs of those in the role could be further identified and supported by educational developers and signposted to senior managers where needed.

In some instances, the forum space created an opportunity for direct dialogue with senior management in a unique way, by enabling the formation of relationships in a face-to-face setting. Creating opportunities for dialogue with PLs is an important aspect of promoting respect for the role. For example, at one forum the incumbent Deputy Vice Chancellor for Teaching and Learning met with the community, and this allowed her to gain insight into the perspective and role of the PL. Similarly, for the PLs, they gained insight into the teaching and learning priorities of a new senior manager and created a pathway for future contact and ease of dialogue.

With this success in mind, following the creation of a new role supporting postgraduate students, we created a subcommunity through the addition of some bespoke fora, aimed solely at those PLs who managed postgraduate programmes. The impact of this more targeted support and networking space is evidenced through the words of one senior colleague:

> For a number of years, I was University Taught Postgraduate Dean, the first appointed at my University. Key for me was building links between PG PLs, to share best practice between themselves, and to provide strong connections between themselves and central professional services (student support, recruitment, International Office, etc.). This activity was best progressed through regular forums, as well as the appointment of PG Leads in each of the University's colleges. Many of the PLs, despite their individual expertise, lacked the capacity and opportunities to work together. Building confidence as mid-management leaders within their Schools, and developing relationships, was thus most important.

Hosting the forum

We found that the forum-based approach can be particularly effective when one forum meeting is hosted by a PL in response to a particular pedagogical need or a request to share practice across the community. For example, one PL contacted us with a request to host a discussion on best practice in managing marking and assessment, which is one of the core challenges of successfully delivering a programme, particularly at undergraduate level. PLs are responsible for a number of quality assurance processes as part of their role, and one key element is that of the assessment literacy of the programme team. Marking and assessment is often raised with PLs as part of external examiner feedback and is regularly identified as an area for improvement in National Student Survey responses. The PL had been inspired to share his practice and request a wider discussion on solutions to the challenges he faced as a result of student concerns about timely feedback and parity of assessment support.

In response to this request and in conjunction with the PL, we designed and delivered a forum event which employed a combination of methods, including online polls, open dialogue and sticky notes, to gather information on the PL community approach to marking and assessment. The forum opened with a presentation from the PL explaining his current practice and contextualising the challenges he faced in marking work, with particular reference to the 15 working days of 'sector-standard' marking policy in place at the University. The discussion was spearheaded by the hosting PL, who explained the methods he had developed and applied to manage marking for a large cohort of over 200 undergraduate students. These methods had allowed him to adhere to good assessment practice while balancing the demands of a heavy workload. This opportunity to discuss and share practice in relation to feedback and assessment proved useful for colleagues and sparked discussion beyond the confines of the meeting. The design of the forum included the use of digital tools as suggested by the hosting PL: colleagues in the room were asked to respond to three questions using live polling software. This was a useful way to quickly ascertain opinions and spark engagement in the room and an opportunity for some to trial the online polling software for the first time. A total of 56 of 62 attendees engaged with the live poll, and colleagues later reported a spike in interest in the use of the software in the wider teaching practice of the group members. This was in itself good evidence of the benefits of sharing practice across an institution.

In addition to using live polling software, we also included a small group discussion as part of the forum, using an online tool which creates virtual sticky notes. Some PLs were comfortable using the tool themselves, while others simply responded as part of a wider discussion, and their comments were added live, projected on screen. The link to this discussion board was communicated to all PLs, and those not in attendance at the forum were asked to add to the responses to support further action following the forum. This approach was designed to collate responses to five key questions concerning the broader topic of marking, assessment and feedback. The responses were then collated and a report on the discussion and suggested policy changes was created for senior management.

Ultimately, the impact of the forum was not sufficient to challenge the existing policy on marking and feedback, with particular reference to the compulsory 15-day turnaround time. However, there was an increased awareness across the PL group of why the policy was implemented across the sector and how different PLs approach assessment and feedback in their practice. The experience of hosting a forum also resulted in identifiable benefits for the facilitator in terms of his development and sense of agency as a PL. He noted that:

> ...it was really useful to challenge the university and see whether the issue could be addressed centrally. When that was not possible it gave more agency (for me at least) to address the issue in more local spaces.

Through his leadership and delivery of one forum, he began a journey of development as a representative of the community of PLs, which had a huge impact not only on his personal practice, but also on the practice in place across the institution:

> Hosting the forum created opportunities for me to develop a staff training programme around 'marking fast and fair' and 'developing quality feedback'. These were delivered six to eight times through staff continuous (*sic*) professional development sessions across the university (as well as a dedicated teaching development session in [my College]). These sessions flagged my interest in improving turnaround time to Directors [of Teaching and Learning] within the College and I've now worked on several successful projects with them which have had a long-lasting impact on the university.
>
> As a result of this engagement and subsequent successes I've found senior managers are more likely to take my voice seriously and support me [in] developing improvement projects. I now feel there is a more robust system in place (supported by assessment calendars, clearer information in module handbooks, reviewed assessment framework) to support staff to achieve 15 day turnaround time on their modules.
>
> This was (and remains) a huge area of improvement for the NSS, but has allowed me to change focus now to improving how the College engages alumni and businesses with their degrees – the key link here is having an existing reputation of success which Directors are happy to support as I turn my focus to a new area.

Challenges of the forum-based approach

The key to the success of the forum described above was undoubtedly the participation and leadership of the individual PL. The opportunity afforded by the forum led to the empowering effect of his direct impact and influence on the teaching and learning community, giving rise to his subsequent delivery of CPD sessions and design of assessment support tools. This work also directly benefited him in terms of his increased confidence in the role. However, it can be challenging to secure hosts for the forum, with PLs citing practical constraints such as busy diaries and heavy workload. Some express concerns that their own practice might not be best practice, indicating that more work is needed to build confidence.

To support more PLs to make use of the opportunity provided by the forum, we are currently working to design a course in academic leadership aimed at our PLs in order to build this confidence. This course will include more face-to-face interaction between senior figures and the PLs. We have found that opportunities to engage with senior leaders in the fora to date have been well received, and this is clearly a useful method in promoting the importance of the role. In addition, in order to replicate the success of the case study above, we feel that the lack of volunteers to host the forum may be linked to a perception of how it was 'not possible' to achieve immediate policy change as a result of the forum. Mechanisms to support change need to be better established, for example, senior leadership support is required should a PL wish to escalate any research or findings from surveying their colleagues and collating their expertise within the forum space.

Another challenge is in ensuring that we maintain the community ethos within the forum meetings. As educational developers involved in various strategic initiatives, it can be difficult to maintain the focus of the forum on the sharing of teaching and learning practice across the institution. By gathering a large number of PLs together in one space, this creates an attractive communication opportunity not just for the PLs themselves, but also for professional services staff who frequently request the ability to communicate ongoing strategy and initiatives or projects to these key stakeholders. We designed the forum to take place every six to eight weeks – regularly enough to form an ongoing community, yet infrequently enough to be realistically sustainable in terms of the time commitments of the educational developers and PLs. Therefore, we often found that at the point of convening the forum, we as educational developers or other professional services teams had an urgent need to communicate with PLs. As a result, there is an ongoing risk of the forum becoming a marketing or communication tool which met the needs of the wider university, but failed to support the community it was created to serve.

Fostering engagement with the forum on an ongoing basis is an important aspect of the sustainable delivery of this approach. It is recommended that sessions which largely comprise transmission of information should be avoided where possible or the information should be circulated in advance of the forum. Where this communication is required, it can be ameliorated through recording and sharing talks or running multiple sessions. If too many fora involve didactic sharing of information, then PLs will begin to disengage from what should be their personal community forum space.

Key learning points

The forum-based approach to supporting PLs, and in many cases asking them to share their expertise or offering them a space in which to share or critique the latest teaching and learning developments, is useful for both PLs and educational developers. A combination of open discussion, the opportunity to host a forum and an avenue for consultation of the PL body on major changes or projects taking place in the teaching and learning community is the most effective design in our context. Through a variation of the content of the forum meetings, the benefits of the forum-based approach to supporting PLs to be led by PLs for the benefit of the PL cohort can be fully achieved, while still ensuring the ongoing function of the community space when there are no volunteer hosts.

The PL body is diverse, and educational developers may find that PLs for postgraduate courses, degree apprenticeships or distance learning programmes find themselves in a liminal space in a forum concerned more with issues relevant to traditional undergraduate programmes. This can be ameliorated by the creation of less frequent bespoke forum meetings, ideally involving senior management to break down hierarchical barriers to development and engagement. However, in line with social network theory, the wider network should remain the focus of the main programme of support and a more open community can be of use to PLs in more specific circumstances. For example, joint degrees require special consideration in terms of supporting and sharing practice, an issue explored in Case Study 5 (Irving Bell) in this book. Here, this diversity of professional experience in a forum which invites over 200 PLs can be an asset. Through the forum-based approach, two colleagues in the process of designing a joint degree successfully used the forum to consult their colleagues on their opinions and seek advice on their intended programme design. In this case, the forum as a space to share practice and create a community of PLs was particularly effective – a model that could be applied in other institutions.

Educational developer colleagues or PLs who plan to trial this or a similar approach may wish to consider the following points:

- Focus the design of the approach to suit the needs of PLs, ideally with PL ownership and/or delivery.
- Try to ensure buy-in from senior management so that their beliefs and assumptions can be 'sanity checked' and the outcomes of the discussion and any additional knowledge gleaned can be escalated to those who should hear it/can do something with it.
- Logistical concerns will directly impact on the realities of PL engagement as academic diaries grow increasingly busier, so consider the benefits and drawbacks of face-to-face and/or online fora for your context through ongoing evaluation and ideally offer a blend of approaches.
- Identify ways to obtain and maintain up-to-date PL lists, use 'push' marketing strategies like calendar invites to make sure everyone is aware of scheduled fora and to facilitate frictionless engagement.
- Avoid using the forum for one-way communication of institutional policy information from colleagues outside of the PL community where possible.
- Align forum topics to appropriate times of the year to maximise the impact of the discussion in terms of changes to practice (see 'Gardeners' Calendar' case study by Eve in the institutional section).
- Pay attention to the needs of less vocal or visible community members, such as those new to their role and those leading more specialised programmes.

Conclusion

Our design for an initiative to better support PLs in their role was for a regular forum meeting which would allow members to move beyond formal engagement with our team of educational developers, towards a peer-based, self-determined and ultimately empowering model. Through this process, we hoped to form a sense of community among PLs and to increase institutional recognition of their importance in underpinning teaching excellence at the university. This recognition became increasingly important as models of teaching changed following the move to online practice as a result of the Coronavirus pandemic.

The benefits of sharing practice and in particular of using the forum as a space in which to consult colleagues were highlighted above. This seemingly simple notion of a collaborative space becomes particularly effective when close attention is paid to the unique needs of this group. The realisation of the importance of communication across disciplinary, hierarchical and spatial boundaries within the institution was our largest gain from the forum-based approach, and we continue to prioritise breaking down silos and creating opportunities for communication where possible to ensure this benefit is maximised. We have embraced the opportunity provided by a move to online practice to explore new ways to deliver the forum-based approach, but note that it is difficult to create opportunities for networking in small groups in a virtual space. We hope to develop our online support to achieve a better balance between communication with PLs and communication among PLs within the forum space. However, for the creation of new links among PLs, it seems likely that in the future, some elements of face-to-face engagement will continue to be incorporated where possible.

It is worth noting that social network approaches more widely have been considered 'advantageous to organizations operating within complex and turbulent environments' (Meuser et al., 2016), as they provide greater access to social capital and other resources, leading to a greater capacity for agile response to the changing environment (Devine et al., 1999). Given the context in which the sector is operating at the time of writing, with the Coronavirus pandemic sweeping the world and having a profound (and likely lasting) impact upon higher education institutions in terms of pedagogy, participation and a host of other aspects, the challenge of avoiding entrapment in the 'death grip of equilibrium' (Wheatley & Kellner-Rogers, 1996, p. 33) has never been more acute. Throughout this chapter, we have shown that by prioritising open communication and collaborative space creation however simple the method, the resulting support mechanisms can easily be adapted to suit a range of needs over time. The authors welcome contact from colleagues interested in creating a similar approach to PL support at other institutions.

References

Anthony, S. G. and Antony, J. (2017) 'Academic leadership – special or simple', *International Journal of Productivity and Performance Management*, 66(5), pp. 630–637. doi: 10.1108/IJPPM-08-2016-0162.

Burke, K. M. (2010) 'Distributed leadership and shared governance in post-secondary education', *Management in Education*, 24(2), pp. 51–54. doi: 10.1177/0892020610363088.

Devine, D. J., et al. (1999) 'Teams in organizations: prevalence, characteristics, and effectiveness', *Small Group Research*, 30(6), pp. 678–711. doi: 10.1177/104649649903000602.

Hammond, M. (1997) 'Developing networked learning within higher education: A case study of an electronic forum for...', *Teaching in Higher Education*, 2(3), pp. 243. doi: 10.1080/1356215970020306.

Hutcheon, R. G., Iorlano, M. and Thomas, M. K. (2010) 'Clinical Status: A daily forum for resident discussion and staff education', *Journal of the American Medical Directors Association*, 11(9), pp. 671–676. doi: 10.1016/j.jamda.2010.02.016.

Kerno, S. J. (2008) 'Limitations of communities of practice', *Journal of Leadership and Organizational Studies*, 15(1), pp. 69–78. doi: 10.1177/1548051808317998.

Kohtamäki, V. (2019) 'Academic leadership and university reform-guided management changes in Finland', *Journal of Higher Education Policy and Management*, 41(1), pp. 70–85. doi: 10.1080/1360080X.2018.1553499.

Laing, C. and Laing, G. (2011) 'The student as customer model and its impact on the academic leadership role in higher education', in Yorke, J. D. (ed.) *Meeting the Challenges: Proceedings of the ATN Assessment Conference 2011*. Curtin University, Australia, pp. 117–123.

Lave, J. and Wenger, E. (1991) *Situated Learning: Legitimate Peripheral Participation*. Cambridge: Cambridge University.

Maslow, A. H. (1943) 'A theory of human motivation', *Psychological Review*, 50(4), pp. 370–396.

Meuser, J. D., et al. (2016) 'A network analysis of leadership theory', *Journal of Management*, 42(5), pp. 1374. doi: 10.1177/0149206316647099.

Mujis, D., et al. (2011) *Collaboration and Networking in Education*. London: Springer.

Pepper, R., Crawford, K. and Sanderson, R. (2018) Developing academic leadership and innovative practice, Leadership Foundation for Higher Education. Available at https://www.advance-he.ac.uk/knowledge-hub/developing-academic-leadership-and-innovative-practice (Accessed December 2021)

Price, E., Coffey, B. and Nethery, A. (2015) 'An early career academic network: what worked and what didn't', *Journal of Further and Higher Education*, 39(5), pp. 680–698. doi: 10.1080/0309877X.2014.971106.

Roberts, J. (2006) 'Limits to Communities of Practice', *Journal of Management Studies*, 43(3), pp. 623–639. https://doi.org/10.1111/j.1467-6486.2006.00618.x

Scott, J. (1998) 'Trend Report: Social Network Analysis', *Sociology*, 22(1), pp. 109–127.

Wenger, E. (1998) *Communities of Practice: Learning, meaning and identity*. Cambridge: Cambridge University Press.

Wheatley, M. J. and Kellner-Rogers, M. (1996) *A Simpler Way*. San Francisco: Berrett-Koehler Publishers.

Practitioner response: Social support for programme leaders – Building an interdisciplinary community

Mayara da Mota Matos, Brazil

The academic environment is filled with competition and isolation as structural questions like lack of funding, emphasis on productivity and heavy workloads do not promote community sense or distributed leadership. In addressing this subject, this chapter has appealing suggestions that could point directions for the adoption by Brazilian universities. Driven by the goal of creating a collaborative space that allows sharing difficulties and innovative solutions, besides the reflection upon their work, the structure of the forum (described in detail in this chapter) makes it possible to be adapted to different cultures and needs.

In Brazilian public universities, PLs are university professors who temporarily assume these roles, frequently due to the lack of others interested in the position. These professors do not lose their other roles in the university when assuming a leadership position. They have to reconcile teaching, research and outreach programs with management activities. Usually, they do not receive any training or institutional support for doing so and taking on those roles has been called a 'sacrifice for the group'. As they lack prior experience and training, having the opportunity to openly discuss practices and solutions could benefit both the professionals and the students that are affected by their decisions. Therefore, the sense of community built by the initiative is much needed and could have a positive impact on the PLs.

Other highlights of the proposal include pointing to the importance of social support for program leaders and the possibility of building this support network based on institutional initiatives and fostering personal agency by letting program leaders themselves identify themes of interest and conduct the activities in a collaborative learning proposal. Since financial resources are usually an obstacle in Brazilian universities, the structure of the forum allows it to be organised without large budgets which can provide a good return for the academic community with a relatively low investment. The forum-based proposal also has the potential to encourage the exchange of knowledge and practices between different fields, which is pivotal since working in an interdisciplinary way has always been challenging because of the way Brazilian universities are organized (i.e. departments separated by field of knowledge). Last, building a sense of community in universities has been linked to reduced stress and anxiety on professors and the proposal of the authors is a complete and manageable way of doing this.

DOI: 10.4324/9781003127413-21

Chapter 8

Empowering programme leaders
Developing relational academic leadership

Sarah Moore, UK

Introduction

This chapter aims to address a key gap in literature, policy and practice around programme leadership – that of building relationships with others. Conversations primarily focus on the knowledge and skills required to carry out the programme leader (PL) role effectively. However, the complex nature of programme leadership means that it is impossible to fully empower those in this role without exploring the relationships that are essential to its success. In this chapter, I draw on findings from interviews with over 20 colleagues from a range of disciplines to identify the multifaceted relationships that PLs cultivate through their role and offer suggestions around how PLs can cultivate effective relationships in practice. I also set out a series of questions that could be used by academic developers to prompt PLs to forge networks with others.

The nature of programme leadership

As highlighted elsewhere in this volume, programme leadership requires a unique set of knowledge and skills. While these are important elements, the significance of affective and relational aspects of the role highlighted in broader management texts have been less well recognised in literature, institutional policy and professional development activity around programme leadership (Cahill et al, 2015; Cunliffe and Eriksen, 2011; Marchiando et al, 2015; Milburn, 2010; Moore, 2018;; Murphy and Curtis, 2013). Recent understandings of leadership have emphasised the way that roles are constructed through everyday interactions between the individual and those around them (Cahill et al, 2015; Crevani et al, 2010; Cunliffe and Eriksen, 2011; Milburn, 2010). Furthermore, building relationships, described by Milburn (2010, p. 93) as a 'concern for people', is at the heart of programme leadership due to the complex nature of the role (Cahill et al, 2015; Murphy and Curtis, 2013). As well as organising the teaching on the programme, PLs need to draw on a wide range of colleagues with specific areas of expertise, not only from their department but across the institution, to ensure the smooth running of their programme (Cahill et al, 2015; Vilkinas and Cartan, 2015).

DOI: 10.4324/9781003127413-22

However, given that much programme leadership is learned 'on the job' (Mitchell, 2015), it is often difficult for new PLs to forge and navigate this network proactively, as they only find out who they need to talk to at the point where they are trying to solve a particular problem. Programme leadership is highly dependent on the local, departmental and institutional context in which the programme and PL operate; so what may work for one programme may not work for others and PLs may need to adapt their approach to different situations (Crevani et al, 2010; Murphy and Curtis, 2013). Unlike other forms of leadership, PLs often do not act as line managers for the colleagues they are working with, so tend to lead by influence rather than exerting authority (Cahill et al, 2015; Irving, 2015; Milburn, 2010; Murphy and Curtis, 2013; Preston and Price, 2012; Vilkinas and Cartan, 2015). These relationships are often sensitive, as while PLs often take on the role for a set period of time, they still consider themselves as part of the academic community (Bryman, 2007; Irving, 2015; Milburn, 2010). However, by virtue of their position, they may also find themselves having to enact decisions made by senior management colleagues, which may be unpopular among their colleagues (Preston and Price, 2012).

Therefore, academic developers can play an important role in helping PLs explore those relationships that can empower them to enact their roles in a way that feels authentic to each individual leader and programme and acknowledges the sensitive and negotiated nature of these relationships. This chapter draws on empirical data collected as part of a research project into the experiences of PLs. The next section will offer a brief overview of the methodology before discussing the findings and their implications for PLs.

Methods

The ideas articulated in this chapter are based on a research project carried out in a single research-intensive institution in 2016. Recognising the difference in roles across the institution, a questionnaire was sent out to senior leaders to circulate to any colleagues with 'programme leadership responsibilities'. This was designed to collect baseline information about how they defined their role and the key tasks associated with the role. Those completing the form were invited to leave their email address if they wished to participate in a follow-up, semi-structured interview about their experiences. Twenty-one PLs from disciplines across the institution were interviewed, with each interview lasting around 45 minutes using a set of open prompt questions. Ethical approval for the project and the dissemination of findings was obtained through the processes of the institution where the project took place.

Initial codes were drawn from the data, and themes were then identified across the codes. While these covered a wide range of aspects of programme leadership, interactions with others was identified as a key theme that could be repeatedly seen in the data, and thus formed the basis for this chapter. Pseudonyms are used throughout.

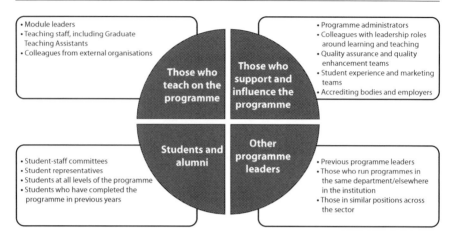

Figure 8.1 Four categories of programme leader relationships

Findings

Through the analysis, four main relationships that PLs had to negotiate were identified as illustrated in Figure 8.1.

The next section will explore how PLs can be supported to nurture each of these relationships using examples from the PLs that were interviewed.

Those who teach on the programme

Getting buy-in from others who teach on the programme such as module leaders and teaching staff, including Graduate Teaching Assistants and external contributors, is especially important for PLs. As Claire, the leader of a postgraduate taught programme, noted, 'That's the key, that's what this role needs, it needs collaboration of people, you can't do this on your own'. PLs bring together colleagues teaching on the programme in a variety of different ways, both formal and informal, to discuss its development (Bryman, 2007).

Bringing colleagues together

Jane's PGT programme was particularly challenging, as it drew on a wide range of modules that were also part of other programmes. Module leads therefore tended to work in silos, so Jane wanted to bring them together in the same room. She sent open invites to all the module leads to attend a series of meetings. At the start of each meeting, she took care to introduce the ethos underpinning her programme's development for those who had been unable to attend previously. She actively encouraged colleagues to voice their opinions and challenges around the programme, so that colleagues felt that they had been heard.

Typically, this involves regular formal meetings of the teaching team, although the make-up of the team and the areas of focus depend on the individual programme. Most include module leads in these meetings, at least. Some teams, particularly those at postgraduate level, are relatively small. Others may be much larger, potentially drawing in colleagues from other departments if their modules are used in programmes across multiple settings and also colleagues who lead on aspects such as recruitment and employability. Considering how to encourage colleagues to take ownership of the programme and its development is especially important.

Engaging colleagues through the meetings

Steven rotated the chairing of his programme team meetings as a way of distributing power among his teaching colleagues and encouraging ownership of the programme.

Away Days and open meetings can act as a catalyst for programme development, whether in the creation of a new programme or generating buy-in for a significant redevelopment of an existing programme.

One of the most common and significant challenges faced by PLs is that of engaging colleagues who teach in the development and delivery of the programme, especially when they do not have line management responsibility for them (Cahill et al, 2015; Murphy and Curtis, 2013). There is potential for the aims and priorities of the PL to be at odds with those set by the line managers of colleagues teaching on the programme, and some PLs find themselves navigating workloads of colleagues who they had previously worked alongside as peers while also ensuring that the programme runs as intended. This often leads to difficulties, for example, if a colleague is suddenly unable to teach their part of the programme that then needs to be filled by someone else (Murphy and Curtis, 2013).

Allowing time for buy-in

Andrew led a large undergraduate programme for three years and valued the different perspectives of his colleagues, many of whom had been teaching on the programme for a long time. However, whenever he tried to suggest changes to the programme, some colleagues became defensive about losing 'their bit'. He also found it difficult to manage their complaints about things he couldn't change. He realised that change would take longer than expected, but that it was important to take the time to ensure buy-in from colleagues before making changes. He allowed space in the meetings for colleagues to talk about their fears, while also being clear about things that could not be changed. He favoured group discussions rather than individual conversations to ensure that conversations were open and fair.

Engaging colleagues who teach on the programme on an ongoing basis, and ensuring that they have the opportunity to voice concerns and take ownership of the programme, is therefore essential in ensuring that PLs gain buy-in.

PRACTICE TIPS FOR WORKING WITH THOSE WHO TEACH ON THE PROGRAMME

- Identify which colleagues need to be involved in discussions, especially those who have little opportunity to talk to each other
- Allow space and time for open discussion
- Acknowledge colleagues' concerns about potential changes
- Revisit the programme's ethos on a regular basis to ensure discussions remain focused
- Be clear about what is and is not within your power to influence
- Consider taking turns to chair programme team meetings

Those who support and influence the programme

PLs also need to consider how they might identify a network of different colleagues from across the institution who can support them in their work (Cahill et al, 2015; Vilkinas and Cartan, 2015). Considered by many as a key part of the programme team, programme administrators are essential colleagues in the running of the programme. This is especially the case for PLs who take on the role for a fixed length of time. Programme administrators have usually been in their posts for far longer, and are a vital source of knowledge around the processes, systems and structures that the PL has to navigate and what they need to do when. Even where there is no dedicated administrator for a specific programme, professional services colleagues working across the department, particularly those whose roles are focused around the student experience, can provide support for PLs.

Working with professional services colleagues to support student experience

Andrew found the expertise and institutional memory of the professional services colleagues he worked with invaluable in supporting him in his role. Over time, he and his colleagues had developed a keen awareness of each other's strengths and tacit knowledge around supporting students on the programme. Andrew was often out of the office due to teaching and research, whereas the student experience office was open during regular office hours. The student experience team could therefore support students with some of their immediate concerns, while Andrew was able to dedicate his time to dealing with more complex issues.

As well as colleagues in their department, PLs also value relationships with colleagues in central professional services, particularly those with expertise that they do not have.

Support for marketing and recruitment

For Jackie's newly created programme, marketing and recruitment were a particularly thorny issue. While she was very familiar with her subject and the rationale for the programme itself, she had little experience of producing a business case or marketing her programme to prospective students. To begin with, she found it difficult to identify who in the institution could help her with this. However, her perseverance was worthwhile, as when she did get to speak to a colleague in marketing, she found their insights incredibly valuable.

Establishing key relationships with one or two individuals from the teams responsible for quality assurance and admissions in the institution, and involving them early on in discussions with the programme team, can make it easier to navigate institutional processes. PLs may also build up relationships with others outside the institution where appropriate, for example, with employers, external speakers and accrediting bodies.

As PLs often do not have authority over those who teach on their programmes, they may be able to use existing departmental structures to establish credibility and authority for their work (Cahill et al, 2015; Irving, 2015; Milburn, 2010; Murphy and Curtis, 2013; Preston and Price, 2012; Vilkinas and Cartan, 2015). Departmental committees can provide a key mechanism for bringing PLs together to share ideas and good practice, though this does depend on the culture of the individual committee.

Utilising committees to support programme development

As well as being the leader for an undergraduate programme, Philip was a member of key committees in his department through the senior role he held. As PL, he identified several significant changes that he wanted to implement, but was aware that to be effective, these changes needed to be adopted by all of those teaching on the programme. He brought his proposals to his undergraduate teaching committee and clearly explained the rationale behind them. Having the support of the committee meant that he was able to convince others of their value, and therefore implement them more consistently across the team.

Senior leaders responsible for learning and teaching can be key figures in providing the clout for PLs to make significant changes to programmes. Nonetheless, senior leaders may also be subject to conflicting priorities between themselves and line managers.

Negotiating priorities

Joe was a senior leader for learning and teaching in a large department and responsible for overseeing the development of a suite of programmes co-ordinated by different PLs. Through his role, he met frequently with PLs to discuss the development of teaching practice within the department and identify common issues across programmes. However, this work did not necessarily align with the objectives set by his colleagues' line managers, including the Head of Department. In some cases, this led to a clash of priorities, and Joe noticed that individuals tended to prioritise the objectives set by their line manager as these were more likely to lead to promotion.

PLs therefore need to develop a network of colleagues, both within their department and across the wider institution, to support them in their role.

PRACTICE TIPS FOR WORKING WITH THOSE WHO TEACH ON THE PROGRAMME

- Include programme administrators in programme team meetings
- Categorise the types of student queries that could be dealt with by professional services staff in the department and those which are more appropriate for PLs to address
- Identify key institutional contacts for areas such as quality assurance, marketing and recruitment and admissions, and include them in discussions around the programme as early as possible
- Consider when and how to involve external colleagues, for example, employers and accreditors
- Identify possibilities for senior buy-in and support for the programme, whether from individuals or committee groups.

Students and alumni

For the vast majority of PLs, the relationships they forge with their students are highly important, both in terms of supporting those on the programme and in engaging students in its design and development. The methods used by PLs to ensure students feel supported while they are on the programme tend to be dependent on the nature of the programme itself, particularly in terms of its size (Cahill et al, 2015; Mitchell, 2015).

Supporting students on the programme

Claire was the PL of a small postgraduate programme with around 25 students. As well as being PL, she was also module leader for two of the modules and personal tutor for half of the student cohort. She therefore engaged in regular informal conversations with students about how they were finding the programme, and while recognising that sometimes they simply needed to express their anxieties, she was also able to respond quickly to issues as they arose. Claire had an 'open door' policy for all students on the programme, regardless of whether they were her tutees. She had tried to set up more formal consultation sessions, but few came; she found that informal approaches worked better.

Philip led an undergraduate programme whose numbers had doubled in a single year. His programme leadership role had included overall responsibility for personal tutoring, which he had relished because he felt it was important to maintain connections with the students. Ultimately, he found this too big a demand on his workload and delegated the personal tutoring part of the role to a colleague to ensure he could continue to have contact with students through teaching on the programme.

A further option that some PLs adopt is to delegate to 'level leaders', where individuals are responsible for the personal and academic support of students across each academic level and report to the PL.

Although less common, students and alumni can be hugely valuable in supporting programme development. Regular student-staff committees and meetings with student representatives are not only helpful in identifying issues as they arise, but also provide unique expertise and perspectives for PLs in the ongoing review and adaptation of their programmes.

Drawing on student perspectives to review and develop the programme

As she had less contact through direct teaching compared to other PLs, in initiating a review of her programme, Natasha circulated a survey and set up a focus group to find out what current students thought. Similarly, alumni can offer insights into what is expected of students after they have completed their programme and the elements of the programme that have impacted on them the most.

Practice tips for working with students and alumni

- Talk to students about their preferred mechanisms for support and ways to feedback about the programme
- For large programmes, consider using a network of colleagues to ensure students feel supported
- Establish processes for working with student-staff committees and student representatives for the programme
- When developing existing programmes or designing new programmes, consider how you might draw on the views of current students and alumni early in the development process.

Other programme leaders

While many institutions across the sector have developed specific professional development activity for PLs, this is not necessarily the case for all institutions. Even where support is in place, professional development for PLs often takes the form of 'informal situated peer learning' (Mitchell, 2015, p. 722). PLs learn much of their role on the job, and given that they are often reactive to immediate crises and issues that need resolving, this can contribute to a lack of confidence. However, other PLs can be a helpful source of support and information, especially in the first year when PLs are yet to see the full 'rhythm' of the programme (Cahill et al, 2015; Mitchell, 2015).

Learning from the previous programme leader

Tom's postgraduate taught programme was accredited by an external body. Knowing he was due to take on programme leadership the following year, the PL at the time invited him to lead on the preparation of accreditation documentation. In doing so, he not only had the opportunity to shadow his colleague, but also developed an invaluable understanding of the ethos, content and structure underpinning the programme before he took on the role.

Although these are often informal and inconsistent across departments, networking, mentoring and shadowing opportunities, whether formal or informal, can be highly beneficial for new PLs as they enable them to apply their learning immediately to their own context.

PRACTICE TIPS FOR WORKING WITH THOSE WHO TEACH ON THE PROGRAMME

- Speak to the previous PL about their experience of the role
- Where possible, arrange a shadowing/handover period with the previous PL
- Explore opportunities for liaising with other PLs across the institution
- Take advantage of any institutional mentoring opportunities that may enable you to pair up with another PL

The final section of this chapter will draw together the findings from this research and explore their implications for those in academic development roles in more detail.

Discussion and questions for practice

Although limited in number and in a specific context, the findings of this project offer insights into how PLs cultivate various relationships with others that are both complex and vital for the successful enactment of their role (Cahill et al, 2015; Crevani et al, 2010; Cunliffe and Eriksen, 2011; Marchiando et al, 2015; Milburn, 2010; Vilkinas and Cartan, 2015). PLs navigate their lack of direct authority through cultivating formal and informal mechanisms to engage their teaching team in programme development, even if that means they have to spend additional time discussing issues to ensure colleagues are on board (Cahill et al, 2015; Milburn, 2010; Murphy and Curtis, 2013). These interactions are often dependent on the context of the programme, with PLs of small postgraduate taught programmes adopting a different approach to student engagement and the formation of the teaching team to those of large undergraduate programmes (Crevani et al, 2010; Murphy and Curtis, 2013). Some utilise existing structures to establish credibility and legitimacy, including senior colleagues and departmental committees. The institutional memory of the programme or departmental administrator is invaluable, but these colleagues are often stretched in terms of their own workload (Bryman, 2007; Irving, 2015). While PLs do build networks of colleagues from across the institution, these tend to comprise those they have worked with before, and they are often unaware of the vast range of expertise across the institution (Cahill et al, 2015; Vilkinas and Cartan, 2015).

Colleagues leading academic professional development play an essential role in helping PLs to understand institutional expectations of their role, the rhythms of academic life and the central processes and systems, as set out, for example, in Case Study 2 (Eve) of this book and elsewhere (Cahill et al, 2015; Mitchell, 2015; Murphy and Curtis, 2013; Preston and Price, 2012). As highlighted, there is significant value in academic developers bringing together programme teams to offer space for them to develop their programmes away from the pressures of day-to-day work. However, while professional development opportunities can go some way to familiarising PLs with systems and structures and offer time for curriculum development, given the complexity of the networks around programme leadership, space must be provided for PLs to consider the types of interactions they will be involved in, who can provide essential support for programme leadership and the power dynamics at play in their interactions with these colleagues (Cahill et al, 2015; Crevani et al, 2010; Mitchell, 2015; Murphy and Curtis, 2013).

As well as offering the opportunity for PLs to consider these issues in the context of their programme team and their students, professional development activity can therefore help PLs to connect with others in a similar position, fostering peer learning and sharing of experiences beyond the immediate and day-to-day concerns (Mitchell, 2015; Preston and Price, 2012). This may not only involve structured networking sessions but could also include the development of shadowing and mentoring activities such as those in Case Study 3 (Johnson and Kalu, this publication); this ensures ongoing support for PLs as issues arise on the job. Questions that academic developers and mentors might use to prompt consideration and the development of solutions to the issues raised in this chapter include:

The teaching team

- How do you help PLs to identify who in their department is included in the programme teaching team?
- How could you enable them to explore mechanisms, both formal and informal, for bringing colleagues in the teaching team together to discuss the programme?
- What might be the purpose of these interactions, and where and how often might they happen?
- Are PLs aware of the challenges and power dynamics inherent in their interactions with the programme teaching team?

Others who support the programme

- What institutional systems and structures are introduced to PLs? Are they aware of the people to contact about each of these systems?

- Could you incorporate an activity that asks PLs to map out all the colleagues outside their immediate teaching team who could support the development of their programme?
- How might PLs identify the senior individuals and structures who can provide authority and credibility for their role?

Students/alumni

- How familiar are PLs with the student support models in their department? What opportunities do they have to reflect on how their role intersects with these models?
- What mechanisms do PLs have to interact with students during the programme?
- Do PLs have the opportunity to consider different models of how they might engage students and alumni in programme design and development?

Other programme leaders

- What opportunities could you facilitate for PLs to learn from others who are or have been in a similar role, including mentoring, networking and shadowing?
- What are the benefits and disadvantages of pairing PLs with others in different departments?

Conclusion

This chapter has argued for the importance of relationships to the PL role. Through everyday interactions with their teaching team, others who support the programme, students and alumni and other PLs, colleagues in programme leadership roles navigate the often immediate requirements of their role. Although this chapter is based on findings from a single institution, it nonetheless offers insight into the significant role that academic developers can play in supporting PLs. By providing space to explore the affective aspects of the role, discuss the relationships that are so integral to its success and enable PLs from across an institution to come together and share good practice, academic developers have the means to be able to empower PLs to develop and cultivate thought-provoking programmes that offer a positive experience to their students.

References

Bryman, A. (2007) 'Effective leadership in higher education: A literature review', *Studies in Higher Education*, 32(6), pp. 693–710. doi: 10.1080/03075070701685114.

Cahill, J., et al. (2015) 'An exploration of how programme leaders in higher education can be prepared and supported to discharge their roles and responsibilities effectively', *Educational Research*, 57(3), pp. 272–286. doi: 10.1080/00131881.2015.1056640.

Crevani, L., Lindgren, M. and Packendorff, J. (2010) 'Leadership, not leaders: On the study of leadership as practices and interactions', *Scandinavian Journal of Management*, 26(1), pp. 77–86. doi: /10.1016/j.scaman.2009.12.003.

Cunliffe, A. and Eriksen, M. (2011) 'Relational Leadership', *Human Relations*, 64(11), pp. 1425–1449. doi: 10.1177/0018726711418388.

Irving, K. (2015) 'Leading learning and teaching: an exploration of 'local' leadership in academic departments in the UK', *Tertiary Education and Management*, 21(3), pp. 1–14. doi: 10.1080/13583883.2015.1033452

Marchiando, L., Myers, C. and Kopelman, S. (2015) 'The relational nature of leadership identity construction: how and when it influences perceived leadership and decision-making', *The Leadership Quarterly*, 26(5), pp. 892–908. doi: 10.1016/j.leaqua.2015.06.006.

Milburn, P. C. (2010) 'The role of programme directors as academic leaders', *Active Learning in Higher Education*, 11(2), pp. 87–95. doi: 10.1177/1469787410365653.

Mitchell, R. (2015) '"If there is a job description I don't think I've read one': a case study of programme leadership in a UK pre-1992 university', *Journal of Further and Higher Education*, 39(5), pp. 713–732. doi: 10.1080/0309877X.2014.895302.

Moore, S. (2018) 'Beyond isolation: Exploring the relationality and collegiality of the programme leader role', in Lawrence, J. & Ellis, S. (eds.) *Supporting programme leaders and programme leadership*. London: Staff and Educational Development Association, pp. 29–33.

Murphy, M. and Curtis, W. (2013) 'The micro-politics of micro-leadership: exploring the role of programme leader in English universities', *Journal of Higher Education Policy and Management*, 35(1), pp. 34–44. doi: 10.1080/1360080X.2012.727707.

Preston, D. and Price, D. (2012) '"I see it as a phase: I don't see it as the future": Academics as managers in a United Kingdom university', *Journal of Higher Education Policy and Management*, 34(4), pp. 409–419. doi: 10.1080/1360080X.2012.689201.

Vilkinas, T. and Cartan, G. (2015) 'Navigating the turbulent waters of academics: the leadership role of programme managers', *Tertiary Education and Management*, 21(4), pp. 1–10. doi: 10.1080/13583883.2015.1082189

Practitioner response: Leadership as collaboration – Taking a less individualistic approach

Oscar Jerez Yañez, Chile

In Latin America, leadership and collaboration, culturally speaking, are seen as opposing processes. However, relationships are core to this same Latin American cultural context. In this sense, strengthening leadership by building on everyday relationships within the educational community is something which should be supported.

The most relevant aspects in this chapter are related to involving in teaching development to others who participate in the programmes. Likewise, coordinating meeting spaces and ensuring their attendance is a recurring theme within university contexts.

In our Latin American context, it is relevant to highlight the importance of meeting and reflecting on teaching, by both academics and students. I think it is fascinating to integrate the experience and points of view of students, especially after completing a programme to find out if expectations align with reality; this is not common practice for us.

Taking on board the previous program leader's experience is also an experience of collaboration that is rarely practiced in this part of the world. Most of the new managers perceive that a new cycle begins with them, without taking into account previous learning. Likewise, connecting and networking with other program managers could lead to better work with greater chances of success.

I believe that the articulated vision as an ecosystem between teachers, teaching teams, support teams, students and other leaders, from a collaborative and constructive perspective, could favour better leadership and transformation of education in the region. A more collective and less individualistic approach could have a positive impact on our results.

An example of this has been the COVID-19 crisis in Latin America. It forced everyone to work collaboratively to move forward in the face of adversity. The challenge is how to sustain it over time beyond the pandemic. And this is precisely the contribution of this chapter, providing guidance and light on moving forward together beyond individual responsibilities within the institution. Why not, with other institutions, strengthen national and regional higher education systems?

DOI: 10.4324/9781003127413-23

Case study 3

Honesty and the power of open approaches that foster trust

Jessie Johnson and Frances Kalu, Qatar

Introduction

Jessie was starting off in a new role as the graduate programme coordinator, while Frances was just beginning her journey as an educational developer within a transnational context. As the graduate programme coordinator, one of Jessie's first tasks was to lead the graduate faculty through a curriculum review. Unsure of where to begin, she knew that it was important that faculty colleagues had confidence that she knew what she was doing as a newly emerged leader. Meanwhile Frances, who had the experience of working with various faculties undergoing the curriculum review process in Canada, was available to teach and guide her through the process.

This case study provides a glimpse into our journey as we learnt to work together out of necessity and due to our roles within the institution. It unpacks the hidden or less obvious gains of collaboration, the value of disciplinary and educational development specialists working together, and the need to acknowledge diverse expertise. Both authors came to this process through different angles, however they both believe that in order to lead you must first be humble enough to follow and learn from others. We use a duo-autoethnographic lens, which is a dialogic methodology (Norris & Sawyer, 2012), to enable us to critically and reflectively examine both of our experiences throughout this process.

Our journey

Frances: As an educational developer specialising in curriculum, I provided consultative guidance for curriculum review projects undertaken by different faculties on our main campus. Moving to the transnational branch of our institution I continued this work with the graduate programme leader Jessie as she led the curriculum review for the graduate programme. This shift by educational developers from working across academic communities, to working embedded in one academic community is something Debowski (2014) has noted. It helps the educational developer to better understand the needs of the community, and provide the targeted support needed. Being embedded within my new

DOI: 10.4324/9781003127413-24

community, I embarked on mentoring Jessie through the curriculum review process. Educational development refers to various forms of support provided to faculty development (Leibowitz, 2014); as educational developers, we are positioned as 'enablers', providing the needed support in various forms.

During our initial curriculum review planning meeting, Jessie informed me that she was new to the process and had never conducted a curriculum review. To allay any concerns she had, it was important to help her articulate her understanding of curriculum, the rationale for, and the importance of this review. I was able to understand what foundational knowledge she had and what she knew as an experienced educator. In addition to establishing buy-in for the curriculum review, our conversations created a space for Jessie to understand how to evaluate programme-level learning outcomes (PLOs), the alignment between the PLOs, course outcomes that make up the programme, as well as the teaching, learning and assessment strategies.

This gave Jessie the confidence needed to lead a curriculum review even though she was new to the process. It was an opportunity to empower Jessie with enough foundational knowledge to be confident in both co-facilitating and eventually facilitating sessions for her peers. Through this process, she was able to be seen as a leader whilst she was learning.

Jessie: One of the most poignant memories I have as the new graduate programme leader was that I had to allow myself to be vulnerable, to embrace the guidance I needed to receive from Frances in order to conduct a curriculum review with a new team of academic peers. I wondered what I knew about curriculum reviews and how I would manage as a newly appointed leader; there was so much to learn. I worried about being able to exude leadership to my peers and yet still express the vulnerability I felt in order to get support. I did not fully understand the process that lay ahead for me.

I decided to be very open to my peers and made it clear that I was being taught to lead a curriculum review. I informed them that I would be working alongside them during some of the process, but other than that I would be actively learning, doing and being guided by Frances. It was a tricky spot to be in. I had not quite realized it at the time, but the educational developer who became my mentor was laying down a leadership style that was both inclusive and transformational as she had me guide numerous workshops and lead sessions on conducting a curriculum review. Each was fraught with a new experience I had to master. There was so much to learn and so little time to do it. As a leader, it was my job to embrace this and learn from it. I had to be ahead of the curve as I taught my peers the process I was learning in situ. As a result my peers were able to see me vulnerable as a leader yet willing to be taught.

The epitome of a leadership role is to not only to provide mentorship to others but to allow oneself to be humble enough to be mentored. Leadership is about 'perception, judgement, skill and philosophy' (Frankel, 2008 p. 23). I believe in fostering leadership that is transformational and based on relationships in a safe environment. My leadership style chimes with my approach as an educator, I recognise the need to create an open, warm, caring environment for learners so that they grow in confidence.

Conclusion

It all began with conducting a graduate programme curriculum review within a transnational context which brought along with it unique opportunities and challenges. This journey brought about tremendous growth in the authors as they worked together through a curriculum review process. It enabled us to build self-confidence within our roles as both graduate programme coordinator and educational developer, and deepen our knowledge within our chosen fields.

It is not easy to either allow oneself to be mentored when in a role of leadership or understand where you fit as an educational developer. Being open to learning from each other, acknowledging the vulnerability created by being in an unaccustomed position, and coming to a realization that the mentee/mentor role can flip depending on circumstance, highlighted the reciprocal relationship between a mentee and the mentor. One of the most important things to be considered here is how one potentiated the other in the journey of mentor and mentee.

References

Debowski, S. (2014) 'From agents of change to partners in arms: The emerging academic developer role', *International Journal for Academic Development*, 19(1), pp. 15–56. doi: 10.1080/1360144X.2013.862621.

Frankel, A. (2008) 'What leadership styles should senior nurses develop', *Nursing Times*, 104(35), pp. 23–24. Available at: https://www.nursingtimes.net/clinical-archive/leadership/what-leadership-styles-should-senior-nurses-develop-29-08-2008/ (Accessed December 2021)

Leibowitz, B. (2014) 'Reflections on research and practice reflections on academic development: what is in a name', *International Journal for Academic Development*, 19(4), pp. 357–360. doi: 10.1080/1360144X.2014.969978.

Norris, J. and Sawyer, R. D. (2012) 'Toward a dialogic methodology', in Lund, D., Sawyer, R.D. & Norris, J. (eds.) *Developing qualitative inquiry. Duoethnography: dialogic methods for social, health, and educational research*. Walnut Creek: Left Coast Press, pp. 9–39.

Case study 4

Reflecting on the transition from traditional to blended programmes
Six critical messages to manage change

Emma O'Brien, Carol O'Sullivan and Gwen Moore, Ireland

Reflections on transitioning to blended programme leadership

As outlined elsewhere, programme leaders (PLs) can act as change agents in the design process through a democratic leadership style (Milburn 2010). This case study reflects on the experience of the authors, who work in a small education and liberal arts higher education institution (HEI) which, in recent years, has adopted blended and online delivery modes more widely.

In 2018, senior management in the HEI recognized the complex, multifaceted nature of blended programme design and developed an Integrated Curriculum Design Model (ICDM) for programme validation and development. It aimed to encourage a systematic yet open approach to dialogue during programme design. This, combined with the need to balance academic rigor with autonomy, was seen as necessary to encourage the adoption of innovative pedagogies within individual disciplines. The ICDM served as a key enabler in the transition to blended programme leadership which features in this reflection.

The ICDM was piloted on the design of a new blended programme in Autumn 2018. The PL, one of the authors of this chapter, began working with a variety of key stakeholders including the institute's Centre for Teaching and Learning (CTL), prior to the submission of the programme for validation (see Figure CS4.1). She began by seeking cross institutional buy-in using the ICDM process to identify key stakeholders for consultation. This process was combined with a participatory leadership approach whereby the PL encouraged sharing of ideas and expertise, successfully urging the programme team to embrace changes to their teaching practices (Sagnak, 2016).

The PL had experience as a Head of Department, but had minimal experience of blended learning. Acknowledging this lacuna, she sought expert advice and support from the outset. She recognised the need to collaborate closely with Faculty from a range of disciplines, many of whom had greater experience of blended learning. Authors who were members of the programme team reflected that this highlights the importance of support through multiple levels in the institution, such as the CTL, the Quality Office, the Research and Graduate School,

DOI: 10.4324/9781003127413-25

Reflecting on the transition 141

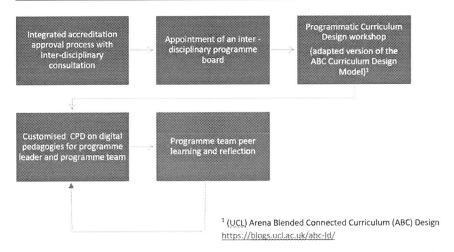

[1] (UCL) Arena Blended Connected Curriculum (ABC) Design https://blogs.ucl.ac.uk/abc-ld/

Figure CS4.1 Multi-level support for traditional PLs transitioning to blended learning leadership

other PLs, and Faculty. The ICDM was a key in securing the provision of such support.

This collaborative approach to programme design ensured a holistic approach to development which involved research, pedagogic, administrative and technological expertise. Programme development and leadership was directed by the three main headings for blended learning design outlined by the Quality and Qualifications Ireland (QQI, 2018)

- Organisational context – ICDM and appointment of an interdisciplinary course board.
- Programme context – programmatic curriculum design workshops and CPD.
- Learner experience context – regular team peer learning and reflection on the student experience.

Including an academic developer with expertise in digital pedagogies on the planning team from the outset was deemed essential to programme development. While the PL's limited experience of blended learning could have been viewed as a barrier, she instead sought to up skill herself and the programme team as part of the process of blended design and development. The expertise and support that she and the other team members received in digital learning, management and validation were critical to the success of the programme.

Reflecting on the approach from both student and staff perspectives, the PL has identified critical elements to success. In particular, the workshop on programmatic curriculum design was a key in bringing the team together to develop a shared vision for the programme. The workshop encouraged collegiality and joint decision making between the programme team and identified key areas for further professional development (PD). An adapted version of the ABC Curriculum Design workshop (Figure CS4.1) was adopted which integrated constructive alignment, principles of universal design for learning and reflective learning activities.

From this blueprint, the digital learning team worked with the PL to identify bespoke PD in digital pedagogies at both individual level and programme level. At these workshops, the programme development team explored changes to their teaching and learning practices through active discussion and engagement. These workshops provided the foundation stone for the programme and initiated the ongoing features of support, active engagement, collaboration and commitment to the process.

Support was provided during the programme implementation through continued inter-disciplinary membership on course boards and iterative team reflection. The PL played a pastoral role, encouraging peer exchange and openness, urging the team to share ongoing experiences which formed a key part of transitioning both the team and the learners to a new learning environment, a key element of participatory leadership.

The impact of the Covid-19 pandemic has illustrated the need for increased leadership expertise in digital and blended learning. The approach adopted in this reflection was instrumental in moving to a fully online form of delivery during the COVID-19 pandemic. The expertise and pedagogical approaches the programme team developed during the design and development stages and the participatory approach to leadership, resulted in the team being agile and resilient in experiencing change.

Potential leaders of blended learning programmes should consider the critical messages outlined below when designing blended or online programmes:

1. The many dimensions of leading a transition from traditional to blended programmes, in particular their role in managing change and encouraging innovative approaches to teaching and learning.
2. Their own limitations and openness to seek assistance when needed.
3. The importance of balancing academic rigor and autonomy through flexible systems which support innovation and creativity. For example the PL should have autonomy in tasks such as selecting the team, consulting stakeholders for buy-in and including team members with specific expertise such as digital pedagogies from the outside.
4. Taking a programmatic approach to design early in the process whereby all members of the team participate in joint decision making, regarding the blend and use of digital pedagogies relevant to meet the needs of the student and learning outcomes.
5. Ensure that the skills of the team are recognised and facilitate a peer-supported approach to professional development, sharing practice and developing skills in digital pedagogy.
6. Provide opportunities for continuous review and adaptation to the evolving needs of students and the programme team.

References

Milburn, P. C. (2010) 'The role of programme directors as academic leaders', *Active Learning in Higher Education*, 11(2), pp. 87–95. doi: 10.1177/1469787410365653.

QQI (2018) *Statutory Quality Assurance Guidelines for Providers of Blended Learning Programmes*. Dublin: Quality and Qualifications Ireland. Available at https://www.qqi.ie/sites/default/files/media/file-uploads/Statutory%20QA%20Guidelines%20for%20Blended%20Learning%20Programmes.pdf (Accessed December 2021).

Sagnak, M. (2016) 'Participative leadership and change-oriented organizational citizenship: The mediating effect of intrinsic motivation', *Eurasian Journal of Educational Research*, 62, pp. 181–194. doi: 10.14689/ejer.2016.62.11.

Case study 5

Leading joint and combined honours programmes
Amplified complexity

Dawne Irving Bell and Sue Morón-García, UK

> **Definition**
>
> 'Joint honours' programmes are made up of modules or courses from two different single honours or subject degrees in which each subject accounts for precisely 50% of study. The difference between a joint and a combined honours programme, where students also take courses originating outside their home department, is the distribution of academic credit between the subjects.

Introduction

Programme leaders (PLs) who lead joint or combined programmes have to address all the practical issues other PLs do with added complexity. They lead programmes that bring together courses and colleagues from different academic units and so have to navigate local cultures and practices with the aim of avoiding a fragmented, incoherent student experience and their own burnout. We wanted PLs to know that they are not responsible for everything, and that while a good working knowledge of the systems and processes that relate to their programme is essential, it does not mean it is their responsibility to undertake and oversee every aspect of that specific activity or task.

The creation of processes and structures for resilient programme leadership

A cross-institutional group of colleagues undertook an investigation to explore the lived experience of PLs and students involved with combined and joint honours programmes. We examined the way the purpose of the degree was articulated to students (and staff) and investigated how students were supported throughout their degree, from recruitment to completion so that they:

- develop the appropriate knowledge, understanding and skills for each subject area,

DOI: 10.4324/9781003127413-26

- integrate their experience across the programme, benefiting fully from the degree, and
- are able to develop their identity both as individuals and as a group

We looked for examples of institutional good practice and identified areas for improvement, working in pairs to hold meetings with key staff informants; not only PLs, but personal tutors, academic registry, recruitment, student support, finance and learning services. Data drawn from regular student consultative forums were utilised and we spoke to alumni, consulted the literature and colleagues in other institutions. Current practice in relation to organisation, management and delivery of these programmes was examined: curriculum development, timetabling, personal tutoring, personal development planning, careers education, information, advice and guidance. The resulting outcomes have benefited all PLs at the institution, not just those leading joint and combined programmes.

Illustrative vignettes

> Students: 'It's the hidden things you don't expect that hold the potential to undermine. Subtle things like differences in teaching between the subjects, or the arrangements for assessment. But perhaps the biggest potential issue is not having a "home" [department] because you could quite easily find yourself feeling a little bit lost and quite isolated'.
>
> Staff: '... the organisation of student and staff timetables, to ensure things run smoothly there needs to be a lot of staff and student dialogue, to ensure good communication. Other challenges can include monitoring students and tracking their progress, and of course gathering and using data. Another consideration must be to ensure that all staff have a good understanding of the programme but are equipped with the necessary knowledge and skills to ensure effective recruitment, admissions and programme delivery'.

We established that two elements, communication and programme structure, were crucial in establishing a sense of cohort identity and mitigating students' feelings of isolation which can arise. Students compare experiences and worry about gaps in experience and knowledge that might come about from a perceived partiality of experience across distinct fields and this is exacerbated if the programme is not clearly understood.

Recommendations and additional outcomes

- Articulate the course identity and value clearly and widely so that all staff and students understand the programme's place alongside single honours courses.

- Have a robust communications strategy that is targeted, timely and personalised.
- Facilitate clear regular messaging between staff and faculties to ensure that teaching, learning and assessment policy operates coherently, that all those involved are informed and that there is timely liaison with year group leads and personal tutors and/or academic advisors.
- Ensure students know who they should turn to when they are in need of support or guidance.
- Establish a designated way for students to "speak" to the programme team about their experience that transcends subject or department boundaries. Meeting as joint or combined honours students as a group is important.
- Pay attention to the context of curriculum design, development and delivery as well as access to resources.
- Communicate and explain differences in teaching approaches, expectations and work on the coordination of assignment deadlines across different disciplines. Ensure that practice in respect of assignment extensions adhere to a common policy and are communicated clearly.
- Ensure that the timetable is coordinated between academic units, through full engagement of both, so that taught session clashes are avoided and opportunities for enhancement are considered, for example, the ability to engage with sports teams or societies.
- Ensure cross-departmental structures and approaches, including administrative practices are consistent. For example, the effective management of student data, from enquiry and recruitment through to graduation to support PL's to management of retention, progression and attainment.

Additional outcomes from our investigation were the development of:

- A student communications strategy that benefitted all students. This is a central communications system that facilitates 'a single source of truth'.
- A series of strategies to support PLs. These are embedded within a series of guidelines we call our threshold standards for the roles and responsibilities of academic and professional service units.

An abridged version of our threshold standards from programme proposal through to delivery are outlined here for information:

Planning consent: academic units involved in the development of combined or joint honours programmes must be able to demonstrate a clear understanding of the implications relating to effective programme delivery and who holds responsibility for issues and consider curriculum design and delivery (staffing), communication, reporting, monitoring and evaluation.

Validation: frameworks were revised to ensure that programme teams are cognisant of the academic and practical implications of any course or module sharing.

Programme organisation: consistent use of institutional course codes or other identifying measures to enable the effective tracking and support robust and reliable student data.

Communication: academic units must provide a clear coherent and comprehensive communication plan. They need to articulate how they will ensure effective communication and coordination between themselves and all the staff and students involved with the constituent parts of the programme. It is important that staff from each part of the programme are able to understand each other's contributions. One way to help this, for example, is by working together on activities such as clearing or open days. This would then be followed up through joint approaches to induction and evaluation.

Ensure that suitable personal tutors/academic advisors are in place with ways of sharing info between academic units.

Ensure representation of different departments at relevant award and progression boards and agree ways to share information about progression.

Dedicated Staff: the academic unit with lead responsibility for the overall programme must appoint a dedicated PL to oversee programme management.

Resourcing: Additional and protected time for the PLs of joint and combined honours programmes to undertake their role.

Staff professional development: a series of best practice recommendations were identified from the standards. These were disseminated via professional development activity on topics including recruitment, induction, transitions and retention. On learning and teaching including innovative pedagogical approaches, arrangements for assessment and innovative feedback.

Case study 6

Taking the lead

Creating an undergraduate environmental science programme to meet the benchmarks and expectations

Bethan L. Wood, UK

This case study illustrates the benefits of listening to student demand, working with students, employers and colleagues to become a programme lead. As a programme leader you must work within institutional frameworks to make your case, build alliances, and take colleagues with you.

My strategic proposal for the 4-year BSc Environmental Science and Sustainability programme was not a sudden idea. Over the course of my teaching at the University of Glasgow, latterly as environmental lead, I had periodically met with students on the MA Liberal Arts (Environmental Studies) and asked for feedback on their programme experience. This, together with information from the student evaluations, feedback, and graduate destination data, sent the clear message that the MA programme was not what they wanted. The students wanted the degree to be a BSc and not a MA, with more core environmental-based courses offered, and an environmental-centred honours project.

Thus armed, I compiled a list of the students' requirements and approached the following for feedback:

- my MSc Carbon Management students,
- my environmental academic colleague, – who was already on board with the overall proposal for a BSc since they also came from a scientific background and had also recognised the need for more scientific content to meet the QAA benchmark for Environmental Science rather than Environmental Studies, and
- local employers who had previously had students on placement or employed graduates from the MA degree – to continue to foster our links and encourage their continued involvement with a new programme.

Scottish undergraduate degrees are typically four years long with time for a dissertation or placement, and an honours project over years three and four. It became clear that the proposal would need to include at the very least: a greater diversity of placement options which were world-wide in reach, an environmental-based honours project in year 4, and a residential field course to foster group work and a sense of community within the cohort. These all fitted well with the new strategic direction of the School into the environmental sector under a new Head of School.

To gain approval for the new programme we needed the support of the Head of School, as they would be our advocate and, crucially, we would need new members of staff to run the new courses involved; there were only two full-time members of staff available at that time to run the degree programme. A meeting was arranged where I explained the plan and highlighted benefits such as increased student numbers, a feeder into our postgraduate taught programmes, and its place in the strategic direction of the School. Support was given. Next, I created the programme plan which contained the list of courses that would contribute to the degree. Environmental-based courses offered by my environmental colleague and I were still running at the campus at the time as they were a key part of the new MA Primary Education with Teaching Qualification. These courses were therefore added to the programme plan. The remaining courses were created by identifying gaps in content that related to the QAA benchmark for Environmental Science programmes and student and employer requests.

The 60-credit placement course, offered in semester 2 of year 3 had run at the campus for many years and was included in the new programme as an alternative to the 60-credit dissertation, albeit the onus was to be put on the student to find their own placement with staff support. Local employers who were consulted about the programme proposal were also keen to commence having students on placement with them again. The fourth and final year was completely new, with a 60-credit Environmental Stewardship Project, the residential field course and two new taught courses: Environmental Policy and Management which would have to be delivered by a new member of staff and Perspectives on the Environment which could be done by an environmental humanities colleague who was keen to be involved with the programme. The programme plan was complete.

Next, we sought approval through the normal University Programme Information Process (PIP). This required me to:

- Complete programme specification and programme support documents for submission to the Learning and Teaching Committees (School and College levels).
- Seek marketing information from the University marketing department.
- Provide evidence of consultations with students, employers, and other relevant University-wide staff. These consultations informed course content.

I was fortunate to have had the experience of going through the same process for my MSc Carbon Management programme. Some sources of help are: exemplars on the University website, contributed by colleagues who have been through the process, and the Chair and members of the School Learning and Teaching Committee.

Once the programme proposal was approved, I evaluated the content of the new and established courses against the QAA Benchmark Statement for Earth Sciences, Environmental Sciences and Environmental Studies. As the first cohort (2010) progressed through the degree, all courses were continually assessed to ensure that they met the requirements of the benchmark; this is still done today as best practice. The resulting BSc programme specification was very much a student-employer-staff partnership that revised the curriculum to create an environmentally focused programme. It is still used by our Senate Office as an exemplar, more than a decade after the programme commenced!

Ten years on ….

Students are drawn to the opportunities provided by the degree programme, especially the placement option, as illustrated by comments from students on their experience of the degree for our programme webpage:

'I chose to study Environmental Science and Sustainability at the University of Glasgow's Dumfries Campus, because the programme was very attractive – a variety of environmental topics …'

'The BSc Environmental Science & Sustainability programme can offer every student an individual pathway. The broad and extensive topics in the classes are there to guide you and broaden your horizons. Many of the assignments can be approached with your own individual interest that you can also pursue throughout the entire programme, as well as the placement (here or abroad) or your final dissertation'.

Our students now travel globally (Australia, Greece, Finland, Borneo, Oman, Sri Lanka), as well as nationally and locally, for their placements. The University's graduate attributes are embedded in the students' personal learning goals which they include in their initial report before going out on placement; this enhances their employability by encouraging them to articulate and use these skills on their CV.

My creation of the programme and its leadership has given me personal success: promotion as well as recognition as a Principal Fellow of the Higher Education Academy. I have contributed to the University's Work-Related Learning Policy and presented at conferences on employability with my students and placement colleagues. In 2016 I stepped down, becoming the mentor for my original environmental colleague who took over. This colleague in turn used their programme leadership to successfully apply for promotion.

Our students leave with graduate attributes which enhance their employability. We know this because of the employment rates of graduates from our programme (our HESA data for 2018 shows 98% in work or in further education), particularly in environmental consultancy. The impact of the programme on the students, through the opportunities offered, manifests itself in their increased confidence as they proceed through the degree. I have witnessed level-1 students who struggled with oral presentations and/or academic writing, blossom into graduates who can critically argue points in environmental debates or research and write A grade final dissertations.

Part 3

The practice of programme leadership

Leading programme teams

Introduction

Rowena Senior, UK

The chapters and case studies that form this third and final section focus on the ways in which Programme Leaders (PLs) can work with their local programme teams (and more widely across departmental and service boundaries) to improve the quality of their student's experiences and the working lives of staff. The section explores different approaches to leading teams, for example, from localised one-to-one support through to a rethinking of the role of PL itself in order to enable the subsequent rethinking of a programme team structure. The section serves to highlight the importance of collaboration and move the PL role away from one of potential overwhelm and isolation to one of connection and meaningful interdependence. The authors focus on the benefits that can be realised from working in this way but also that authentic collaborative working requires long-term commitment from those involved. We can see that PLs need to engage with the resources and expertise that exist within their immediate team and beyond but recognise that in order to do this they need the space and time themselves to create links and devolve responsibility among team members. The case studies in particular use this space to demonstrate how some of these resources can be deployed. The chapters on the other hand, provide a more strategic consideration of the role of teams within the sphere of Programme Leadership.

The practice of programme leadership: Leading programme teams will be of interest to

PLs and those wishing to develop support structures to facilitate the work of PLs be they departmental Heads, Senior executives or academic/educational developers.

Chapter and case study relevance to specific tasks and activities

1. **Developing collaborative approaches within programme Teams**
   Chapter 9. The collaborative programme leader: Embedding meaningful collaboration into a programme culture. Evelyn Jamieson.

DOI: 10.4324/9781003127413-29

Case study 8. Leading successful programme transformation. Sharon Altena and Karen Theobald.
Case study 10. Facilitating educational leadership: Building and sharing an understanding amongst the programme team. Eva Malone and Stephen Yorkstone.

2. **Addressing poor scores in student evaluation measures**
Case study 9. Co-ordinating programme design through 'Assessment Therapy'. Dominic Henri.

3. **Mobilising the programme team to targeting a specific area of the programme for development**
Case study 9. Co-ordinating programme design through 'Assessment Therapy'. Dominic Henri.
Case study 8. Leading successful programme transformation. Sharon Altena & Karen Theobald.

4. **Developing quality enhancement or transforming the curriculum**
Case Study 7. A team-based retreat for programme development. Sarah Moore.
Case study 8. Leading successful programme transformation. Sharon Altena and Karen Theobald.

5. **Professionalising the role of Programme Leader**
Chapter 10. In pursuit of excellence: A collaborative and interdisciplinary framework for reconceptualising programme leaders. Jacqueline Hamilton and Christopher Donaldson.
Case study 10. Facilitating educational leadership: Building and sharing an understanding amongst the programme team. Eva Malone and Stephen Yorkstone.

6. **Working across institutional departments to improve quality enhancement**
Chapter 10. In pursuit of excellence: A collaborative and interdisciplinary framework for reconceptualising programme leaders. Jacqueline Hamilton and Christopher Donaldson.
Case study 10. Facilitating educational leadership: Building and sharing an understanding amongst the programme team. Eva Malone and Stephen Yorkstone.

7. **Utilising existing resources within the Programme Team to capitalise on development opportunities**
Case Study 7. A team-based retreat for programme development. Sarah Moore.
Chapter 10. In pursuit of excellence: A collaborative and interdisciplinary framework for reconceptualising programme leaders. Jacqueline Hamilton and Christopher Donaldson.

Chapter 9

The collaborative programme leader

Embedding meaningful collaboration into a programme culture

Evelyn Jamieson, UK

Introduction

This chapter is a highly reflective and personal account of my approach to the programme leader's (PL's) role in the performing arts, which I achieved by working with the programme team and, where relevant, bringing students on board. My goal is one of desired collaboration, developing an environment in which everyone is a co-creator *in* and *of* the programme (Bovill and Woolmer, 2019). However, it is important to say at this early stage that we should be careful not to use the word collaboration as a 'catch-all' term (Schrage, 1990). There are several definitions, approaches and models regarding what collaboration is depending on, for example, the particular field of study, discipline or context.

In the case of the performing arts disciplines such as dance, drama or music, intensive collaborative working is found at the very heart of ensemble practice (Britton, 2013). It requires time to learn to be as one – a completely shared 'voice'. True collaboration (John-Steiner et al, 1998) is about learning to listen and negotiate a constant mutual understanding and respect for each other as well as having time to develop a high level of skill in working as a unified group in performance (Zarrilli, 2013). This chapter stems from and emphasises the value of such collaborative practice. My own artistic practice in collaborative-making and ensemble-performing of dance has informed my role as a collaborative PL in higher education (HE). What has become an embodied understanding as an ensemble player in performing arts practice has transferred directly to how I work with my colleagues in facilitating teaching and learning with HE students.

Often I feel trepidation towards collaborative practice exists due to fears of potential risks, for example, around a lack of time to build trust, respect and a shared way of working. However, from experience as a PL over some 30 years, it is my view that collaborative practice as a means of achieving co-creation within a programme is essential. By outlining a case for collaboration and, in particular, for working effectively as a staff team, what is being proposed is a horizontal approach to programme leadership. In fact, in dance production we often take this approach for granted as it is the key and habitual way that we work together. The goal of this chapter is to demonstrate how, led by the PL, developing strong

DOI: 10.4324/9781003127413-30

collaborative practice (as a programme team and with students through a horizontal approach) is a highly effective means of fostering a successful learning and teaching environment. I feel the principles behind the approach outlined below are readily transferable to other disciplines within the HE context.

This chapter explores the concept of how a team evolves and then investigates how collaborative practice has had a major impact on creating a research-based learning synergy within a postgraduate taught curriculum. As I will go on to explore, I feel this approach has contributed to optimising the student experience. The involvement of professional arts partnerships (management and practice-focused), alongside the input from lecturing staff who are artists-researchers (Doughty and Fitzpatrick, 2016), inform the curriculum design, content and delivery of the Master of Arts Dance programme (MA). It is this programme that is used as the focus of this chapter. First, however, we need to look in detail at the gains that can be achieved through taking a collaborative approach.

Why should programme leaders collaborate?

In HE today, it seems there are many challenges and tensions that are not confined to any one specific discipline, department, faculty or institution, but are found more generally in daily operational practices ranging from teaching, learning and research to managerial strategic planning and senior executive management. The value placed on collaboration for educational leaders within a university in terms of getting departments and faculties to work together has been found to be of great benefit (Beattie, 2020) or, indeed as is my view, a necessity even though we must recognise that it may also be incredibly challenging (Alix et al, 2011).

It is critical, however, that collaborative practice is enacted, not just transmitted. A survey, symposium and consequent report demonstrated a number of exciting collaborative approaches/models with a range of case study examples. What became evident is that in the performing and creative arts, teaching staff are 'not *teaching* collaboration but collaborating' (Alix et al, 2011, p. 19). Thus, adopting the act itself in the art-making process becomes part of their teaching practice. Although the challenges of working with others are complex, we learn from each other the more we take part in such practices. John-Steiner, who has written and theorised about the power of creative collaboration in the arts, business and science, maintains that in:

> ...collaborative work we learn from each other by teaching what we know; we engage in mutual appropriation. Solo practices are insufficient to meet the challenges and the new complexities of classrooms, parenting, and the changing workplace.
>
> (2000, pp. 3–4)

Ultimately, if we want to collaborate, then the rewards will be far greater than what could have been achieved alone (Sawyer, 2007). Therefore, collaboration as co-creation is a way to effect real discovery and innovation (John-Steiner, 2000). In the sections that follow, I explore and reflect upon the key elements and acts of co-creation that I have found to be necessary elements in building collaborative practices with staff and students.

a. An underpinning desire to work truly collaboratively

Although seemingly obvious, I feel that it is critical that collaborative practice is underpinned by a true desire or overarching philosophy to work in this way. Here, it is important that we separate the notion of enforced collaboration through organisational (or even reorganisational) imperative and the more profound notion where collaboration is truly wanted and thus actively pursued.

In terms of my own professional journey as an artist, someone working in community contexts and as an academic in HE, I have consistently emphasised the pursuit of active collaboration in my leadership practice. On a macro-level, my practice in professional dance, community arts and HE does form the essential connecting tissue for my role as a PL. This connectivity occurs because these three fields of endeavour are all interlinked and, importantly, dependent upon each other (Jamieson, 2016). Linking academe with the professional world and society at large has given me a holistic overview and, in so doing, provided me with experience relevant to the PL role. For example, in the design of the curriculum, the ongoing changes to teaching and learning approaches in modules, the monitoring of processes and improvements made thereof, and the opportunity to provide enhancement opportunities with students and staff alike.

A PL therefore should both hold and enact a desire to work with colleagues within and beyond their immediate team. Such meaningful interaction with both the dance profession and creative dance practice research has remained a consistent element in my role and means that when I approach the various tasks of a PL, they are done so with these three interconnecting spheres in mind. Indeed, students have remarked both in forum discussions and module feedback on the innovative research areas covered by the staff on our programme and visiting artists as well as the areas covered by way of our partnerships with artists and professional dance agencies.

If you are thinking about enhancing collaboration within your leadership practice, consider the ways in which you can connect with the wider context in which your programme exists. Connections could be made with those in the profession, with organisations that utilise the skills you teach, in conducting research in areas that apply your disciplinary teachings or other relevant practices.

b. An authentic part of professional leadership practice

I feel the PL is ideally placed as a *primus inter pares* to effect collaboration through co-creation as an authentic part of their leadership practice. Indeed, my quest is to work with my HE colleagues and students in the same way that I do as a dance artist, namely in pursuing a shared creative endeavour (Jamieson, 2014). This horizontal approach is central to my working strategy as I feel it creates a collaborative advantage (Huxham and Vangen, 2005), which is of particular importance in resource-deprived sectors of HE.

The core principles of co-creation for a PL and his/her team are, as John-Steiner, Weber and Minnis outline, that they 'not only plan, decide, and act jointly, they also think together, combining independent conceptual schemes to create original frameworks' (1998, p. 774). This approach has been operationalised in my own practice via two complementary positions on collaboration which have served me well in bringing authenticity to my role as PL. First, when no one person has a dominant view, 'authority for decisions and actions resides in the group, and work products reflect a blending of all participants' contributions' (John-Steiner et al, 1998, p. 774). Indeed, I feel the perception of rank in the context of a PL is actually misplaced. The PL in my experience is not senior to any of his or her colleagues on the team. The key element here is that everyone respects each other and has a desire to work together in pursuing a shared goal. This approach also forms the basis of desired as opposed to imposed (or necessary) collaboration. Second, Betz, describing his career as an artist and HE educator, states that collaboration is 'a combination of all-present at the same time, and an embrace of the different expertise in the project ... full participation from beginning to end...' (2018, p. 64). He believes everyone has to be prepared to move out of 'their comfort zone' nurturing the 'new discovery of *becoming*, which is shared and reaffirmed by the group and raises the value of this collaborative approach' (p. 64). Ultimately, everyone engaged in the collaborative act has to participate.

I foster this environment of co-creation within the MA Dance curriculum design and delivery by ensuring that postgraduate students are regarded as dance artists and teaching staff as innovators alongside them. For teachers, this can often emerge as them not being afraid of letting go of 'the reins' (the vertical) with respect to taking a collaborative approach or as a fear that an aspect of the module may 'fail'. The MA students whom we attract already possess a good deal of experience in the profession; others are lecturers and teachers of dance and some come from undergraduate courses. The diversity of student experience is celebrated as each one has an important part to play. My philosophy has always been about co-learning and sharing a process, which applies equally to how we as a MA teaching staff team learn from each other. We are all part of a shared journey of discovery becoming motivated to learn and trust each other, take risks and explore new horizons.

To develop collaboration as an authentic part of your leadership practice, think about what principles underpin your approach to leadership. Do you see yourself as a co-learner in a process of shared discovery, whether it is with staff or students? How can you empower everyone involved? Do they trust you, each other and feel secure enough to be on this journey? Are they unafraid to take risks (does this include yourself as a PL)?

c. Acceptance that true collaboration takes time

It is important to explore the time it takes to achieve true collaboration within a programme team. Indeed, it seems the willingness to partake in such longitudinal activity is often held back by underpinning concerns around potential risk and, ultimately, failure. More broadly, Spillane (2018) outlines fear and risk as underpinning our ability to be effective and creative in working with others. Spillane refers to Halberstam's *The Queer Art of Failure*, stating that 'creativity is envisioned as collaborative endeavour that begins with failure and moves forward together into unchartered territory where new meanings are made' (2018, p. 10). Dixon rightly places a positive spin on this: 'what's most valuable is the risk, surprise, and mystery involved' (2018, p. 86). However, we must be prepared to take such risks as a key part of building trust and uncovering innovation over time (John-Steiner, 2000; Sawyer, 2007). Often, the affordance of time (which we have little of in HE), and especially in the PL's role, is the crucial factor in building collaborative practice.

The need to take a longer-term view contrasts with today's climate of 'instant fix'. PLs are often expected to adapt with great speed within the ever-changing HE landscape (Van Veggel and Howlett, 2018). Of course, the balance for senior management is undoubtedly not easy, especially at the time of writing this chapter during the COVID-19 pandemic. Senior leadership must manage the tension between 'central university administration and the aspirations of their academics' (Beattie, 2018, p. 612), meaning that what is imposed from above may clash or interfere with the 'slow burn' of collaborative practice described here. Importantly, the tension between the imposed and the desired is contingent on trust. Creating the time to build a desired level of trust in and between staff and students must be at the forefront of practice. Specifically, in order to waylay feelings of fear in the programme team that may emerge, for example, by some of the rapid changes mentioned above.

In our MA creative practice module, the sessions move from being staff-led to students leading them as part of a formative assessment strategy. This takes time. It also involves a negotiation between staff and students concerning the scoping criteria of assessment, produced and written jointly. This process facilitates shared knowledge, for example, 'I (student) know what I am doing and how to get there (assessment)'. Here, our students and the teaching staff are co-creators in their roles as 'co-constructors of knowledge' (John-Steiner, 2000). Working collaboratively in the teaching, learning and assessment process, they have to trust each other and equally uphold and protect the time it takes to do that.

Therefore, the notion of time is threefold: firstly, to excite, enliven and grow a shared desire to collaborate and ideally to include senior management in this process not just a programme team; secondly, to find the time for the team to share ideas and sometimes facilitate 'blue sky' thinking in order to develop excitement and passion about new possibilities; and thirdly, to give everyone (including management) enough time to fully understand, analyse, shape and implement work as co-creators.

d. Awareness of the critical intersection between vertical and horizontal organisational structures

Huxham and Vangen (2005) purport that achieving success through teamwork (what they term 'collaborative advantage') has many challenges that emerge as part of the process. In the HE context, I suggest that such difficulties can occur when the vertical line of management and horizontal line at a programme or course level do not always see eye to eye. Therefore, the intersection of vertical and horizontal is an important area of consideration. A PL's role can be additionally complex in managing a variety of complications, often left unacknowledged by vertical senior management (Murphy and Curtis, 2013). Working in HE has become 'the perpetual requirement to produce more, and faster' (Morrish, 2019, p. 45). However, I feel that by applying care to engagement with vertical management, imposition can be replaced by constructive negotiation.

A question for PLs to consider is how can we build a more trusting relationship with our senior managers? (Actually, the reverse should be the proper order in this question.) Do we know why policies that are cascaded down the vertical chain of command to programme level have been put to us? Do we understand enough about each other's role and what we have to do? Has a communication loop been affected and, if not, can we as PLs help to achieve this?

The barriers that arise for the PL as a facilitator relate to the core principle of acting jointly (Carnwell and Carson, 2009). Often the directive is passed down the chain, frequently without time for either the senior manager or PL to think together before there is an expectation that, at a programme level, it will be implemented. Assumptions are often made from senior management that the PL will tell the programme team (read: impose their objective) which runs the risk of disempowering a programme team.

As discussed, the vertical and horizontal acting jointly is key. Therefore, it is important to consider if the context is in place to enable this to happen. For example, do we have open channels of communication where we can build trust at whatever level we are working at? Can we find solutions together, whether it be with senior management and the programme team or programme team and the students who study with us? Ultimately, the 'we' and the 'with' are essential and form the basis of meaningful, creative and successful practice.

e. Enabling staff to work in their area of expertise

Within HE, lecturers and students deserve to feel secure in working together. As a PL, I feel the ability to build a team should be an essential experience requirement for taking on the role. Like the dance, theatre or music ensemble, we practise over and again to get better at our metier (Britton, 2013) and get to know how to work with others with skill through experiential learning (Moon, 2004). Starting with really getting to know the team and working on gaining respect for each other has always been the essential first step. As creative practitioners, we need to consider: are we truly interested in each other's artistic work? What kind of dance practitioners are we? What is special about each one of us? Have we ever been in the same dance studio together? Do we ever watch each other apart from peer teaching evaluations each year or share a session for students? Ensuring these questions are considered builds upon how we then share our teaching practice on the various modules within a programme. The staff should be able to share and respect the work that they are involved in and, in so doing, buy into the philosophy of the course.

Research-informed teaching (RIT) through creative practice has been at the centre of ensuring that MA Dance programme team members work within their area of expertise. Through RIT, each member of the teaching staff brings their own specialised area of research, including practice as research (PAR) (Nelson, 2013). The design offers an emphasis on a process-orientated curriculum, whereby students have the opportunity to follow areas of interest and need (Fraser and Bosanquet, 2006).

The MA modules offer students the opportunity to learn how to propose and carry out a PAR investigation that has strong theoretical underpinning related to key cultural and aesthetic frameworks in creative practice. Various modes of teaching allow for different learning approaches through tutor-directed and student-led learning. Students engage in problem-solving as they develop their PAR through continuous reflective practice (Moon, 2004). The programme team is able to engage in the teaching of compositional approaches extending our own PAR, specifically reflecting upon our own teaching of creative practice with students (Schön, 1984). This process leads to the students being able to develop their own learning in sharing their creative practice as PAR with each other. In addition, they can present such findings at a regional professional dance symposium with national and international professional dance artists gaining confidence as they do so. For example, one of the students was investigating bodily memory and embodied knowledge. When a guest artist at the symposium spoke about the 'body being like a book', the student was delighted to have her own premise reaffirmed. Furthermore, staff took part in the symposium as panel members, presenters and participants sharing from their own areas of expertise in research. Good satisfaction levels (as reported in module evaluations) are to be found when everyone – staff *and* students – feel they have been acknowledged, respected and grown through the process together.

It is important to consider how we can continue to not just value our colleagues' specialisms and research practice, but also to enable the implementation of it as a driving force in the curriculum we lead. This reflection is extremely important in order to build a shared vision for the programme and in the journey of developing an exciting, dynamic and excellent curriculum with highly motivated staff and students. Taking this approach makes them co-creators *of* and *in* the process.

f. Recognition that true collaboration is a holistic process

Building a strong team involves the acknowledgement that everyone's contribution through trust and respect has a part to play in good interpersonal relations

(Carnwell and Carson, 2009). Therefore, the PL has to have the respect and trust of all colleagues in the teaching team and, equally importantly, take into account what and how the students contribute. The PL cannot be the font of all knowledge; consequently, good programme leadership should recognise that 'my way' is not the only way (Alix et al, 2011). Again, we have to ask ourselves as PLs these questions not just once but as an ongoing process.

In commencing a new academic year or at any other time, have you as a PL – as a facilitator – given the opportunity for everyone in that team to have an expert voice regarding the key strategies that affect the planning and delivery of the programme? Have the team had sufficient time to listen, consider and offer other ways forward? Is the staff team speaking with one cohesive voice, are they unified in their support of the programme philosophy, and thus able to communicate it effectively to everyone within the team as well as with students? Ultimately, I feel a dysfunctional staff team does not engender trust in students.

Conclusion

Success for an HE PL is about developing a creative, innovative and dynamic programme with a unified voice, a shared vision (John-Steiner, 2000), one which involves respect in bringing together a group of complementary staff and students in a cohesive, planned and effective way. Collaborating as a group and developing into a team over a period of time does involve a strong sense of trust (Sawyer, 2007). As John-Steiner et al state (1998), this collective effort is achieved 'through a synergy of collaborative connections and dialogue that engenders group creative pursuit that leads to innovation' (p. 774). In fact, John-Steiner claims that most of the greatest discoveries have been made through collaborations (2000).

For a PL, desired co-creation develops into collaborative practice between the PL as gatekeeper, the teaching staff (as lead learners) and the students, each having a voice and ownership of the syllabus. Through collaborative practice between staff and students, one can see that student enhancement and increasing engagement is a consistent feature. Co-creation in the curriculum provides the vehicle to shape teaching and learning with students in real time. The teaching staff through their research areas are working with (not at) the students, looking at what they, the staff, are researching and how, for example, they might expand upon specific areas of practice and research. Sometimes we, staff and students, identify key practitioners as partners near the onset of a new academic year and, at other times, enhancement opportunities arise due to external conference events or artists coming into the region.

The PL, as outlined above, should offer all involved time through trust to have and share a creative voice. This creates an opportunity as a team to explore and discover something new, something quite unique, something exciting and of real quality.

References

Alix, C., Dobson, E., & Wilsmore, R. (2011) *Collaborative arts practices in HE: Mapping and developing pedagogical models*. Available at: https://www.heacademy.ac.uk/sites/default/files/collaborative-practice-report-final-july2011.pdf (Accessed: 11 January 2021)

Beattie, L. (2018) 'Educational leadership: a nirvana or battlefield? A glance into higher education in the UK using Bourdieu', *International Journal of Leadership in Education*, 21(5), pp. 608–620. doi: 10.1080/13603124.2017.1330490.

Beattie, L. (2020) 'Educational leadership: Producing docile bodies? A Foucauldian perspective on higher education', *Higher Education Quarterly*, 74(1), pp. 98–110. doi: 10.111/hequ.12218.

Betz, S. (2018) 'Why collaborate at University?', in Shields, M.K. & Spillane, S (eds.) *Creative collaboration in art practice, research, and pedagogy*. Newcastle upon Tyne: Cambridge Scholars Publishing, pp. 63–77.

Bovill, C. & Woolmer, C. (2019) 'How conceptualisations of curriculum in higher education influence student-staff co-creation *in* and *of* the curriculum', *Higher Education*, 78, pp. 407–422. doi: 10.1007/s10734-018-0349-8.

Britton, J. (2013) 'Forming ensemble some approaches to training: Introduction', in Britton, J. (ed.) *Encountering Ensemble*. London: Bloomsbury, pp. 273–312.

Carnwell. R. & Carson A. M. (2009) 'The concepts of partnership and collaboration', in Carnwell, R. & Buchanan, J. (eds.) *Effective Practice in Health, Social Care and Criminal Justice: Working Together*. Maidenhead: Open University Press, pp. 3–21.

Dixon, M. (2018) 'On the spectrum: Stories of collaboration and its pedagogy', in Shields, M. K. & Spillane, S. (eds.) *Creative collaboration in art practice, research, and pedagogy*. Newcastle upon Tyne: Cambridge Scholars Publishing, pp. 79–87.

Doughty, S. & Fitzpatrick, M. (2016) 'The identity of hybrid dance artist-academics working across academia and the professional arts sector', *Choreographic Practices*, 7(1), pp. 23–46. doi:10.1386/chor.7.1.23_1.

Fraser, S. P. & Bosanquet, A. M. (2006) 'The curriculum? That's just a unit outline, isn't it?', *Studies in Higher Education*, 31(3), pp. 269–284. doi: 10.1080/0307507600680521.

Huxham, C. & Vangen, S. (2005) *Managing to collaborate: The theory and practice of collaborative advantage*. London: Routledge.

Jamieson, E. (2014) 'Touching the ineffable: Collective creative collaboration, education and the secular-spiritual in performing arts', *Dance, Movement & Spiritualities*, 1(2), pp. 271–282. doi: 10.1386/dmas.1.2.283_1.

Jamieson, E. C. (2016) *From dance cultures to dance ecology: a study of developing connections across dance organisations in Edinburgh and North West England, 2000 to 2016*. PhD thesis. University of Chester. Available at: https://chesterrep.openrepository.com/handle/10034/620561 (Accessed: 23 November 2020).

John-Steiner, V., Weber, R. J., & Minnis, M. (1998) 'The challenge of studying collaboration', *American Educational Research Journal*, 35(4), pp. 773–783. doi: 10.3102/00028312035004773.

John-Steiner, V. (2000) *Creative Collaboration*. New York: Oxford University Press.

Moon, J. (2004) *A handbook of reflective and experiential learning: Theory and practice*. London: Routledge.

Morrish, L. (2019) *Pressure vessels: The epidemic of poor mental health among higher education staff*. Available at: https://www.hepi.ac.uk/wp-content/uploads/2019/05/HEPI-Pressure-Vessels-Occasional-Paper-20.pdf (Accessed: 15 March 2021)

Murphy, M. & Curtis, W. (2013) 'The micro-politics of micro-leadership: Exploring the role of programme leader in English universities', *Journal of Higher Education Policy and Management*, 35(1), pp. 34–44. doi: 10.1080/1360080X.2012.727707.

Nelson, R. (2013) *Practice as research in the arts: Principles, protocols, pedagogies, and resistances*. London: Palgrave MacMillan.

Sawyer, K. (2007) *Group genius: The creative power of collaboration*. New York: Basic Books.

Schön, D. (1984) *Educating the Reflective Practitioner: Toward a New Design for Teaching and Learning*. New York: Jossey-Bass.

Schrage, M. (1990) *Shared minds: the new technologies of collaboration*. New York: Random House Inc.

Spillane, S. (2018) 'Fear and Risk', in Shields, M. K. & Spillane, S. (eds.) *Creative collaboration in art practice, research, and pedagogy*. Newcastle upon Tyne: Cambridge Scholars Publishing, pp. 9–15.

Van Veggel, N. & Howlett, P. (2018) 'Course leadership in small specialist UK higher education: a review', *International Journal of Educational Management*, 32(7), pp. 1174–1183. doi:10.1108/ijem-09-2017-0250.

Zarrilli, P. (2013) 'Psychophysical training and the formation of an ensemble', in Britton, J. (ed) *Encountering ensemble*. London: Bloomsbury, pp. 369–380.

Practitioner response: Using our disciplines to improve our leadership approaches

Lucía Piquero Álvarez, Malta

As a PL in dance studies, this chapter is essential to the way we work. Jamieson does not refer to anything we are not already familiar with in the performing arts (collaboration *is* at the heart of our creative work); however, the chapter shows us how to use our own practical knowledge towards the delineation of our programme design. The work is thus a homage to the discussion of our disciplines and the knowledge they produce. Arguably, through this process, we not only improve our own leadership but have the potential to train leaders in other disciplines, empowering their leadership approach.

I have been fortunate to work as part of a dedicated team of lecturers (active in practice and research) within the School of Performing Arts at the University of Malta. Although collaboration and interdisciplinarity have been at the heart of our work, we continue to strive towards new ways of implementation. Jamieson's suggestion that collaboration takes time is accurate to develop a trusting team. Collaboration outside of the School is also key for us. As Jamieson states, there is an intense need to 'connect with the wider context in which your programme exists'.

It seems that engaging stakeholders at different **levels** from students to senior management is also important. An institution can be considered to be formed by all its agents. Understanding, collaborating and most especially listening to both management and students have been the main point of learning to me as lecturer and as PL. As Jamieson explores, there is no other way to develop a programme than to think of the journey as shared. Her argument is beautifully put; the team needs to be 'pursuing a shared creative endeavour'.

Of course, not all is easy and risk-free. Even if one is happy to embrace risk, then the most difficult thing to face can be what Jamieson brings up as 'becoming' together, which in a way implies putting forward and letting go of different parts of oneself (whilst being strengthened by the possibilities of collaboration).

Other key points of note include the need for a longer-term view and the importance of thinking as 'we' and 'with'. Both have been made immensely difficult by the COVID-19 pandemic; indeed, quick fix solutions and safety protocols had to take over most thinking. Jamieson offers a solution: when nobody is certain how to proceed, having knowledge from many perspectives might co-construct the best possible solutions. Her suggested questions for PLs will certainly be on my mind in the future.

Case study 7

A team-based retreat for programme development

Sarah Moore, UK

Introduction

> *You need mental space, people to challenge you and people to answer questions. The workshop provided that space.*
>
> Retreat participant/programme team member

Building positive relationships with colleagues is at the heart of good programme leadership, with programme leaders (PLs) needing to work not just with their immediate teaching team, but also others from across the institution and beyond (Cahill et al, 2015; Lawrence and Ellis, 2018; Milburn, 2010; Murphy and Curtis, 2013; Vilkinas and Cartan, 2015). As noted in the above quote, the process of programme development can require space for difficult and complex discussions among colleagues. However, in the context of heavy workloads and the need to prioritise immediate and urgent concerns, opportunities to focus on the more strategic and visionary aspect of curriculum design are not easily created and PLs often find themselves working in isolation from others who can support them (Knight and Trowler, 2000; Milburn, 2010; Moore, 2018; Preston and Price, 2012; Chapter 8 this publication, Moore). While professional development opportunities including workshops, resources and mentoring might be available for PLs in some institutions, such provision tends to vary across the sector. Even in institutions where these opportunities do exist, they tend to be offered to and accessed by, PLs as individuals. It is therefore important for those supporting PLs to consider how they might provide opportunities for teams to collaboratively explore difficult, complex issues of programme development.

This case study sets out the underpinning rationale and implementation of a retreat designed to support PLs, their teams and other key staff across the institution to engage collaboratively with the messiness of programme development. I begin by setting out the ethos of the retreat and how it worked, before highlighting the lessons learnt that might be useful to others supporting PLs.

DOI: 10.4324/9781003127413-32

The retreat

The underpinning principle of the retreat was to get programme teams and colleagues from a range of areas across the institution to sit around the same table at the same time to develop their programmes in a way that would not have been possible within the constraints of normal departmental practice. The design of the retreat was influenced by models more commonly used to support academic writing that combine structure and individual goal-setting with the feeling of being part of a community (Murray and Newton, 2009). Rather than a traditionally packed workshop agenda set by the facilitator, the retreat adopted a participant-centred ethos of space, allowing programme teams to set their own agendas and progress their curricula at a pace that suited them.

In advance of the retreat, interested programme teams were asked to articulate what they wanted to get out of the session, and identify at least three people from their team who would attend. This participant-centred approach was important for several reasons. Firstly, identifying the specific issue(s) that they wanted to address meant that each programme team took ownership of how they would develop their programme in the time available, and could therefore hopefully continue this work beyond the retreat (Murray and Newton, 2009). Secondly, requiring the PLs to bring at least three colleagues along with them ensured that the programme development was conducted collaboratively through teams rather than PLs working in isolation (Crevani et al, 2010; Milburn, 2010; Moore, 2018). Thirdly, the facilitators could invite colleagues from professional services with particular expertise around the issues that the teams hoped to explore, thus tailoring the support to each team and drawing on knowledge from those situated elsewhere in the institution, including curriculum development specialists, quality teams and colleagues in student engagement roles (Irving, 2015; Moore, 2018; Vilkinas and Cartan, 2015). Programme teams themselves also invited colleagues beyond the immediate teaching team, including students, alumni and peers from cognate departments who could offer their perspectives on the programme.

Facilitators worked with three programme teams from different disciplines and at different stages of developing their curriculum. Inspired by Murray and Newton (2009), the structured day-long retreat started with a short introduction to the purpose and approach of the workshop, followed by a discussion among each of the teams about what they hoped to achieve during the session. Teams then had two hours of unstructured time to discuss their programmes, allowing for the depth of conversation required for the complex, strategic issues of programme development, before providing a brief update to the room before lunch as a way of reflecting on where they had got to (Murray and Newton, 2009; Milburn, 2010; Moore, 2018, Preston and Price, 2012; see also Chapter 8 this publication, Moore). In the afternoon, there was a further two-hour discussion followed by some dedicated time for concrete action planning and final sharing of what each team had achieved. During the discussions, facilitators asked colleagues from professional services to move between groups if they felt that a particular team could benefit from specific expertise (for example, around student engagement), thus adapting to the needs of each team as conversations progressed.

Feedback

Feedback was provided through two means. Participants were asked to note down their immediate thoughts anonymously on post-it notes at the end of the session in response to the following questions:

- What have you got out of today's session?
- What could have been done differently?

A feedback form was also circulated to participants after the session. As highlighted in the literature, inviting colleagues both within the teaching team and beyond supports programme development by bringing together different perspectives and voices (Cahill et al, 2015; Lawrence and Ellis, 2018; Milburn, 2010; Moore, 2018). Participants highlighted this as one of the main benefits of the retreat, as it gave them an opportunity to work with colleagues who would not normally be in the same room at the same time. For example, there was an *'excellent range of backgrounds and opinions around the table* [which] *created varied discussion'* (retreat participant/student).

The views of students and peers present at the retreat were especially valued by those teams who had invited them. Some attendees reported that they would have benefitted from more interaction between the teams themselves in order to learn from each other, thus building further on Murray and Newton's (2009) emphasis on community as a motivation and support. One of the most beneficial aspects from the workshop was the space and time to focus on the strategic and visionary aspects of curriculum design and development rather than day-to-day concerns. Nonetheless participants also appreciated that the activities resulted in a specific action plan that could be taken forward beyond the retreat (Milburn, 2010; Moore, 2018; Preston and Price, 2012; see also Chapter 8 this publication, Moore). For one PL who had thought their curriculum was relatively well-developed, challenging discussions within the team led them to revisit and reshape particular elements. The retreat therefore surfaced questions that would not necessarily have been raised without the depth of conversation it enabled:

> *That was very challenging work - lots of hard thinking, but some of the moving pieces have been pinned down and this is great progress.*

Conclusion

This case study has outlined an approach to supporting programme teams with developing their curricula. There were two key principles to its success. The first was the focus on building relationships, both within teams and with others including colleagues from across the institution, students and alumni, and peers (Milburn, 2010; Moore, 2018; see also Chapter 8, Moore). Secondly, the provision of structured but participant-centred space allowed them to engage in strategic and visionary aspects of curriculum development (Milburn, 2010; Murray and Newton, 2009; Preston and Price, 2012). It is hoped that this case study will provide a simple but valuable model for academic developers to implement with programme teams in their own institutions.

References

Cahill, J., Bowyer, J., Rendell, C., Hammond, A. and Korek, S. (2015) 'An exploration of how programme leaders in higher education can be prepared and supported to discharge their roles and responsibilities effectively' *Educational Research*, 57(3), pp.272–286. doi: 10.1080/00131881.2015.1056640.

Crevani, L., Lindgren, M. and Packendorff, J. (2010) 'Leadership, not leaders: On the study of leadership as practices and interactions' *Scandinavian Journal of Management*, 26(1), pp.77–86. doi: 10.1016/j.scaman.2009.12.003.

Irving, K. (2015) 'Leading learning and teaching: An exploration of 'local' leadership in academic departments in the UK' *Tertiary Education and Management*, 21(3), pp.186–199. doi: 10.1080/13583883.2015.1033452.

Knight, P. and Trowler, P.R. (2000) 'Department-level cultures and the improvement of learning and teaching' *Studies in Higher Education*, 25(1), pp.69–83. doi: 10.1080/030750700116028.

Lawrence, J. and Ellis, S. (2018). *Supporting Programme Leaders and Programme Leadership*. (London: Staff and Educational Development Association), SEDA Special, 39, pp. 11–14.

Milburn, P. (2010) 'The role of programme directors as academic leaders' *Active Learning in Higher Education*, 11(2), pp.87–95. doi: 10.1177/1469787410365653.

Moore, S. (2018) 'Beyond isolation: Exploring the relationality and collegiality of the programme leader role' in Lawrence, J. and Ellis, S. (eds) *Supporting Programme Leaders and Programme Leadership*. London: Staff and Educational Development Association.

Murphy, M. and Curtis, W. (2013) 'The micro-politics of micro-leadership: Exploring the role of the programme leader in English universities' *Journal of Higher Education Policy and Management*, 35(1), pp.34–44. doi: 10.1080/1360080X.2012.727707.

Murray, R. and Newton, M (2009) 'Writing retreat as structured intervention: Margin or mainstream?' *Higher Education Research & Development*, 28(5), pp.541–553. doi: 10.1080/07294360903154126.

Preston, D. and Price, D. (2012) '"I see it as a phase: I don't see it as the future": Academics as managers in a United Kingdom university' *Journal of Higher Education Policy and Management*, 34(4), pp.409–419. doi: 10.1080/1360080X.

Vilkinas, T. and Cartan, G. (2015) 'Navigating the turbulent waters of academia: The leadership role of programme managers' *Tertiary Education and Management*, 21(4), pp. 306–315. doi: 10.1080/13583883.2015.1082189.

Case study 8

Coordinating programme design through 'Assessment Therapy'

Dominic Henri, UK

Introduction

In 2017, I was asked to lead the BSc Zoology programme to address bottom quartile scores for overall satisfaction in the National Student Survey (NSS); an annual survey completed by UK finalist undergraduates gathering student perspectives on the quality of their degree. One of the key areas to address was low satisfaction with assessment (68% 3rd quartile). Below I explore a three-stage process to overcome common challenges to coordinating programme-wide curriculum design, focused on improving student satisfaction with assessments and staff marking workloads.

Prior to becoming PL, I had recently improved Module Evaluation Questionnaires (MEQs) on a number of my modules after adopting an Assessment-as-Learning philosophy (as well as improving my quality-of-life with streamlined marking loads). This approach is designed to encourage assessment and feedback literacy in lecturers and students through iterative assignments and active reflection (Boud and Falchikov, 2007; TESTA, 2015; Scott, 2017). I hoped that helping module leaders apply these principles to reduce, refine and streamline assessment across our provision would improve both their workloads and our NSS scores.

The first challenge resulted from the complexity of the BSc Zoology programme. Specifically, BSc Zoology runs as part of a shared provision of biological degrees. Our students pick from a large selection of options, with limited compulsory modules, hampering individual academic oversight of what assessments a student might have to complete at any stage. This situation prompted me to question how module leaders could make assessment design decisions without knowing what other assessments students were doing? To address the lack of clarity over assessment profiles, I collated all assessment information into a single infographic that staff could refer to when planning their assessment strategy (Figure CS8.1). This stage was also important for me as PL as it revealed a new perspective on my programme. The infographic informed where my efforts needed to be directed; for example, one module in Figure CS8.1 has six separate elements of assessment and another is assessed entirely through Multiple Choice Question (MCQ) exams.

DOI: 10.4324/9781003127413-33

Coordinating programme design 171

58127	MCQ*	Habitat Guide	Stats report	Essay	WB	PDP
58129		MCQ*		Work book	Work book	MCQ*
58130		MCQ*		Drawings	Class tests	
58131		MCQ*		Practical MCQ	Practical MCQ	
58135		MCQ*		Poster	Practical report	PDP
58030		Exam*		Field drawing	Portfolio	
58031		Exam*		Scientific report		MCQ*
58022	Essay		Essay	Practical exam		
58023	Portfolio	Presentation	Essay			

Figure CS8.1 An excerpt of the Assessment Audit Infographic for year one of study that outlines the assessment strategy for a number modules side-by-side; includes the type of assessment and the weighting (relative size of blocks adds up to 100%). PDP denotes personal development plan, WB denotes workbook, MCQ denotes multiple choice questionnaire, * denotes those assessments under exam conditions. Note in the original output a full-spectrum of colours were used to denote each assignment type.

One of the most common challenges for PLs is the need to engender change as part of a non-hierarchical team (Massie, 2018). While team-based curriculum design can have significant long-term benefits (Burrell et al, 2015), it can be difficult and may require fostering 'buy-in'. Willingness to actively support curriculum reform requires individuals to believe efforts will be beneficial and that they can deliver the resulting structure (Brownell and Tanner, 2012; Shadle, Marker and Earl, 2017). In this project, success relied on convincing staff that they would benefit by being involved. This reticence was addressed through a process of problem realisation. In practice, initial invitations to take part were sent via a short email to the whole Biology department with the support of the Departmental Head. The invitation highlighted several potential benefits: reduced marking loads, more time for research, improved MEQ scores and help responding to external examiner comments. The idea of helping staff to resolve problems was reinforced by formatting the invitation as a survey asking participants to articulate key issues in their modules; the most common response related to staff/student workloads (Figure CS8.2).

As a PL and an education-focused lecturer, I wanted to be able to inform changes to assessment strategy. However, this desire also sits within the sector-wide context of the so-called research/teaching divide (McCune, 2021). Here, this final challenge describes the often highly localised nature of pedagogic expertise which commonly rests with a few individuals within each University and who can struggle to bring their expertise to bear at the programme level (Tierney, 2016). As part of completing the initial survey, staff booked a one-hour face-to-face session, with me performing the role of 'Assessment Therapist'. Sessions were used to overcome uncertainty in individual staff in relation to their pedagogical expertise and discuss issues in detail, develop new assessment strategies, and collaboratively finalise the quality-assurance paperwork. Discussions started by asking staff what they thought solutions might be, which were then refined through brokerage of my experience of disciplinary education research (Tierney, 2016). Most commonly we focused assignments into 'bite-sized', iterative assessments that built together towards a large final component (TESTA, 2015).

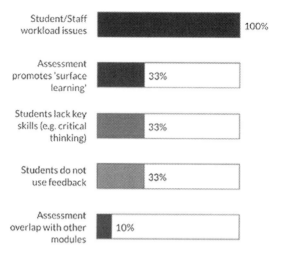

Figure CS8.2 Percentage of respondents that identified with common key issues within their modules.

Outcomes of the three-stage process

In total, I held therapy sessions with nine different staff that covered 13 modules across all levels of undergraduate provision, making significant changes to key modules on the Zoology programme. A clear positive comment from staff undertaking 'therapy' was that they felt encouraged that an 'expert' supported their solutions to their issues. I feel this is particularly important because a commonly cited barrier to the implementation of broader, student-centred teaching is low pedagogic self-efficacy among lecturers (Brownell and Tanner, 2012; Fraser, 2016).

> ...*given his expertise in scholarship, I was **reassured** that Dr Henri supported my proposed new assessment.*
>
> Senior Lecturer in Biology

On average, we saved an estimated 10 hours of marking time per staff member per year. Some staff felt that changes allowed students to focus on particular assignments, complete them to a better standard and improved student use of feedback within the module.

> ***Time spent marking was reduced, freeing** up time to utilise elsewhere...–*
>
> Senior Lecturer in Ecology

My reflection

As the above shows, staff were impacted positively, however, I am unsure of the impact on students. In the future, I suggest the setup of specific survey evaluation tools as part of the process and not to rely on this information being collected

Table CS8.1 BSc Zoology NSS scores on focal questions related to the 'Assessment Therapy' programme

Question	2017	2018	2019
Overall satisfaction	80%	96%	89%
Assessment and Feedback	68%	74%	80%

through MEQs and staff feedback. While I am unsure about the relative importance of this specific set of actions described in this case study, I believe that they contributed to our BSc Zoology experiencing a dramatic improvement in NSS scores (Table CS8.1); including finishing in the Top 10 in 2018.

References

Boud, D. & Falchikov, N. (2007) *Rethinking Assessment in Higher Education: Learning for the Longer Term.* Oxon: Routledge.

Brownell, S. E. & Tanner, K. D. (2012) 'Barriers to faculty pedagogical change: Lack of training, time, incentives, and … tensions with professional identity?', *CBE—Life Sciences Education*, 11(4), pp. 339–346. doi: 10.1187/cbe.12-09-0163.

Burrell, A. R., Cavanagh, M., & Young, S. & Carter, H. (2015) 'Team-based curriculum design as an agent of change', *Teaching in Higher Education*, 20(8), pp. 753–766. doi: 10.1080/13562517.2015.1085856.

Fraser, S. P. (2016) 'Pedagogical content knowledge (PCK): Exploring its usefulness for science lecturers in higher education', *Research in Science Education*, 46(1), pp. 141–161. doi: 10.1007/s11165-014-9459-1.

Massie, R. (2018) 'The programme director and the Teaching Excellence Framework: How do we train the former to survive the latter?', *Higher Education Quarterly*, 72(4), pp. 332–343. doi: 10.1111/hequ.12169.

McCune, V. (2021) 'Academic identities in contemporary higher education: sustaining identities that value teaching', *Teaching in Higher Education*, 26(1), pp. 20–35. doi: 10.1080/13562517.2019.1632826.

Scott, G. W. (2017) 'Active engagement with assessment and feedback can improve group-work outcomes and boost student confidence', *Higher Education Pedagogies*, 2(1), pp. 1–13. doi: 10.1080/23752696.2017.1307692.

Shadle, S. E., Marker, A. & Earl, B. (2017) 'Faculty drivers and barriers: laying the groundwork for undergraduate STEM education reform in academic departments', *International Journal of STEM Education*, 4(1), p. 8. doi: 10.1186/s40594-017-0062-7.

TESTA (2015) *Best Practice Guides.* Available at: http://testa.ac.uk/index.php/resources/best-practice-guides (Accessed: 22 July 2020).

Tierney, A. (2016) 'Communities of practice in life sciences and the need for brokering', *F1000Research*, 5, p. 280. doi: 10.12688/f1000research.7695.1.

Chapter 10

In pursuit of excellence

A collaborative and interdisciplinary framework for reconceptualising programme leaders

Jacqueline Hamilton and Christopher Donaldson, Canada

Introduction

In the current higher education (HE) landscape, curriculum development and management require a collaborative and interdisciplinary approach to lead and support continuous change within programmes (Voogt et al, 2016). In our experiences we have seen programme leaders (PLs) take on a coordinating role within their units, with a focus on planning and management of academic programming as well as bringing curriculum changes forward on behalf of the faculty. Here, we explore an alternative model to traditional programme leadership in the Academic Manager. This model is based on a collaborative and interdisciplinary approach focusing on teamwork and relationship-building. It is seen as a means to effectively meet stakeholder needs while also fostering increased faculty engagement in the curriculum process.

In our setting, Academic Managers are normally professional staff members who oversee the curriculum and quality assurance management of programmes or suites of programmes within academic units. They differ from the traditional PL model, as they do not necessarily perform a teaching and/or research function in relation to the programmes or suite of programmes, and instead are focusing on curriculum development and the management of academic quality. The role of the academic manager in our context mirrors the role of PL and is responsible for supporting an academic unit (i.e. a College or Faculty). We play a critical role in the development of new programmes and the coordination of changes to existing programmes in addition to other educational development activities. Academic Managers function as curriculum project managers, fulfilling the role of institutional and educational experts. They know who the key players are in academic departments and central reporting units as well as institutional policies, quality assurance protocols and institutional quality assurance frameworks, and what resources are available to achieve common objectives. The traditional PL is thus reconceptualized to be an interdisciplinary role that functions across traditional academic units and central supporting offices. For HE practitioners in educational development and management, historically continuous programme

DOI: 10.4324/9781003127413-34

improvement is based on providing documentation and correcting gaps in how a programme fulfils its intended learning outcomes, based on data and feedback from multiple stakeholders (Brodeur & Crawley, 2009). While this definition can certainly tell us what encompasses this trend, it may be more valuable to focus on the spirit and intention of quality assurance initiatives. We feel that authentic strategic engagement with a breadth of stakeholders across an institution (including instructors, other staff and learners) allows us to all strive to work together to continually improve our programmes and curriculums for future generations. Indeed, internal quality assurance processes feature the shared basic values, purposes and directions of an institution (Daromes & Ng, 2015). This holistic philosophy sits at the heart of how we embody the role of Academic Managers and how we apply the definition of continuous improvement throughout this chapter.

In this chapter, we will explore how Academic Managers can support curriculum development work by bridging the gap between institutional quality assurance and programme improvement initiatives, and faculty on the front lines of teaching and learning. We will explore how this alternative inception of the PL role can facilitate curriculum development in a more efficient and evidenced-based manner, one that reduces demands and pressures on faculty workload and resources. The above is achieved by considering the benefits of reconceptualising and repositioning the role of the PL with specific reference to their potential as 'boundary spanners' (Rudhumbu, 2015) within and across stakeholder groups, and as relationship builders encouraging collaboration rather than conflict.

Benefits to reconceptualising programme leadership: Connecting with stakeholders

From our experience, effective curriculum development and management requires the input of several stakeholder groups across an institution, effectively a very large team which includes faculty and academic staff, educational developers and quality assurance leaders as well as learners and student groups. A potential challenge is that the needs and motivation across groups vary and reaching consensus is required for moving change forward. In practice, this is challenging to do without explicit intention, clear expectations or effective planning (Hunt et al, 2006). It seems that with so many internal and external stakeholders involved, roles, responsibilities and processes can become confused and disjointed. Leading and moving initiatives forward that are focused on continuous programme improvement therefore benefit when an Academic Manager is facilitating a co-ordinated approach in support of curriculum development at various levels, including course design, curriculum renewal and programme development. In our context these Academic Managers are located within disciplinary units, so are part of the same team as the academic units they support. In addition, they also form a team unto themselves, meaning they can work effectively as a community of practice (Wenger, 2011) to debrief and support each other, keep each other apprised of institutional practices and sometimes also collaborate effectively across academic units.

As external stakeholders, established quality assurance bodies within an institutional framework are generally not intending to police how curriculum development and management is applied in individual academic units across the institution. Instead, these bodies provide defined frameworks to help ensure there is alignment in the programming individual institutions offer, which then further align with accountability purposes within the goals of the organisation (Morley, 2003). That said, we recognize there are institutional and system differences in how quality assurance frameworks are applied, but also see their value in how they afford the opportunity to improve academic programming on a recurring or cyclical basis. Faculty have several competing needs at various points in a typical academic year with respect to their role as instructor, researcher, supervisor and what service commitments they hold. Their academic departments house academic programmes that undergo cyclical programme reviews, audits and other internal and external quality assurance processes. The PL tends to triage and prioritize curriculum development not only based on institutional quality assurance protocols and cyclical requirements by external stakeholders, but also supports best practices in curriculum design and curriculum innovation. We feel the ability of Academic Managers to engage with stakeholders inside and outside of the academic units is possible in different institutional contexts, including centralized and decentralized centres of teaching and learning excellence.

Academic Managers can support faculty in curriculum development initiatives by being well versed in relevant quality assurance protocols as well as being practitioners in educational development. They are able to effectively facilitate or provide a framework for managing curriculum projects, navigating across campus stakeholders that may otherwise be siloed within larger institutional contexts and serve as faculty liaisons to enrich teaching and learning within and across the academic areas they support (Sharif et al., 2019). Academic Managers are often the first point of contact for faculty when engaging with curriculum initiatives, where they handle inquiries on best pedagogical approaches in programme design, while ensuring that the resulting curriculum plans align within the institutional quality assurance framework. In our experience, as they are part of the same team as those they are supporting, there is more trust and openness to these conversations. Faculty, for example, will often reach out to us and see us as a key member of their team rather than as an enforcer of quality assurance processes. To be the most effective, however, Academic Managers need to build positive relationships across various stakeholder groups, both internal and external, to the academic areas on campus.

Creation of interdisciplinary teams: The approach

We have observed that an effective Academic Manager must be able to network and build positive team relationships with other institutional units outside their own team. Of course, positive relationships in any environment are a valuable way of working with others, accomplishing tasks and moving initiatives and projects forward. As part of this, collaborating with stakeholders on a particular project or activity can be a powerful means of ensuring everyone's needs are being met. In addition, greater value is developed when stakeholders engage in co-creation on projects or initiatives, particularly because there is diversity amongst stakeholder groups (Le Pennec & Raufflet, 2018). As Academic Managers, we have experienced a range of interest and ideas from instructors (i.e. those engaged in teaching as well as participating in other department activities such as curriculum development), from intensive support (e.g. "Can you send me a completed draft?") to step-by-step advisement and consultation (e.g. "How do I do x, y, z in my own teaching practice?"). While both approaches reflect interest in curriculum work, both present unique challenges. For Academic Managers, collaboration is not just an important tool, it is an essential one. Given their role as middle managers and the ways in which they can serve to connect with multiple stakeholders (Rudhumbu, 2015), having the ability to develop positive working relationships across stakeholders with diverse needs we feel is a critical skill.

When it comes to curriculum development, as previously discussed, we have found a diverse set of stakeholders exist such as instructors, students, Academic Managers, administrators and institutional quality assurance staff. Each of these stakeholders will likely have a different set of priorities, a different preferred engagement strategy and will also likely have their own thoughts and ideas to bring forward. For the faculty member who wants to see a completed draft, challenges may occur when it comes to long-term engagement and actioning the change; it is difficult to action something you did not have a hand in developing yourself. When it comes to a faculty member who is more fully involved, the challenge of engagement can be replaced by workload management concerns. Instructor engagement in the curriculum process is important in order to enact meaningful changes and curriculum reforms (Alsubaie, 2016; Handler, 2010). Thus, a type of self-fulling prophecy emerges, where due to lack of engagement with the process, faculty may not see curriculum reviews and development as a productive use of time, and instead may become an exercise in satisfying the minimum of institutionally defined requirements.

Collaboration as conflict resolution

Despite the positive potential the shift to authentic quality enhancement and improvement can have on curriculum development and its various stakeholders, we would be remiss not to acknowledge some of the more challenging implications. These include faculty and staff workload considerations, training and development and navigating institutional policies and practices that are often historical in nature. Faculty are subject matter experts within a disciplinary area and asking them to also become disciplinary experts in the field of education (for those trained outside of the field of education) can create a significant increase to their workload. This may prevent them from maintaining an appropriate ratio between their research, instruction and service commitments. A common distribution of effort (DOE) for faculty in Canadian HE is 40% research, 40% teaching and 20% service to the university or local community (Jonker & Hicks, 2014). Academic Managers therefore have the opportunity to support and lead continuous programme improvement through collaboration and teamwork.

Similar to the discussion in Chapter 9 (Jamieson), the process of collaboration itself is one that is more nuanced than perhaps anticipated at first glance, for example, proper collaboration is much more than simply sharing information and asking for feedback. From our professional experience, there are numerous instances of people or stakeholders who have raised concerns or experienced misunderstandings because didactic communication rather than true collaboration has occurred. This situation can be indicative of a more dualistic approach to working on curriculum changes. Such an approach, by its very nature, makes it difficult to examine the nuances of power and conflict within curriculum change processes (Ylimaki & Brunner, 2011). Conflict is arguably an inevitable part of any process where different individuals are coming together to try to make a decision and build consensus. We feel it is important, however, that conflict is not overly managed or ignored when it comes to curriculum development. Specifically, to ignore or minimize conflict in the process indicates participants are not expressing their honest views, and authentic participation is required for meaningful change to occur (Ylimaki & Brunner, 2011).

Given the central role of conflict and stakeholder engagement required for successful and high-quality curriculum development, Academic Managers are uniquely positioned to provide support. We recognize the different organisational structures that exist across academic institutions, and therefore recognize that frameworks for curriculum change processes may vary accordingly. In our setting, Academic Managers are positioned within specific units, usually academic colleges or faculties, and support curriculum development work in a disciplinary context. Functionally, as Academic Managers, we do very similar work to individuals in centralized teaching and learning offices, but with additional disciplinary depth. This approach allows us to build meaningful relationships within our respective units, navigate roles and translate requirements to others to avoid confusion. Trust is central to strong relationships in education (Ali, 2014) and at times this can be difficult to build with a central office. Academic Managers, however, have a more specialized and smaller group of stakeholders where they can then build stronger relationships and have a stronger understanding of the nature of department politics and preferences, existing projects that may relate to proposed curriculum changes and be aware of a missing stakeholder group or individual when a new initiative is brought forward. This places them in a critical role where relationship-building is key. In addition, Academic Managers can also triage and refer stakeholders to different institutional supports where appropriate. This process further facilitates positive changes to macro level curriculum changes, such as course redesign, supporting creating new assessments, implementing a new educational technology and other more in-depth but potentially out of scope needs that might emerge from stakeholders in curriculum conversations.

The new role in practice: The interdisciplinary programme leader in action

In practice, with so many stakeholders involved, it is easy to see how roles and processes could become confused and disjointed. As presented in Figure 10.1, in our context Academic Managers sit in the centre of institutional stakeholders

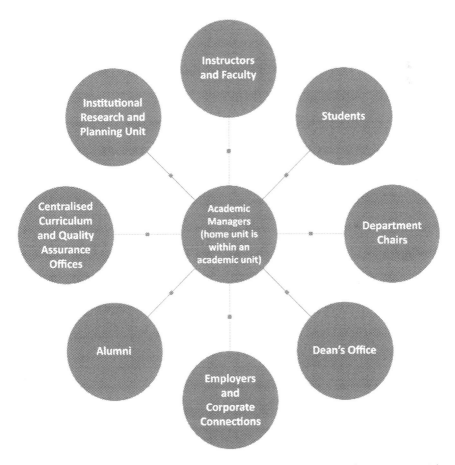

Figure 10.1 Stakeholders in the curriculum development process that connect with Academic Managers. The permutations for how Academic Managers can connect with various stakeholders are vast and provide a great opportunity to connect resources to those who need them.

who engage in curriculum development work and have a boundary-spanning role. Instead of needing to know who to connect with for each stage or part of the process, faculty can inquire through a primary point of contact. Depending on the nature of the inquiry, we take the same approach as a triage nurse in an emergency room. If the inquiry is quick and can be dealt with effectively and efficiently by us, we may choose to provide direct support ourselves. Alternatively, if the inquiry is more complex in a way that makes it out of scope of our role or perhaps requires more resources than one individual can provide and is a longer-term project, we are then able to make a referral.

As Academic Managers, we have seen firsthand the positive impact of making meaningful referrals. Informal theory describes the informal practices and decisions professionals form as a result of their own work and experience, referring to mental maps or tacit-theories-in-use that we all have and use to inform our actions and decision-making (Love, 2012). Drawing on our own informal theories, we realize the challenge of navigating institutional bureaucratic channels that exist in academia. We have found that making a referral helps both the faculty and the stakeholder who receives the referral. It connects the support to where it is most needed at the time, and anecdotally, many additional partnerships have emerged between faculty and other areas on campus because of these referrals. We feel that Academic Managers in general need to be well connected and aware of institutional changes; by connecting as a team across campus, there is support and onboarding for new hires that would not ordinarily happen if they were siloed within their academic units and unable or unaware they could connect with one another.

Practitioner spotlight: Effective referrals

While working with a business faculty member in 2019, Jackie attempted to make a referral to the educational technologies unit to support the integration of more active educational technologies into the program's curriculum. The faculty member was hesitant to accept this referral. Upon further discussion, it was discovered they had been going to the wrong unit on campus for educational technology support and were getting responses that sent them to different stakeholders, causing confusion. The faculty member's frustration at not getting support at first point of contact was understandable, as they disclosed, they felt like they were bouncing around and never getting the support they needed. With some convincing, the faculty member agreed to try the referral. The experience this time was radically different. The faculty member got a response they found helpful within 24 hours and expressed surprise that it had been that easy to get support.

Furthermore, we have found our ability to triage and prioritize requests from faculty supports workload management for everyone. Faculty risk inadvertently contacting the wrong unit or even the incorrect individual within the right unit. We have frequently had discussions with other institutional units about how to develop awareness and engagement with instructors about their resources and services. By serving as the middle manager, our roles sit at the centre of this challenge and have the ability to positively influence the experiences of both sets of stakeholders (Rudhumbu, 2015).

We have found that central to the success of this model is Academic Managers establishing trusting and knowledgeable relationships with faculty within the academic unit they support and across campus stakeholders. As previously discussed, (see also Chapter 9, Jamieson and case study 7, Moore), collaboration and relationship-building are important skills for our roles. In the absence of meaningful relationship-building, any framework under discussion is very likely to fail. As such, we feel it is important to have a strong mechanism to support onboarding of new Academic Managers as well as establishing a method to stay in touch with campus stakeholders. In our institutional context, central to our success is that we formed a community of practice (Wenger, 2011) with other campus Academic Managers who meet regularly. This approach is not only supportive, but also helps to share information and brainstorm ideas for interdisciplinary collaboration.

Practitioner spotlight: Supporting curriculum across teams

The value of teamwork is demonstrated by collaboration from the authors, where their teams intersected. The chair of the political science department asked us to facilitate a curriculum retreat (a further example of this can be found in case study 7, Moore). Through the Academic Manager team, one author reached out to a counterpart to co-facilitate the event as someone external to their academic unit. In doing so, we created a productive space for faculty across the department to share their perspectives as it related to their undergraduate programming. There were contrasting ideas heard about where the department should go as it relates to their undergraduate programming, and was an authentic reflection of the current climate in the department. Through the facilitation of the retreat, we were able to summarize key ideas and themes raised by faculty members in order to establish a curriculum roadmap informed by consensus in new major level learning outcomes. Based on anecdotal feedback from several faculty members, faculty expressed surprise at the value they got from the retreat and were more willing to engage in meaningful conversation about the curriculum because they already had a relationship with their Academic Manager, someone from their own team. Essentially, a trusting relationship already existed. This is a great example of how having Academic Managers participate and identify as members of multiple teams adds value.

The value of context in the work of the programme leader

We are not suggesting that our roles are identical across academic units; in fact, having Academic Managers within different academic units allows them to offer a nuanced and customized support approach. For example, faculty in geography and environmental studies may require technical support for geospatial technologies and other software used within their laboratory sections. The Academic Managers can then help facilitate and support the connection between pedagogy and educational technologies. Conversely, a business faculty member may require support getting Bloomberg licenses and be uncertain of where to start. In that way, the power of the depth of relationship-building that we as Academic Managers engage in because of our placement within disciplinary units is revealed. Again, this is not to say that deep relationship-building does *not* occur in centralized or other campus units. In our experience, it is difficult for central offices, such as teaching and learning centres and library licensing services, to do this with many faculty members across campus simply due to the volume of their service workload.

We then act as catalysts. We work with a smaller group of faculty and instructors, and therefore are naturally spending more time developing relationships and learning about the unique needs of the discipline. Therefore, through their relationship-building, Academic Managers are developing social capital that is formed as a result of the trust in their competence and abilities (Ali, 2014). We have attempted to capture the nuances of this model in Figure 10.2.

We feel there are benefits to centralized and decentralized approaches to educational development. The model presented is applicable in both instances as well

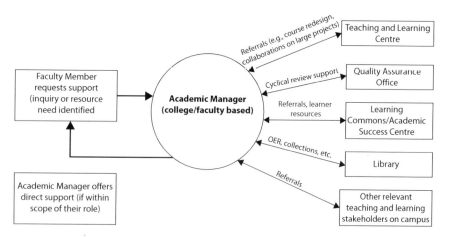

Figure 10.2 Academic manager framework for supporting faculty inquiries, OER denotes open educational resources.

as in hybridized variations. Institutions that hold formalized centres dedicated to academic excellence and educational development usually consist of a team that may include curriculum managers, educational developers, instructional designers and those well versed in the application of pedagogy regardless of their particular disciplinary backgrounds. Academic units are then able to request support from the centre to support curriculum development, cyclical programme review, instructional skill development and more granular course-level support. This transactional model supports faculty across the institution but can be fragmented when there are no Academic Managers to support the liaison between the faculty member and the areas of support. The Academic Manager, by contrast in the way we conceptualize the role, can focus on transformational leadership in directing curriculum development efforts to be in alignment with institutional goals and objectives as well as meeting the needs of the individual faculty member and is in the spirit of continuous programme improvement.

We feel a decentralized approach relies on faculty to be experts in their field of study while also experts in the pedagogical application of their field in their teaching and learning practices. In this model, individual academic units may use their departmental resources to hire a professional staff person, such as an Academic Manager, to fulfil the role of an educational development practitioner and faculty liaison available for the faculty in their department. There are benefits to having a dedicated staff member or staff team to support programme-level curriculum development, ensure consistency in how pedagogy is applied across the programme, ultimately supporting both teaching and learners. This approach, however, may be challenged by an academic unit operating in a silo, namely they become disconnected from other pedagogical innovations that happen in inter- and multidisciplinary collaborations across academic units and are focused on what is happening within the framework of their academic upbringing. In either context, we feel the intentionality in establishing a community of practitioners in small- and large-scale institutions is critical in transforming HE. This model requires the buy-in from senior administration and leadership to ensure the true value (as outlined above) is achieved. The dedicated resources allocated to funding the Academic Managers' roles can be a substantial investment to foster excellence in teaching and learning across academic areas.

Conclusion

The role of the traditional PL is one with many complexities and nuances. Due to unique institutional, disciplinary and professional contexts, it can be difficult to offer a comprehensive definition of the role of a PL. Attempts to do so often result in something that is so vague that, while it applies across contexts, it is meaningless in its ambiguity. This chapter, with a strong focus on supporting curriculum development work, offers a model or framework that we believe encompasses flexibility with meaningful contributions to practice.

By fostering positive and trusting relationships, engaging in collaboration that embraces constructive dialogue and change as well as serving as a connector between faculty and campus stakeholders, we feel Academic Managers can help foster authentic and efficient curriculum work. Furthermore, due to their location within academic units, they have the space to engage more deeply with those stakeholders. The model presented in this chapter is a practitioner-focused approach that provides a framework for how to do this successfully. By supporting faculty and curriculum change, we as Academic Managers support continuous improvement of student learning experiences and as such we feel are critical in creating high-quality programmes and positive campus communities. While the model can be adapted across institutional contexts as needed, at the heart is the importance of team collaboration, human connection and the desire to support others – an approach that should resonate regardless of discipline, location or institutional models.

References

Ali, N. (2014) 'Trust as a Social Capital: a Critical Input Underlying Economic Growth and Educational Development. An Indian Experience', *Rocznik Pedagogiczny, 37*, pp. 151–160.

Alsubaie, M.A. (2016) 'Curriculum Development: Teacher Involvement in Curriculum Development', *Journal of Education and Practice*, 7(9), pp. 106–107.

Brodeur, D.R. & Crawley, E.F. (2009) 'CDIO and Quality Assurance: Using the Standards for Continuous Program Improvement', in Patil, A. & Gray, P. (eds) *Engineering Education Quality Assurance*. Boston: Springer, pp. 211–222.

Daromes, F.E. & Ng, S. (2015) 'Embedding Core Value into the Internal Quality Assurance Systems in Higher Education', *Procedia - Social and Behavioural Sciences*, 211, pp. 660–664.

Jonker, L. & Hicks, M. (2014) *Teaching Loads and Research Outputs of Ontario University Faculty Members: Implications for Productivity and Differentiation*. Toronto: Higher Education Quality Council of Ontario. Available at: https://heqco.ca/wp-content/uploads/2020/03/FINAL-Teaching-Loads-and-Research-Outputs-ENG.pdf (Accessed: 14 December 2021).

Handler, B. (2010) 'Teacher as Curriculum Leader: A Consideration of the Appropriateness of that Role Assignment to Classroom-Based Practitioners', *International Journal of Teacher Leadership*, 3(3), pp. 32–42.

Hunt, L., Bromage, A. & Tomkinson, B. (2006) *The realities of educational change in higher education interventions to promote learning and teaching*. Oxon: Routledge.

Le Pennec, M. & Raufflet, E. (2018) 'Value Creation in Inter-Organizational Collaboration: An Empirical Study', *Journal of Business Ethics*, 148(4), pp. 817–834. doi: 10.1007/s10551-015-3012-7.

Love, P. (2012) 'Informal Theory: The Ignored Link in Theory-to-Practice', *Journal of College Student Development*, 53(2), pp. 177–191. doi:10.1353/csd.2012.0018.

Morley, L. (2003) *Quality and Power in Higher Education*. UK: McGraw-Hill Education.

Rudhumbu, N. (2015) 'Managing Curriculum Change from the Middle: How Academic Middle Managers Enact their Role in Higher Education', *International Journal of Higher Education*, 4(1), pp. 106–119. doi:10.5430/ijhe.v4n1p106.

Sharif, A., Welsh, A., Myers, J., Wilson, B., Chan, J., Cho, S., & Miller, J. (2019) 'Faculty Liaisons: An Embedded Approach for Enriching Teaching and Learning in Higher Education', *International Journal for Academic Development*, 24(3), pp. 260–271. doi: 10.1080/1360144X.2019.1584898.

Voogt, J.M, Pieters, J.M., & Handelzalts, A. (2016) 'Teacher Collaboration in Curriculum Design Teams: Effects, Mechanisms, and Conditions', *Educational Research and Evaluation*, 22(3–4), pp.121–140, doi: 10.1080/13803611.2016.1247725

Wenger, E. (2011) *Communities of Practice: A Brief Introduction*. US: National Science Foundation.

Ylimaki R.M. & Brunner, C.C. (2011) 'Power and Collaboration-Consensus/Conflict in Curriculum Leadership: Status Quo or Change?' *American Educational Research Journal*, 48(6), pp. 1258–1285. doi: 10.3102/0002831211409188.

Practitioner response: The importance of framing the curriculum as a living system

Catherine M. Millett, USA

Reading the Hamilton and Donaldson chapter at an inflection point in HE around the world made me stop and think about five storylines I see in the US. One is the increasing diversity of our student populations (e.g. age, gender identity or expression, racial and ethnicity identity and political and ideological perspectives). The second storyline is the important skills and knowledge that learners will need, which typically focuses on hard and soft skills. Third is the growing awareness that curriculum needs to encompass areas beyond disciplinary knowledge such as social and emotional learning and civic engagement and awareness. Fourth, comprehensive learner records and digital wallets are going to multiply the types of materials that students will present to demonstrate their learning experiences. Finally, in a global pandemic, institutions are reviewing their enrolment rates and income streams, both of which may be declining. In spite of possible gloomy fiscal forecasts, after reading the Hamilton and Donaldson chapter, I could lay out a compelling case for why the PL position can play a crucial role.

The strength of Hamilton and Donaldson is their skill in framing the curriculum as a living system in a department and institution that merits continuous attention to be relevant and contemporary. My own scholarship (Nettles and Millett, 2006) focused on the experiences of doctoral students in the US concluded that doctoral education training has privileged the acquisition of research skills over teaching skills. This framework respects disciplinary differences while seeing the opportunity to connect with other disciplines. Hamilton and Donaldson's framework for the PL role as an academic manager who supports and leads curriculum change development and management is a viable model for tending to the curriculum while maintaining the faculty's ability to manage their multiple responsibilities, creating linkages to other areas with similar priorities such as the teaching and learning centres and managing change both from internal and external forces.

Currently, I am not a faculty member. Nevertheless, I participate in meetings that consider how to include social and emotional learning and civic learning and democratic engagement in the curriculum at the department level. Often, during these discussions, I envision the faculty with a 'teaching backpack' that

DOI: 10.4324/9781003127413-35

we keep adding more course goals and content areas for them to carry. Having a PL in their department would allow them to redistribute the backpack weight by handing some pieces to a colleague.

Reference

Nettles, M.T. & Millett, C.M. (2006) *Three Magic Letters: Getting to Ph.D*. Baltimore: The Johns Hopkins University Press. (Translated to Chinese in 2019).

Case study 9

Leading successful programme transformation

Sharon Altena and Karen Theobald, Australia

Introduction

The Bachelor of Nursing is a flagship undergraduate programme at Queensland University of Technology, with 3500 students studying for the degree at any one time. This case study describes how two programme leaders (PLs) from different areas within the university formed a partnership to lead and empower a team of academics in delivering long-lasting, transformational curriculum change. The learnings presented here will benefit PLs wishing to achieve sustainable, holistic, student-centred changes to teaching practice at their institutions. The curriculum renewal was not a 'business as usual' approach or 'a box ticking exercise'. Instead, renewal was a deliberate attempt to undertake an in-depth examination of the existing curriculum and to fundamentally redesign and invigorate.

The two PLs appointed to implement the new curriculum were the Director of Academic Programmes and a Learning Designer. The former had existing relationships with academic staff and a thorough knowledge of the curriculum, external accreditation and industry requirements. The latter brought expertise in curriculum design, pedagogy, student-centred learning and digital technologies. Blending these areas of knowledge was essential for this bold curriculum transformation to be successful.

The Five Practices of Exemplary Leadership framework guided our approach to the process as we sought to model the way, inspire a shared vision, challenge the process, enable others to act and encourage the heart (Kouzes & Posner, 2011). Below we explore the actions we took in each of these areas to show how such leadership models can be applied in practice with programme teams.

Modelling the way

Our approach to leadership involved 'modelling the way' through our actions and words. We remained consistent and passionate about the vision, maintained an openness in communication, authentically invited opinions, and accepted feedback. Importantly, we demonstrated the benefits and outcomes of working in partnership by setting an example for others to follow and explicitly showing

DOI: 10.4324/9781003127413-36

how harnessing different skill sets and working together could bring about extraordinary results.

Inspiring a shared vision

During an on-site retreat, we shared a vision for a holistic, future-focused, student-centred and digitally enhanced programme. This shared vision was consistently communicated to our academics at every opportunity, it became the mantra of the School of Nursing and, in many ways, took on a 'life of its own'.

> *the process was sort of the bringing together of all the academics, to get them onto the same page... I felt that that was so important for us to... remind ourselves about our purpose as educators.*
>
> Academic C

Challenging the process

To achieve a holistic curriculum, we found it was critical to 'challenge the process' and facilitate new ways of working. We, as PLs, guided staff in relinquishing their control over individual courses, resulting in shared ownership of the curriculum, where courses were 'owned' by the School. Although this was challenging for some, belief in the vision seemed to move the team through this.

Enabling others to act

The central means by which we enabled others to act emerged from organising academic staff into three course streams. Each stream had a leader who was empowered and mentored by the programme leads to think differently, elevate their thinking to 'whole-of-course' consistent approaches, and examine all aspects of programme implementation through a student-centred lens. The stream leads 'modelled the way' for their teams, by being the first to redesign their course.

> *From when I started, to now, is worlds apart. We very much worked on our own when we first started ... once the streams came in, it became really clear who we needed to be working with, and how we could help each other.*
>
> Academic A

Encouraging the heart

We felt it vital to provide opportunities at a School forum for early adopters to showcase examples of the innovations incorporated into their courses. This showcase sparked interest, further enlisting academics to deliver the implementation vision. When the first group of courses was released, the overwhelming positive reaction of students built further engagement and commitment, as academic staff could see the vision come to life.

Applying the five practices approach

Taking the five practices approach (Kouzes & Posner, 2011) to leading programme transformation has broken down academic teaching silos, fostered collegiality and united a team of academics behind a vision to strive for excellence in active, engaging, digitally enhanced and student-centred nursing education. Through a belief in the vision, academics relinquished some control over their courses to create a holistic, integrated curriculum that offered a consistent student experience. These consistent approaches have been noticed by students, who have responded positively to the changes:

> *The layout of the Blackboard (Bb) page for this unit is excellent - very clear and easy to navigate. I love how Bb has been set out, with pre-learning/post-learning activities.*
>
> Student A

Importantly, follow-up interviews with academics after three years have revealed longevity and sustainability of the changes in teaching practice. However, programme transformation was not without its challenges. Development of new courses occurred at the same time as a full teaching/research load with no release time. The entire curriculum was changed all at once rather than progressively, resulting in student experiences changing part-way through their programme. In the spirit of innovation, new technologies were introduced and trialled as part of programme transformation, however, discontinuation of funding for these technologies by the university resulted in much frustration and disappointment by affected academics.

Conclusion

Key lessons were learned through this process. PLs need to have a clear vision and paint a compelling picture of the future. The equal partnership and blending of the expertise of the two PLs was instrumental in achieving the vision. Finally, creating opportunities for early adopters to shine was a turning point by providing a vehicle to showcase innovations that inspired those next to embark on the journey, and helped even the resistors to engage.

Reference

Kouzes, J. M. & Posner, B. Z. (2011) *The five practices of exemplary leadership.* San Francisco: Pfeiffer.

Case study 10

Facilitating educational leadership

Building and sharing an understanding amongst the programme team

Eva Malone and Stephen Yorkstone, UK

Introduction

This case study explores how we worked as a cross-institutional team to produce a Programme Roadmap for a suite of five undergraduate programmes. The Roadmap is a document designed to distil the activities of the programme leader (PL) and programme team to increase visibility of the tasks, create a shared sense of responsibility and increase collaboration within the group. The production of the Roadmap evolved iteratively over several phases which, although 'messier' than presented here, ensured that input to the document was shared and feedback acted upon.

Setting the roadmap in motion

Based in Edinburgh Napier University (ENU), a modern university in Scotland, I (Eva) lead a suite of five undergraduate programmes accredited by the Royal Society of Biology. We have around 500 students enrolled across the suite at any one time and a portfolio of 37 modules.

Before embarking upon this project, I had completed one academic year as PL which had quickly enlightened me on the complexities of the role. Throughout this first year I had adopted a hands-on approach, I was accessible and available to both students and the programme team. However, this approach meant I felt responsible for all the various intricacies of the programme and as a result I felt overwhelmed. When I reflected on that year, and looked ahead, the thoughts of doing it again, in the same way, did not energise me. I felt there had to be a more efficient, effective way to go about the role, but at that time I could not see it. This is where colleagues from the ENU Business Improvement service came in. The role of this service is to enhance how people, processes and systems work together across the University.

Steve leads Business Improvement at ENU. He has a background in applying lean management and extensive experience in coaching and facilitation around such processes. Lean management consists of improvement approaches rooted in both continuous improvement and respect for people. This approach originates

DOI: 10.4324/9781003127413-37

from the Toyota Production System and how it has been translated into other organisations (Netland & Powell, 2016). Indeed, Lean approaches are increasingly being seen in Higher Education (Yorkstone, 2019).

Steve's team in ENU hosts a community of practice for people interested in applying continuous improvement within the higher education (HE) setting. For this community, there is a seminar series with invited external speakers. Importantly for me, it was in one of these seminars where I met Vincent Wiegel, an academic, engineer and expert in applying lean in HE. Vincent spoke of how he had transformed the marking process for his programme. This sharing of effective practice ultimately sparked the idea of Steve, me, and colleagues, working to develop a heuristic model for assigning marking on a challenging research project module. The initial connection, and ensuing project, were a gateway to my appreciation of more practical, applied and iterative approaches to problem solving. It also meant I had someone to discuss the programme leadership role with and seek support for developing a solution to the amorphous nature of the position.

Constructing the roadmap

Although, as PL, resources were available to me, for example, I had a role descriptor and a PL's checklist (Edinburgh Napier University DLTE, 2021), I still required more. I needed to create clarity around the tasks that were to be completed and focus on what was required and when: this is what became the Programme Roadmap. However, it was an exceptionally busy time, so I needed to secure support for the project. There was a discussion that the project might place a burden on an already busy workload, but I passionately believed that the investment up front would pay back later. The project received the support needed and so we began. With Steve's help we started the job of making the programme tasks explicit, without critical judgement, so we could see the nature of the problem and make iterative, practical improvements towards working through how to manage these tasks.

Together, we brainstormed, listed all the tasks and all the roles or teams involved with the delivery of the programme suite. Importantly, we did this quickly without overthinking it. We realised we needed more input to ensure the list was representative of others' views. For example, Adam Satur, our programme administrator, brought a different and valuable perspective to the discussions, understanding how the administrative tasks and teams intersect over the entire year.

The spreadsheet provided a matrix structure, which allowed us to identify levels of contribution for each task. In so doing, we followed an established project management approach and used a RACI (Responsible, Accountable, Consulted, Informed) matrix (Project Management Institute, 2013) but found the addition of two further elements particularly helpful within the programme management context. First, we added an 'Uninvolved' category, second, a 'Participating'

Table CS10.1 Adapted RACI definitions (see also, Project Management Institute, 2013, p. 262)

Involvement	Description
Accountable	Ultimately answerable for the task, delegates work to those responsible
Responsible	Leads on and acts to do the task
Participating	Opinions sought, two-way communication, and acts to do the task
Consulted	Opinions sought, two-way communication, and does not act to do the task
Informed	Kept up to date, one way communication
Uninvolved	Not involved in or informed of this task

category, this enabled us to add more granularity and for one person to be responsible but allow other team members to participate in completion (Table CS10.1).

The spreadsheet was further developed to add details of when tasks should be completed. Also, an option to record when they were completed was added to enable us to monitor how work progressed in reality against the original plan. Tasks were also grouped together too to enable a simpler view. Sort and filter functions could be used to pull up related tasks or look at tasks for individual roles.

This, now highly evolved version of the matrix, was shared at our Board of Studies (a bi-annual review meeting involving programme stakeholders such as the programme team, students and support services) and a follow-up drop-in session to enable us to obtain feedback from the programme team. We received valuable comments in relation to the complexity of the matrix and how it could be difficult to engage with. We responded to this input by adding guidance on how best to use the tool; clarification on what the tool was intended for (to assist the programme team in understanding what tasks are to be done by whom and when); and the tool's limitations. The feedback served as a useful reminder on the inherent complexity of the role but also enabled us to make this complexity visible to the other programme stakeholders. These refinements gave us the final version of our Programme Roadmap.

Outcomes

At the time of writing, we have been using the Roadmap for 5 months. It is a resource to which I can turn to inform meeting agendas and as an aide memoire regarding who is participating in tasks. I feel less overwhelmed, there are fewer surprises, and I am continually reminded I work as part of a dedicated team. I no longer need to remember everything and that frees up my headspace for more creativity and innovation within the programme leadership role. Of course, we still need to refine and adapt our Programme Roadmap, indeed, I see it is a live document that will improve the more we use it and will be invaluable particularly when the time comes for succession planning.

This creative process has shifted the emphasis away from me and my perceived limitations onto a much more solutions-focused approach. As a PL, both the process and output of building the Roadmap have helped me to 'manage the management' so I can now shift my attention onto educational leadership. You may have someone in your institution that can help you do this too should you want to. Reach out to find them.

References

Netland, T. & Powell D.J. (2016) 'A Lean World' in Netland, T. & Powell, D.J. (eds.) *The Routledge Companion to Lean Management.* New York: Routledge.

Yorkstone, S. (2019). *Global Lean for Higher Education: A Themed Anthology of Case Studies, Approaches, and Tools.* CRC Press (Taylor and Francis Group)

Edinburgh Napier University DLTE (2021) *Programme Leader Operational Checklist 2019/20.* Available at: https://staff.napier.ac.uk/services/dlte/PL/Documents/PL%20Checklist%20FINAL.pdf (Accessed 12 May 2021).

Project Management Institute (2013) *A Guide to the Project Management Body of Knowledge (PMBOK Guide)* Project Management Institute.

Conclusion

Championing programme leadership for success in higher education

Rowena Senior, Sue Morón-García and Jenny Lawrence, UK

Introduction

This book is testimony to how higher education institutions (HEIs) that invest in programme leaders (PLs) may enjoy student, departmental and institutional success. Others before us (e.g. Burgess et al, 2018, in their discussion about the National Student Survey in the UK) have pointed out how the organisation and management of a programme is a critical factor in driving student satisfaction scores. Such areas are squarely within the purview of a PL and impactful with respect to institutional reputation. As this book shows, success is built by taking a strategic, scholarly approach to the development of programme leadership and by designing developmental opportunities for and with PLs, trusting in their academic agency and in their ability to lead.

This conclusion outlines what we have learnt about programme leadership, through our work in institutions and with the authors who have contributed to this book. Clearly, there are variations in practice that relate to contextual differences in the institutional and regulatory environments within which our international contributors work, but overwhelmingly there are many similarities and connections in what has been explored here. We discuss how it is important to focus on these parallels in order to provide an outline for a comprehensive support framework. In so doing, we propose a 'manifesto for sustainable programme leadership' based on four central themes. We finish with a set of reflective questions to aid those who wish to create their own framework for successful and valued programme leadership in their institutions.

Travelling through a changing landscape

This book has been a very personal journey for all of us and has taken us from 'normality', recognising the ever-shifting context of higher education (HE), through COVID-19 times and, hopefully, out to the other side. As we elaborated in the introduction to this book, our journey, championing the role of the PL in higher education, began, was defined and consolidated from 2017 onwards. We recognised the need for support and development work for this often neglected

DOI: 10.4324/9781003127413-38

group of colleagues and saw increased demand in our institutions. Early work that brought educational developers in the UK together at the Aston University symposium (Senior, 2018a) that gave rise to the SEDA Special (Lawrence & Ellis, 2018; Senior, 2018b) and focused on ways to support the development of PLs gave us great impetus for the book as well as certainty that it was needed. Our focus was always, and remains, on the provision of practical wisdom to those in HE who undertake and support the role.

We know that the complexity and time-consuming nature of the PL role has historically arrested a traditional academic career (Cahill et al, 2015), with the immediate priorities of programme leadership often superseding research activity. It seems this has traditionally made these roles less desirable and worked to the detriment of the busy PL, as research is often the most valued currency of academia.

However, we have noticed more recently that institutions are reshaping academic roles in response to a changed focus and creating teaching-focused contracts which, when done well, recognise the contribution of those focused on the support of an institution's teaching endeavour. Forward-thinking institutions have created career pathways equitable in standing, opportunity and remuneration to the traditional mixed focus, research and teaching contract. This is to the advantage of PLs, who have started to be justly rewarded and recognised for integrating their disciplinary expertise with academic and educational leadership (Lawrence, 2021).

We note that for many early to mid-career academics, who have only ever studied and worked in a professionalised HE sector, programme leadership can be a central component to an academic career. Leadership of a successful programme of study can be a creative and rewarding experience, and this is something that shines through the many case studies in this book. This leadership should be comparable to a research colleague's contribution to knowledge, especially in institutions where, on the whole, the main income comes from the teaching offered. This work seeks to drive forward the advancement of support in this most essential group of academic leaders.

A manifesto for sustainable programme leadership

We call upon institutional leaders to recognise and understand how to create environments within which PLs can flourish. Institutional leaders cannot simply focus on outlining what PLs must do in order to have the transformational impact desired; they must instead involve PLs themselves in the creation of the supportive environments and structures that they need to grow and thrive. PLs are actors within a highly contextualised environment, of a particular institution, in a specific national landscape and within disciplinary communities; they are often best placed to help identify what is needed to survive and prosper. We know that experienced practitioners have a wealth of practical wisdom that they can share, given the right environment and that these environments are best developed through dialogue.

We argue that socially mediated development activity is more effective and sustains higher levels of engagement from those involved. Only other PLs understand the unique hybridity of the role, the necessary intersection of disciplinary, academic, educational and administrative expertise as well as the personal and professional challenges. Through this type of activity, it is possible to provide both practical solutions, empathetic support and acknowledge PL expertise. Indeed, you will have read many examples in this book.

We feel it is important to create an environment where PLs can develop their own academic agency. They have disciplinary and pedagogic expertise and need to be trusted to lead in consultation with other curriculum stakeholders, including colleagues in the programme team. By lead, we mean design and manage their programme to ensure an excellent student experience, including the engagement, challenge and enrichment that lead to successful outcomes.

Institutions must now take what is discussed herein and elsewhere (e.g. Lawrence & Ellis, 2018; QAA Scotland, 2019) to create environments that encourage PLs to use their agency in the creation of excellent student experiences, meaningful work for their programme team and the development of their own leadership role. We argue that four central themes should be adopted as foci when creating a framework for programme leadership development. Currently, we find that programme leadership is not sustainable for the PL, as many of our authors have discussed. As such, we argue that in order to support programme leadership, institutions must attend to the following interlinked areas:

1. Organisational culture
2. Connection and collaboration
3. Holistic support
4. Recognition

These four themes form the basis of our manifesto for sustainable programme leadership, and below we offer instructional insights to institutions on how to take these forward. It is important to remember, however, that these areas are everyone's responsibility. If we are to create successful HE environments, we must all contribute to and support the endeavour of those in programme leadership roles.

Organisational culture

The oft-cited trope that no one-size-fits-all is very applicable in the development of support for PLs. We feel a critical factor in getting that support right that is embedded, integrated and meaningful is ensuring that the organisational culture in which the PL sits is understood at institutional, faculty and department level.

There must be clarity about the expectations the institutional leadership has of those who hold the role and of those who support the day-to-day operation of that role. Reporting structures should be made clear. The mission and values of the institution, the customs and practice, the hierarchies and the relationships that exist within it will all affect this. For example, an institutional Programme Directors' Network-based approach, such as Lawrence and Scott discuss in Chapter 5, is likely to support medium- or small-sized organisations with flatter management structures, better than large institutions where practice could be more diffuse and faculties may work more autonomously. Whereas a retreat-based approach such as the one Moore took (see Case Study 7) may suit a more bounded team than a context where many shared modules exist across a larger number or suite of programmes.

We feel that it is essential to state the aims of any developmental support provided for PLs, in the same way that you would create a programme philosophy in a curriculum design context; this enables those involved and others in the institution to better understand the purpose and the roles and responsibilities of those involved. Those in institutional leadership positions are in a space where they can drive cultural change that embraces PLs as active agents of such positive development and put in place the recognition, opportunity, resources and instructions that PLs should have to be able to do their jobs well. It is important for institutions and their leaders not to adopt a deficit model in programme leadership, as this is unlikely to encourage the dedicated innovators that we need in these boundary-spanning roles.

Our manifesto deliberately starts with a call to action in relation to organisational culture as the values of an institution form a platform upon which the other areas rely. As such, it is this first theme that provides a foundation for the growth of the other three themes detailed below.

Connection and collaboration

Connection and collaboration permeate all three parts of this book. It is perhaps this year (2020–21) more than any other that we have felt acutely the need for the community that connection and collaboration bring to our working and personal lives. Connection and collaboration can be at their most powerful when they are meaningful and rooted in a common purpose that comes from a sense of community. A sense of community can aid understanding. Better sharing reassures (see e.g., Chapter 7, O'Dwyer and Sanderson) and can lead to greater clarity. We feel that it is when people feel listened to that innovation, development and ideas can flourish.

It is important to foster and encourage connection and collaboration through specifically targeted PL development opportunities (see e.g. Chapter 4, Petrova). These connections, across disciplines and departments, the institution and wider sector networks, are enriched due to their diverse membership and will enrich a local community in turn. The social networks (see e.g., Chapter 7, O'Dwyer and Sanderson) that we foster through these connections can lead to extended learning, better understanding of context and, in turn, can foster ever more meaningful collaboration. For example, the creation and adoption of PL-specific networks or forums serve to recognise the community that carries out this role and give members a collective voice, or at a minimum space, through which to speak to the power brokers in their context. This platform reinforces their sense of agency and ability to see themselves as the leaders they are (see e.g., Chapter 6, Parkin).

As this book has shown, the ability to work with and manage the programme team is also critical to the success of programme leadership. This is understood as connection and collaboration on an immediate, local level. In order to support the focal mission, PL institutional documents such as a PL role descriptor and a specific support structure should be developed in collaboration with those affected (see Chapter 2, Forsyth & Powell; Chapter 3, Maddock, Carruthers & van Haeringen,). This process should co-locate the responsibility and accountability for the tasks set out among the PL, academic team members and other contributors in professional services. Indeed, Malone & Yorkstone (Case study 10) explain how tasks and processes essential to the successful running of a programme and the success of its students can and should be shared by the programme team, while Hamilton & Donaldson (Chapter 10) tell us about a different model of programme leadership through the Academic Manager role.

The role of a PL involves being a facilitator and coordinator; it can be emancipatory. Encouraging the programme team to take shared ownership of the programme leads to a greater appreciation of the complexity of the role and a better understanding of the programme. As Parkin states (Chapter 6), leadership only works when relationships do. There are numerous examples in this book where PLs have benefitted from involving their team in developing a programme (see e.g. Case Study 3, Johnson & Kalu; Case Study 10, Malone and Yorkstone).

Holistic support

We feel that taking a holistic approach to supporting PLs involving all parts of the institution and providing support for the development of academic, educational and administrative leadership, not just one aspect of the role is critical. It involves building connections within teams and across intra-institutional boundaries and can foster a greater sense of recognition (as discussed below). Indeed, we have structured this book so as to provide examples of how practice has been enacted and enhanced with respect to a focus on the institution, the individual and the team. By organising the book in this way, we highlight the range of approaches that can be used to provide what should be holistic support that addresses the arenas PLs work in.

We recognise that institutional leaders will tailor these approaches to suit the context in which PLs need to be supported, but at the heart should be an underlying philosophical approach that sees the PL as valuable and central to the effective functioning of a programme. The support pathway that takes a PL from novice through to succession planning needs to be strategic and purposeful (see, e.g., Chapter 3, Maddock, Carruthers & van Haeringen,). The holistic approach will, likely of necessity, be designed with the institutional context and culture in mind, but it should be communicated through places where accountability and action are visible, for example, via committee structures and through visible senior leadership sponsorship. Forsyth et al. (Chapter 2) highlight the need to problematise the space before designing solutions. This may be an effective method to begin the conversation in some institutions, while others may well be more interested in using data, such as satisfaction scores, league tables or other metrics, as a starting point.

It is important to recognise that the creation of a holistic, multifaceted suite of development and support is not without challenges that also encompass the ever-changing roles of educational developers in our institutions. However, if we do want to move perceptions away from fears about programme leadership being a career killer (see for e.g. Vilkinas and Ladyshewsky, 2012), these brave steps are necessary.

Recognition and reward

This book continues the reimagination of programme leadership as integral to an academic career where reward and recognition is not only monetary through the possibility of promotion, but also about investment in the personal and professional development of those who are a talented and crucial element of both disciplinary and institutional leadership. As Parkin (Chapter 6) rightly points out, we need to do more to recognise and celebrate PLs: there is a mismatch between the pivotal nature of the role in relation to organisational success and its recognition.

Recognition does not sit apart from taking a holistic approach and the importance of connection and collaboration discussed thus far. We feel that it is through taking a holistic approach to programme leadership support that meaningful recognition can be built into and across the institution and have an impact on organisational culture. Recognition that filters through institutional procedures and practices can be achieved in a number of ways and in a number of different places. For example, as already mentioned, individually through formal promotion pathways or as a substantial part of annual performance reviews. Institutionally, it can be expressed in the form of considered and contractual time allocation.

Further examples of ways programme leadership can be recognised and, by implication, valued, include specific continuing professional development opportunities, honorariums, administrative support and a competitive process to attain the role. Acknowledgement of the importance of programme leadership for an institution will be conferred by a meaningful budget allocation, inclusion in criteria that need to be met to apply for senior roles, the existence of internal awards for leading well and the possibility of being championed for external awards. Kudos will likely accrue for the PLs if they are given a reduction in expectations in other areas of practice, are able to access additional opportunities because of service undertaken and are supported to engage with the sector more widely. For example, showcasing institutional and disciplinary work at conferences, network-building opportunities or links to the learning and teaching arm of a relevant professional and statutory regulatory body.

It is important that institutions implement as many of these as their resource base allows, in order to feed into a culture that enables PLs to thrive and grow, to share and disseminate innovative practice; champion a PL and they will become a champion for the institution. PLs are focused on educational leadership and are often one of the largest academic role groups in institutions; yet, few institutions have a space in which PL expertise and needs can be communicated to the senior leadership and in which they can be nurtured to help move the institutional vision forward.

Conclusion

This book brings together a wealth of experience and examples that we hope you will find useful in creating developmental support for PLs in your institutions. We suggest that collaborative community spaces should be facilitated and organisational structures that assist PLs should be reviewed and bolstered. We used the four manifesto themes as lenses through which to view PL needs and to indicate a framework that could be used to develop support for PLs in your context. This support should be holistic, take account of and, where necessary, change organisational culture. It should provide opportunities for connection and collaboration with peers, institutional leadership and those with other relevant roles as well as build in recognition as an integral element.

We offer the following reflective questions to guide your thinking in the creation of PL support and development in your context:

- What is your organisational context, what existing structures could be used to most effectively embed planned development and support, what structures might need to change to facilitate this support and how will this be orchestrated?
- Where do PLs have the opportunity to make meaningful connections and foster valuable collaboration with their colleagues and students, how is this supported and what changes need to be made?
- What will holistic support look like in your context, which significant layers within the institution should be included in your context (e.g. departments, cross-institutional professional services, individuals, programme teams and/or senior leadership)?
- Where and how will you recognise PLs so that it is evident how significant the role is to the institutional mission? How will you relate this to career progression and job fulfilment for those undertaking the role?

References

Burgess, A., Senior, C. & Moores, E. (2018) 'A 10-year case study on the changing determinants of university student satisfaction in the UK', *PLOS ONE*, 13(2), pp. e0192976. doi: 10.1371/journal.pone.0192976.

Cahill, J., Bowyer, J., Rendell, C., Hammond, A. & Korek, S. (2015) 'An exploration of how programme leaders in higher education can be prepared and supported to discharge their roles and responsibilities effectively', *Educational Research*, 57(3), pp. 272–286. doi: 10.1080/00131881.2015.1056640.

Lawrence, J. (2021) 'Thriving on the winds of change: repositioning programme leadership as a career thriller'. QAAS Enhancement Themes Collaborative Cluster on Programme Leadership. Available at: https://www.enhancementthemes.ac.uk/docs/ethemes/resilient-learning-communities/thriving-on-the-winds-of-change.pdf?sfvrsn=57abd681_6 (Accessed: 14 December 2021)

Lawrence, J., et al. (2018) 'Supporting Programme Leaders and Programme Leadership'. [Workshop] University of Hull, 13th September.

QAA (2019) *Enhancing Programme Leadership*. Available at: https://www.enhancementthemes.ac.uk//en/completed-enhancement-themes/evidence-for-enhancement/optimising-existing-evidence/enhancing-programme-leadership (Accessed: 14 December 2021).

Senior, R. (2018a). Programme Directors CPD symposium. Aston University.

Senior, R. (2018b) 'The shape of programme leadership in the contemporary university', in Lawrence, J. & Ellis, S. (eds.) *Supporting programme leaders and programme leadership: Vol. 39 SEDA Specials*. London: SEDA, pp. 11–14.

Vilkinas, T., & Ladyshewsky, R. (2012). 'Leadership behaviour and effectiveness of academic program directors in Australian universities', *Educational Management Administration & Leadership*, 40(1), pp. 109–126. doi: 10.1177/1741143211420613.

Index

Note: Italicised page numbers refer to figures, **bold** page numbers refer to tables.

Aamodt, P. O. 52
Abel, M. 104
academic leadership 111; dimensions of 95–7
academic manager, role of: coordinating institutional stakeholders 179, *179*; curriculum and quality assurance 174; curriculum project managers 174–5; development of new programmes 174; institutional community of practice 175, 181; institutional policy advisors 175; programme leader workload, reduction of 175; stakeholder liaison and engagement 175–6
academic manager, skills of: adapting to local context 182; collaboration 177–8; conflict resolution 178; curriculum team building 177; relationship building 175, 178, 181; source of advice and referral 177, 180, *182*
action learning: enhancement and programme leadership 18; online meeting 18; programme leaders panel 19; virtual support network 18; workshop 18; writing retreat 20
action research 30; 43–4
Adams, P. 21
Åkerlind, G. S. 64–5
Ali, N. 178, 182
Alix, C. 156, 162
Allais, S. 72
Alsubaie, M.A. 177
Anderson, J. 108
Anderson, M. 51
Anthony, S. G. 111
Antony, J. 111
Appreciative Inquiry 29, 37, 74–5
Argyris, C. 48
Assessment as Learning 170
Assessment Audit infographic *171*
Assessment Therapist 171

Aston University (UK) 4, 196
Atkins, L. 75
Australia 41, 71, 188
Australian Universities Quality Agency 55

Barnett, R. 60
Bass, B. M. 43
Bath, D. 51
Beattie, L. 156, 159
Becher, T. 29
belonging, sense of 115
Betz, S. 158
Billot, J. 65
Blackmore, P. 15, 18, 79, 87
Blackstock, C. 84
blended learning 140–2; advice on design of 142; leadership of *141*
Bolden, R. 4, 42, 96
Bolman, L. G. 95
Bosanquet, A. M. 161
Boud, D. 43, 170
Bovill, C. 63, 155
Bowen-Jones, W. 70
Bowyer, J. 68, 82, 169, 202
Brazilian comparative experience 123
Brew, A. 43, 66
Britton, J. 155, 160
Brodeur, D. R. 175
Bromage, A. 184
Brownell, S. E. 171, 172
Brunner, C. C. 178
Bryman, A. 42, 126, 132
Building Programme Leadership Strategy 41, 42; 53; evaluation of 46, *47*; successes with 46; value of observing and modelling leadership practice 48; value of sharing and discussing experience 48
Buissink, N. 84
Burgess, A. 195

Burke, K. M. 111
Burrell, A. R. 171
Burt, H. M. 80
Business Improvement Unit 191

Caddell, M. 17, 22, 25
Cahill, J. 4, 43, 60, 66, 74, 78, 81, 89, 124–5, 127, 128–33, 166, 168, 196
calendar of programme activities 86; communal creation of 86, example *88*; impact of 86
Calleja, P. 50
Cameron, A. 41
Cameron, R. 50
Campbell, S. 51
Canada 137
Cape Peninsula University of Technology (SA) 40
Cardell, E. 50
Carnwell. R. 160, 162
Carruthers, S. 44, 46
Carson A. M. 60, 162
Cartan, G. 3, 60–1, 66, 124–5, 128–9, 132–3, 166–7
Carter, H. 173
Cavanagh, M. 173
Chan, J. 185
change agents 43, 140
change-making, difficulties with 190; overload of work 190; new technology, withdrawal of support 190; whole programme change at once 190
change-making, leadership of: encouragement, by student response 189; good practice, by modelling 188; leadership devolved and shared 189; shared ownership, by challenge 189; shared vision, by inspiring 189
Chapleo, C. 3
Checkland, P. 30, 32
Chilean comparative experience 136
Cho, S. 185,
Clark, J. 51
Clarke, A. 82
Clarke, C. 82
Cleaver, E. 74
Clegg, S. 65
Coates, H. 51
Cockell, J. 75
co-creation 155–7, 162; core principles 158; diversity of student experience 158
Coffey, B. 122
collaboration 140–2, 155–6, 165; as daily practice 156; definitions of 155; embracing risk 165; with managers 160; as professional practice 156; role of failure in 159; time, importance of 159, 165

collaborative cluster 15–16, 19, 23, 24; benefits of 23; multi-institutional 16; national project 16
Collington, V. 75
communication and structure, importance of 146
community building, social space 115
community of practice 77–9, 81; difficulties with 112
constructive alignment 142
constructivist / interpretive epistemology 74
Cooperrider, D. 32, 75
Costley, C. 84
Covey, S. R. 97, 99
COVID-19: 3, 19, 63, 74–5, 78, 85, 136, 142, 159, 165, 195
Crawford, K. 122
Crawley, E. F. 175
Cresswell, J. W. 74
Crevani, L. 124–5, 132–3, 167
Cullen, R. 37
Cunliffe, A. 124, 132
Cunningham, C. 16, 21
curriculum design, team based 171
curriculum redesign and transformation 188–90
curriculum review 137–8
Curtis, W. 4, 15–16, 32, 60–1, 66, 68, 89, 124–5, 127, 129, 133, 160, 166

Daromes, F. E. 175
data landscape: complexity of 18–21; PL role in navigating and brokering 22, 24
Dearing, R. 4
Debowski, S. 137
Delaney, D. 46
Devecchi, C 38
development programme: accredited development module 36; challenging questions, 201; change management skills 61; collaboration 60; context, recognition of 61; continuous adaptation 63; curriculum design and management 61; definition of purpose of 34; design principles 61; developmental activities 44–5; environment scanning 61; grounded in scholarship 67; institutional expertise 62; leadership development 61; managing a range of duties 61; relevance to all staff 62, 64; sharing of experience 65; welcoming practitioner expertise 66; workshop design 63; workshop topics and literature 62
Devine, D. 121
Dewey, J. 65
dialogic methodology 137
Diamond, P. 85
difficulties: career progression, lack of 34; conflict with institutional framework and

priorities 33; heavy workloads 166; hidden labour 15; induction, lack of 113; isolated 166; lacking in prestige 15; leadership without authority 125; little institutional recognition of 15; powerless as managers 33; role, temporary 125; team building, impossible 33; time, insufficient 166; undervalued 15; university administration, standardisation of 33; university management policies 125; unsupported 113; working in silos and disciplines 113; workload allocation of colleagues 33
digital pedagogies 141–2; *see also* blended learning
disciplinary tribes 111
diversity 186
Dixon, M. 159
Dobson, E. 156
Doughty, S. 156
duo-auto-ethnography 137

Earl, B. 171
Edinburgh Napier University (UK) 191; DLTE 192
educational development: embedded 137; as "enabler" 138; mentored 138–9
educational leadership, literature on 42
Edwards, R. 64
Ellis, S. 3–5, 16, 61–2, 66, 73–4, 76, 81, 103, 166, 168, 196–7
England 3
enhancement: bespoke workshops 61; continuous 62; conversations 25; culture of 21; development of teams 21; enhancement planning 20–1; four interconnected spheres of 16, *17*
Environmental Science and Sustainability BSc 148; strategy of development of, 148–50
Eraut, M. 63, 65–7
Eriksen, M. 124, 132
evaluation, Kirkpatrick's model 46
Eve, J. 70

Falchikov, N. 170
Fanghanel, J. 30
Fitzpatrick, M. 156
Five Practices of Exemplary Leadership 188
Flavell, H. 43
Fook, J. 75
Forman, D. 104
Forsyth, R. 37, 70
forums, implementation of 114–17; advice about 120; challenges with 118; collaborative space 112; digital support for 117, 121; hijacked by other agencies 118; hosting of 116, 118, 123; insufficient to make policy change 118; non-hierarchical approach 112

Framework for Programme Quality and Programme Review 42
Frankel, A. 138
Fraser, S. P. 161, 172
Freire, P. 84
Frolich, N. 52
Fullan, M. 97, 106
Fyffe, J. 51

Gallos, J. V. 95
Gantogtokh, O. 62
Gardner, A. 65
Gentle, P. 107
Gibbs, G. 42, 72
Giles, D. 82
Glaser, B.J. 75
Gosling, J. 50, 107
Greece, comparison with 53
Griffith University (AUS) 41, 55
Grounded theory 75
Guba, E. 30

Haddow, C. 16, 18, 20
Hagan, B. 82
Hallas, J. 85
Hammond, A. 68, 82, 169, 202
Hammond, M. 112
Handelzalts, A. 185
Handler, B. 177
Harkin, D. G. 19
Harris, A. 42
Hartley, P. 62
Harvey, M. 51
Haslam, S. A. 97
Healy, A. H. 19
Herrick, T. 73
Hicks, M. 178
hooks, B. 6
Howlett, P. 159
Hubball, H.T. 73, 80
Hunt, L. 175
Hutcheon, R. G. 112
Huxham, C. 158, 160

influence 95
Integrated Curriculum Design Model 140–2
Iorlano, M. 122
Irving, K. 73, 125, 129, 132, 167

Jamieson, E. 157–8
John-Steiner, V. 155–6, 158–9, 162
Johnston, V. 32
joint or combined programmes 144–7; advice for programme leaders 145–6; issues of leadership 144; students' essential requirements 145; threshold standards, elements required 146–7

Jones, S. 42
Jones-Devitt, S. 21
Jonker, L. 178

Kandiko, C. B. 15, 18, 79, 97
Kaplan, R. E. 102
Kellner-Rogers, M. 111, 121
Kember, D. 44
Kemmis, S. 44, 45, 48
Kerno, S. J. 112
King, H. 62, 64, 66
King, M. 20
Kirkpatrick, D. L. 46
Knapper, C. 50
Knight, P. 166
Kohtamäki, V. 111
Kopelman, S. 83, 135
Korek, S. 50, 68, 82, 169, 202
Kotter, J. 43, 99
Kouzes, J. M. 188, 190
Koya, K. 100
Krause, K. 4, 43, 105
Kung, S. 75

Ladyshewsky, R. 42–3, 200
Laing, C. 111
Laing, G. 111
Lave, J. 66, 77, 112
Lawrence, J. 2–5, 16, 61, 73, 166, 168, 196–7
Le Pennec, M. 177
leadership, administrative 104–6; developing networks 98; establishing legitimacy 99; integrating with other models 105; investing in relationships 98; orchestrating tasks 105; planning 104
leadership, embodied 100–1, 106; developing spheres of influence 99; ethical dimension 101; living the change 101; relational 98–9, 106; shared or distributed 97; social identity 97, 109; visibility 100
leadership, enabling 102–4, 106; authority of the group 158; developing collective commitment 103–4; fostering connections 102; horizontal 155, 160; through influence 105; using creative approaches 103
leading change 171
leading without authority 4
Lean Management 191–2
learner records 186
LeBihan, J. 21
Lefoe, G. E. 3, 51
Leibowitz, B. 138
Lester, S. 84
Lewin, K. 30
Lincoln, Y. 30
Lindgren, M. 135, 169

Lintern, M. 74
Lizzio, A. 42, 43
Loesel, I. 84
Louw, I. 43
Love, A. 50, 180
Lund, D. 139
Lyubovnikova, J. 21, 22

Maddock, L. 44, 46
Maddox, M. 84
Malone, E. 98
management, vertical 160
Manifesto for Sustainable Programme Leadership 196
Marchiando, L. 74, 124, 132
Marker, A. 171
Marshall, S. G. 43
Marshall, S. J. 42
Mårtensson, K. 42–3
Maslow, A. H. 115
Maslow's hierarchy of needs 115
Massie, R. 171
Maxwell, J. C. 105
Mayne, J. 46
McAlpine, L. 64–5
McArthur-Blair, J. 75
McCune, V. 191
McDermott, R.A. 83
Mcintosh, E. 4
McLinden, M. 74
McTaggart, R. 51
Mertova, P. 21
Meuser, J. D. 121
Mezirow, J. 48
Milburn, P. 16, 60, 124–5, 129, 132, 140, 166–9
Miller, J. 185
Millett, C.M. 186
Minnis, M. 155, 158
Mitchell, R. 1, 16, 32, 61, 66, 74, 125, 130–1, 133
Module Evaluation Questionnaire 170–3, 172
Mok, K. H. 3
Moon, J. 160–1
Moore, S. 3, 4, 66, 73–4, 76, 80, 89, 100, 124, 166–9
Moores, E. 202
Moos, L. 97
Morley, L. 176
Morón-García, S. 5, 62
Morrish, L. 160
Mortiboys, A. 89
Mujis, D. 113
Murphy, M. 4, 15–16, 32, 60–1, 66, 68, 89, 124–5, 127, 129, 133, 160, 166
Murray, R. 167, 168, 169
Myers, C. 83, 135, 185

Index

Nair, C. 21
National Student Survey (NSS) 18, 22, 37, 78–9, 87, 116, 118, 170, *173*, 195; importance of organisation 195
Nelson, R. 161
Nethery, A. 122
Netland, T. 192
Nettles, M.T. 186
networks 44, 46, 54; benefits of 77–9; career progression 79; central formal network 75–7; communities of practice 73; distributed leadership 111; formal 73; guide to building 73; local informal network 77–8; recognition and professional standing 79; relationships 111; six-point guide to building 81; social network theory 111–13; strategies to improve 76–7; types of 73
Newton, M. 167–9
Ng, S. 175
Nimmo, A. 3, 62, 66, 74, 76, 81
Nixon, R. 51
Norris, J. 137
Nutt, D. 4

O'Carroll, A. D. 84
O'Neill, G. 61
organisational culture, importance of 197; differences between institutions 198
organisational structure 160
Orrell, J. 51
Outram, S. 30

Packendorff, J. 135, 169
Paechter, C. 69
Parkin, D. 30, 76, 78, 95, 98, 102, 104
pastoral role 142
Pearson, A. 50, 80
Pepper, R. 114
performing arts 155
Petrov, G. 50, 107
Petrova, P. 69
Piccinin, S. 50
Pieters, J.M. 185
Platow, M. J. 107
Porcelli, M. 98
Posner, B. Z. 188, 190
postgraduate programme leadership 116
Potter, J. 38
Poulter, J. 30, 32
Powell D.J. 192
Powell, S. 70
Pratt, D.D. 82
Preedy, M. 69
Preston, D. 125, 129, 133, 166–9
Price, D. 125, 129, 133, 166–9
Price, E. 112
Probert, B. 72

professional learning ecology 45
professional service colleagues 128
programme development, elements to consider 148–50
programme focused curriculum design, Australia 81
programme leader development: awareness of cultural differences 84–5; building relationships 84; collaboration 198; connection 198; disciplinary context 81; educational developers 73, 133; forum-based approach 111–12; holistic support 199; institutional support 80; mentors 74, 134, 166; networks 74, 134; on the job 125; peers 73; previous leaders, learning from 136; recognising varied experience and contexts 74; relationships between 115; resources 166; retreats 166–9; shadowing 134; shared ownership 199; sharing best practice 114; social network 199; strategic, not 2; surveys of 74; training, as 2; workshops 45, 166
programme leader development programme *see* development programme
programme leader difficulties *see* difficulties
programme leader networks *see* networks
programme leader relationships *see* relationships
Programme Leader Research Project 125
programme leader role 15; Canadian comparison 27; complex 29; concerns with 32; contested 29; critical position of 15; database of tasks 36, 40; definitions of 1; disciplinary differences between 29; enhancing student learning 24; formal description, lack of 32; in context,1; role descriptor 2–4; skills 3; varied 29
programme leader, role specification 56; broad role (excerpt from statement) 57; detailed responsibilities (excerpt from statement), 58; essential document 199; influence of 66; impact on perceptions of leadership role 59; need to recognise the role 200; recognition and reward 200–1; role statement 44, 54; support for 66; tasks 192–3
programme leaders, institutional position: evaluation of success of 37; influence and efficacy, factors affecting 42; institutional profile, raising of 36; responsibilities of institutional leaders 196, 198
programme leadership; coordinating module assessment 170; four dimensions of 95, 98; model of 98; support for 197; team development 171; undervalued 2
Programme Level Learning Outcomes 138
Programme Roadmap 191–2

programme teaching team, formation of 126–7; advice on 128; line management of 127; workload allocation 127; ensuring cooperation 127
Project Management Institute 192

QAA Benchmark Statements 150
QAA Scotland 197
Quality and Qualifications Ireland 141
quality assurance 44
Quality Assurance Agency Scotland 15, 17; enhancement themes 15, 20
Queensland University of Technology (AUS) 188
Quinlan, K.M. 62

RACI (Responsible, Accountable, Consulted, Informed) Matrix 192–3, *193*
Ramsden, P. 43, 64, 66
Raufflet, E. 177
Rawlings, C. 84
referrals 180
Reicher, S. D. 107
relationships 84; advice on 132; as agents of change 43; building a community 43; committees 129; four categories of 126, *126*; importance of 124; learning from others 131; other programme leaders 131; senior managers 116; supporters and administrators, 128–30
Rendell, C. 50, 68, 82, 169, 202
research informed teaching 161
retreats, benefits of 168
retreats, design of 167; group participation in 167; participant centred 167; professional contributions, role of 167; timetable, one day 167
reward and recognition 18, 22, 196, 200; promotion pathways, 18, 22; performance related pay 18, 22; supporting transition into PL role 18
Riggio, R. E. 43
Ringan, N. 37
Roberts, J. 112
Robinson, K. 103
Robinson-Self, P. 3, 29, 79, 80, 81
Roxå, T. 43
Royal Society of Biology 191
Rudhumbu, N. 175, 177, 181
Ryland, K. 51

safety, sense of 115
Sagnak, M. 140
Sanderson, R. 122
Sawyer, K. 156, 159, 162
Sawyer, R. D 137
Schein, E. H. 99
Scholarship of Teaching and Learning 3

Schön, D. A. 50, 65, 161
Schrage, M. 155
Sciascia, A. D. 75
Scotland 148, 191
Scott, G. 2, 5, 43, 69, 113, 170
SEDA (Staff and Educational Development Association) 4–5, 89, Special 196
self-leadership 95
Senge, P.M. 43
senior leaders 7
Senior, C. 202
Senior, R. 5, 15, 21, 60–1, 66, 80, 196
Shadle, S. E. 171
Sharif, A. 176
Sharpe, R. 74, 81
Shulman, L. S. 81
Sice, P. 108
Simms, C. 3
Sinek, S. 104
Snyder, W. M. 83
social support, importance of 123
Soft Systems Methodology (SSM) 29–32, 37
Soler, J. 69
South Africa 40
Spencer, D. 51
spheres of influence and action *17*
Spillane, J. 42, 159
Srivastva, S. 32
Staddon, E. 69
Stensaker, B. 41, 51
Stewart, H. 50
Strauss, A.L. 75
Stubbs, M. 37
student consultative forums 145
student engagement 161
student experience 3; diversity of 158
students and alumni 130; advice on 131; engagement activities 131; relationships with 130; use of committees 131
Swann, J. 85

Tanner, K. D. 171–2
team building 160
terminology 1
TESTA 170, 171
Thomas, M. K. 122
Thomas, S. 51
Tierney, A. 171
timetable: institutional activity 87; programme leaders' activity 86; student life cycle 86–7
Tomkinson, B. 184
transactional model 183
triage 180–1
trial and error, reliance on 71
Trowler, P. R. 29, 30, 166

Index

Ukraine, comparison 109–10
UNESCO 84
Universal Design for Learning 142
University of British Columbia (CAN) 27
University of Glasgow (UK) 148
University of Hull (UK) 73
University of Malta 165
University of Queensland (AUS) 71
University of West of England (UK) 60
USA, current and future developments in HE 186

Van Veggel, N. 159
Vangen, S. 158, 160
vignettes 145
Vilkinas, T. 3, 42, 60–1, 66, 124–5, 128–9, 132–3, 166–7, 200
Voogt, J.M. 174
Vygotsky, L.S. 45

Wallace, S. 75
Walumbwa, F. O. 98
Wareham, T. 30
Weber, R. J. 155, 158
Welsh, A. 185
Wenger, E. 46, 66, 77, 81, 112, 175, 181

West, M. A. 21, 22, 96
Westwood, J. 32
Wheatley, M. J. 111, 121
Whitfield, R. 62
Wilcox, P. 89
Wilder, K. 16, 21
Wilder-Davis, K. 22
Willey, K. 65
Williams, J. 65
Wilsmore, R. 156
Wilson, B. 185
Winch, C. 66–7
Winn, S. 89
Wood, P. 22
Woolmer, C. 155
Workload, academic 170–2
Workshop based CPD, doubts about 72

Ylimaki R.M. 178
Yorkstone, S. 192
Young, S. 173

Zarrilli, P. 155
Zoology 171, *173*
Zuber-Skerritt, O. 43, 44, 45
Zutshi, A. 3

Printed in the United States
by Baker & Taylor Publisher Services